Freeport Public Library

314 W. Stephenson
Freeport, IL 61032
815-233-3000

Dearest Ones

Dearest Ones

A True World War II Love Story

Rosemary Norwalk

John Wiley & Sons, Inc.

New York • Chichester • Weinheim • Brisbane • Singapore • Toronto

Copyright © 1999 by Rosemary Norwalk. All rights reserved.
Published by John Wiley & Sons, Inc.
Published simultaneously in Canada.

All photographs are courtesy of the author.

This publication is designed to provide accurate and authoritative information in regard to the subject matter covered. It is sold with the understanding that the publisher is not engaged in rendering professional services. If professional advice or other expert assistance is required, the services of a competent professional person should be sought.

Library of Congress Cataloging-in-Publication Data:

Norwalk, Rosemary
    Dearest ones : a true World War II love story /
Rosemary Norwalk.
        p.   cm.
    ISBN 0-471-32049-8 (cloth : alk. paper)
    1. Norwalk, Rosemary. 2. World War,
1939–1945—Personal narratives, American. 3. World
War, 1939–1945—War work—United States. 4. England—
Social conditions—20th century. 5. American
National Red Cross—Biography. 6. World War,
1939–1945—Women—United States. 7. Women—United
States—Biography. I. Title.
D811.5.N715   1999
940.54'8173—dc21   98-33652

Printed in the United States of America

10 9 8 7 6 5 4 3 2 1

For Bob and our children, Martha and Tom, and the family
and
for the wonderful Red Cross women who
dropped everything to serve overseas

Contents

Acknowledgments

To Anna Cottle and Mary Alice Kier, my literary agents, in deep appreciation for their enthusiasm, efforts, and time, especially Anna, whose brilliant editing skills helped to shape the book.

To Hana Umlauf Lane, my editor and champion, who so carefully and skillfully guided me through the publishing process.

To Barbara Pathe, American Red Cross Volunteer Manager of the Archives at Hazel Braugh Center, for her frequent, skilled, and gracious assistance.

To Isabel ("Ski") Seaton Carver Baum, Eloise Reilly, Harriet Scudder, Alice Finney Gabbard, Kari Lund Fougner, Barbara Hayes Van Winkelen, Bettie Brodie, and my many other former Clubmobile crew friends who generously shared their time, their jokes, and their memory banks in the interest of accuracy.

To my writing group friends at the Women's University Club of Seattle, who supported me with humor and good suggestions as the manuscript developed.

To my fellow author and friend Professor Emeritus Leon Standifer of Baton Rouge, whose GI perspective proved invaluable.

Preface

World War II was the defining period of my generation. It was our war, now often called the last good war because our country was united in believing it necessary and just. It was also a turning point in life for the women who volunteered for service overseas with the American Red Cross. Ever since 1946 when I returned, I've wanted, with growing urgency as too many years flew by, to share my experience of working with other young women who were liberated long before the term was coined. We were called girls then and it was an expression of affection and respect.

For years life intervened—marriage, career, family—and my old footlocker sat in the attic, full of "letters home" that Mother had pasted in scrapbooks along with photos, notes, orders, and newspaper articles. Journal notes, which I had scrawled on tablets or any piece of paper handy when I wanted to remember an experience, were stuffed into the bottom of the footlocker, exactly where I had tossed them. Most were too explicit to pass censorship or too personal to share with my family.

It was only in 1994, when television and news stories heavily featured the fiftieth anniversary of D day and my husband and I were moving from a house we'd lived in for many years, that I opened the footlocker in the attic. The contents were crumbling with age, the paper flaking, the ink faded. The process of typing the letters, some 600 single-spaced pages, took some time. In the meantime the media rediscovered World War II and celebrated troops, generals, divisions, GIs, battles, and victories in magazines and newspapers and on TV. Then they rediscovered famous women entertainers who had performed valiantly wherever they were sent, and eventually, the brave work of the Army nurses and the challenges they had faced. But in all the coverage of trials, disasters, and triumphs, very little was said of the efforts of volunteers who served overseas with the American Red Cross (ARC).

Red Cross National Headquarters is still not sure how many women volunteered for overseas duty. Documents list every penny spent on supplies and services to the troops during the war, and state that over 15,500 ARC volunteers served abroad. But at that time no details were kept of sex or race: it was enough that we were simply American citizens volunteering to help speed our country's war effort. The best guess is that about 2,000 were male field directors and the rest—12,000 to 13,500—were women. Today, at a new state-of-the-art record center at the national headquarters, efforts are underway to recover and clarify the old records.

We were sent to all the theaters of operation: the Pacific, the CBI (China-Burma-India), the ETO (European theater of operations), the Mediterranean, everywhere the war was being fought. Many of us ended up in highly unexpected spots, from steaming jungles in New Guinea to frigid outposts in Iceland. We managed Red Cross Clubs, which provided social activity and sleeping accommodations for troops on leave. We worked in rest homes for battle-weary troops, in hospitals, on hospital ships and trains, in dugouts. We led excursions and drove jeeps, Bedford or GMC Clubmobiles full of the latest popular records, hot coffee and doughnuts, and gum and cigarettes to share with the troops in the field.

Always, wherever we were sent, we were expected to be the friend, the girl next door, the kid sister, the funny aunt, Mom, adviser, sympathizer; to listen, commiserate, cajole, and cheer up the guys; to write notes for the wounded and arrange for emergency leave in family crises. We were not nurses; our job was to nurse morale.

But a widespread misconception that all Red Cross girls were nurses lingered from the First World War, where nursing service on both sides of the conflict was performed by Red Cross nurses. In our war, that was the Army's responsibility. Actually, only 8 Red Cross nurses served abroad, overseeing health at staff headquarters.

We volunteered for Red Cross duty so we could go where the war was being fought. Women officers in the WACs and WAVES, at the time I joined the Red Cross, were limited to stateside service. As volunteers we were not considered official members of the armed services; nor were we eligible for GI benefits, insurance, or tax deductions. We also had to sign releases not to sue in case of injury or loss of life. We wore ARC uniforms and battle dress and were issued dog tags, helmets, and gas masks—and honorary officer rank in the event of our capture by the enemy.

My personal experience was typical of that of so many others, no matter the huge contrasts in climate and challenges of our various locales. We left as girls, we returned as women, for we soon discovered how relatively sheltered our lives had been. Most of us were college graduates and considered ourselves capable, even sophisticated in the ways of the world, mature enough to handle anything. We were to find out quickly how much we still had to learn in a world of men at war.

Yet I've never discovered anyone who regretted going. We were vitally alive, living at full speed, working together for a cause we believed in. It was a time of very special togetherness.

The letters are edited for length and excess adverbs and adjectives (a malady of the young), and the documents and notes edited from the originals, journal notes reconstructed from tablet notes not sent home. Only two or three names have been changed to prevent embarrassment all around.

Rosemary Norwalk
Seattle, Washington
May 1998

Author's note: The lifelong efforts of Clara Barton, who rescued and nursed wounded soldiers during the Civil War, led to the founding of the American Red Cross in 1881. Today ARC Headquarters estimates there are 1,400,000 active volunteers.

Part One

Off We Go,
Destination Unknown

By 1944, World War II had reached a critical stage. Although San Francisco lay equidistant from the fighting fronts, the war seemed very near to those of us who lived or worked in the city. Since 1938 we'd heard horror stories from an influx of refugees fleeing the Japanese in Asia and Hitler in Europe. After the Japanese bombed Pearl Harbor in 1941, we watched with eagle eyes the hospital ships, troop ships, and warships that sailed into and out of San Francisco Bay. Servicemen from every Allied nation crammed the vibrant city, partying for one last time before going on to action or home on leave.

By 1944, Britain had been at war for five years, the United States since the attack on Pearl Harbor. Everyone had relatives or friends in service and studied the latest editions of newspapers for news of loved ones and battles. Wall maps decorated many homes, marked with flags and colored tacks designating battle lines or locations of family members.

Japanese incursion in Asia and the Pacific had finally been stopped and the Allies were slowly retaking, at great cost in lives, the islands Japan controlled. But the Japanese still held Singapore, most of Burma, and much of southern and eastern China.

In the Pacific, General MacArthur's forces were preparing to retake the Philippines and would land in Leyte in October. After finally defeating Axis forces in North Africa, American, British, and Canadian forces were facing fierce German resistance in the Mediterranean as they fought their way up through Italy.

Allied troops poured into Great Britain preparing for an expected invasion of the continent. On June 6, 1944, the combined Allied forces crossed the English Channel and took the Germans by surprise, landing in Normandy.

1

Chapter One

AMERICAN RED CROSS

PACIFIC AREA
CIVIC AUDITORIUM
SAN FRANCISCO, CALIFORNIA
ZONE 1

May 4, 1944
SPECIAL DELIVERY

Miss Rosemary Langheldt
Sacramento Street
Berkeley 2, California

Dear Miss Langheldt:

It gives me great pleasure to offer you an appointment as Staff Assistant for an overseas assignment with the American Red Cross. The salary is $150 per month and maintenance, and is effective on the day you report for training.

You are scheduled to report for training at National Headquarters, Washington, D.C., on Monday morning, June 12, 1944. After a period of training and probation you will be assigned, as needs require, somewhere abroad. The location cannot be determined in advance. However, the Red Cross reserves the right to release or transfer to domestic duties any person who, during the training period, fails to meet the Red Cross or Army requirements for overseas duty.

Expenses of travel and maintenance in connection with the training program in Washington will be assumed by the Red Cross. You should call at this office on the day of your departure, June 8th, for your check and further instructions.

Upon arrival in Washington on Monday morning you are to report directly to Hurst Hall, Campus American University, Mass. & Nebraska Ave., N.W. for registration. . . .

3

We congratulate you on your appointment and wish you every success in this important work.

> Very truly yours,
> (Miss) Esther Bristol
> Assistant to the Director, Personnel

❧❀☙

> June 8, 1944, 10:40 PM
> *The Challenger*—eastbound!

Dearest Mother and Dad,

At last the goodbyes are over and I'm on my way. I still can't believe it despite the clicking of the wheels on the track. For a while in the station tonight I was afraid the train never would get to Berkeley and was touched so many friends showed up to see me off. I couldn't look at either of you without starting to brim over and that's why I kept going out of the station to peer down the track. The gang from the store who rushed up just as the train finally did whistle in was all that saved me from becoming an emotional blob. It's a miracle they managed to get away from work and make it over the bridge from the city during rush hours and probably accounts for their hilarity. But I still felt pretty weepy.

That's why you both got such quick hugs and I hopped aboard almost before the porter had time to put down his stool. I raced back through the cars planning to wave gallantly from the observation car platform as the train eased out of the station—just as it's done in all those war movies. I should have known the *Challenger* doesn't carry an observation car in wartime, worse luck. But I waved furiously from the rear window of the club car and hope you recognized your daughter—you know, the one with the red eyes and runny nose dripping all over her navy suit with the white piping. I sure saw you, etched in my mind already, standing so straight and handsome, the two dogs beside you, backed up by so many others I love, cheering me off to life overseas, God knows where, with the Red Cross.

I accidentally on purpose forgot to pat the dogs and I'll never know why I insisted we bring them to the station. I couldn't bear to look at either Bing or Clipper while I was packing. Obviously, Bing knew I was leaving. Tell them for me to keep their tails up and in good wagging order for my return, please.

Mom and Dad, I can't thank you enough for your understanding and support of my decision to leave a job I love, in the city I love, to join the Red Cross. So many think I'm crazy to volunteer, but you understand and I'll always be grateful. If you had disapproved it would have made a difficult decision horrible. I hope that the invasion of Europe the day before yesterday may mean I'll be sent to the Pacific area and come through San Francisco on my way. Wouldn't that be wonderful! But there are no guarantees with this job—just remember my only regret is that I didn't turn twenty-five sooner so I could have volunteered sooner. Wherever they send me, every day is bound to be challenging, but don't worry. I'll write as often as possible to share this experience as we've always shared others.

Sacramento's approaching so I'll get off to mail this and "stretch my legs" as we always used to do in those magic summers of childhood when we started east to visit our relatives. Remember how Sis and I loved the Southern Pacific station soup? Now that I'm actually on my way I think my appetite's coming back. Maybe I'll go see if the soup's as good as my memory of it.

I'm so glad to be started. All my love to the best parents in the world.

Roses

P.S. Am sending back my official Red Cross acceptance letter as it's cluttering up my purse and I'm sure they already know I'm coming. Keep it for me, please, as proof that I didn't join up for the money.

≈≈◎≈≈

June 8, 1944, 1:30 AM—The Challenger
Oops! It's already the 9th

Mrs. Willis Camp
Boylston Avenue N.
Seattle, Washington

Dearest Marty,

Sleep is out of the question, Sis, despite the hour as I'm still pretty wound up from the excitement of the last few days. Besides, this lower berth reminds me of you, or don't you remember all those berths we shared in childhood, with me always complaining that *you* were squashing me against the fishnet strung between the windows and *making* me kick your clothes out? You deserve to be here now to see me get my comeuppance for having been such a bratty little sister. You'll be delighted to learn that I've managed to create havoc all by myself.

Of course, the gorgeous Val-Pak the store gave me at the surprise party they threw for me Tuesday after work helped create the problem. It's a new type of canvas and leather luggage (sea blue canvas with brown leather trim) and full of pockets on the outside and opens to hang clothes inside. Unfolded in the berth, there's barely room for me, and in trying to stuff in the gifts that turned up at the station, I accidentally dropped a box as I was removing the gift card. Blue Grass dusting powder exploded all over the berth, the opened luggage, and especially all over my I. Magnin suit you've so admired. Blue Grass over navy blue sharkskin lends an angora effect, in case you care to know. It also takes about forty minutes in the ladies' room to remove. Funny, I was very conscious of an overpowering smell as I snuck back to my berth in my new pajamas and robe which also reek of guess what? Was thankful everyone else in the Pullman seemed to be asleep.

Am enclosing a few pictures of the party at Ransohoffs which the store photographer brought me at the station. Aren't they good? You can see how surprised I was when Mr. James called me into his office and everyone was there waiting with all those gorgeous gifts. The stockings (eight pairs of scarce-as-hen's-teeth nylons, not lisle cotton!) and cashmere sweaters and travel robe and pj's are going to war and the marvelous watch Mr. James presented (a handsome new type that is shockproof, waterproof, has a second sweep hand, and glows in the dark—I love it and may wear it forever). The lovely lingerie trimmed with Alençon lace and a few other very unwarlike presents I left behind to await my triumphal return. It was reassuring to find the bonus check, vacation pay, and a request to hurry home in one pocket of the Val-Pak, particularly as the new personnel manager I've just finished breaking in is not only attractive but seems very capable.

How I wish you could have seen me being ushered out of Ransohoffs elegant entrance into a waiting limousine, door held open by a liveried driver, as Post Street shoppers stared. Me in the backseat, arms loaded with two dozen American beauty roses and surrounded by gifts. I felt like a princess as we swept over the Bay Bridge just at sunset.

From now on will probably just write one letter home with the details for you all to share. If I happen to end up stranded on a lonely atoll in the Pacific, however, you and Willis, and Marcy, Steve, and Bobby can expect long personal tomes. But tonight I just wanted to tell you, Sis, how much it means to me that you're so enthusiastic about my going. After all, I'm single and most of my friends are already involved and scattered over the Pacific. My career will wait and this war is affecting my whole generation. I want to be a part of it. Somehow, helping run a luxury store whose main purpose is selling designer clothes, mink coats, Lily Daché hats, and Delman shoes made me feel I was losing out on the most important event of my life. Say, Marty, can't you get a sitter for the kids and join me for a year or so? Don't answer that—I can hear Willis screaming already.

Love to you both and hugs to the children,
Rosie

❧

Friday, 6:35 PM
June 9, 1944—Great Salt Lake

Dearest ones,

A note before we arrive in Ogden. We're sitting at Midlake waiting for the westbound *Overland Limited* to pass us. I'll bet *it* still has an observation car on it!

Two other Red Cross girls are aboard—one from San Francisco and one from Berkeley. The blond one, Marjorie, has been to Europe several times, the attractive dark-haired one, Joan, around the world, so this is definitely old hat to them, but they're fun and very nice. Mom, the huge packed City of Paris lunch you gave me in case the diner was too crowded proved a big hit. We opened it the middle of the day, even though we had consumed a great breakfast this morning after only a five-minute diner wait. The three of us sat with a pregnant Army wife whose husband has just shipped out and we invited her to share the lunch basket with us. Joan had some fruit so we really had a spread.

You've never seen so many children as aboard this train. I counted thirty-seven between here and the diner, most of them very young and very cute. The train is full of Army and Navy wives and Army and Navy generally.

When I got off the train in Sacramento last night a shore patrolman came up to me and asked if I hadn't worked at the San Francisco World's Fair in 1940. I looked at him and he was one of the Fair policemen when I had the summer job after graduation. The young one who worked with Joe A.—that attractive cop who kept sending me cards, remember? Had big talk so no time to try the soup.

Owe so many thank you notes I'd better get going. If I write to everyone I'll have to send about seventy-five. Am bound to run out of stamps or continent before I finish—but I'm trying, Mother.

Best love,
Roses

Journal

June 9, 1944

A joy, a real sense of freedom—is it the sudden release from so much responsibility?— has been growing in me all day. Think it's just hit me that for the first time since college I won't be trying to juggle three or four balls at once. This seems to be a fresh start in every sense of the word, with everything prior put on indefinite hold. Of course, watching the old familiar scenery glide by only adds to my state of mind. Am so darn glad I'm a railroad man's daughter and caught his love of trains early—any train, going anywhere, as long as I'm on it.

Feeling mellow too, I'm sure, because I finally had time to answer the letters that piled up this past hectic week and gave me a guilty conscience, one thing I didn't need with all the other last minute pressures. Eight came from Bob B. so I tackled him first. How was I to know he'd be back this month to pick up a new minesweeper? He said he was going to surprise me as he'd have a leave before going on to Florida to get his new command. He seems to think I can just say, "I can't go this month, Red Cross, it's inconvenient. Try me next month." It makes me so mad as I wrote him in May and explained everything. I thought he'd understand, at least, and maybe even applaud.

His surprise is no doubt why his folks have been so much in evidence lately, applying not-so-subtle hints about how much wiser it would be for me to stay in my wonderful job. When that failed they even turned up at the station with the Blue Grass gift set with a card from Bob on it. This was another surprise as Mrs. B. dropped by (a fairly long drop from Piedmont) as I was frantically packing the night before (remind yourself, Rosie, to leave work more than twenty-four hours before departing for the next war, will you?). She brought me a small leather Bible with a sweet note on the flyleaf, including her favorite verses. It really was dear of her and we all sat down for a cup of coffee—and added a post-midnight hour to my packing. I am grateful for the Bible; it went right into the Val-Pak, but I am not grateful for the strings attached.

Nor for any strings. Got a disappointed letter from Bob L. too. He's finally coming home on leave before going on to Seattle to be Exec. on a new attack transport. And he's built up our prospective reunion beyond belief. When Albert's letter came I considered not opening it until I was safely out of reach—like assignment to the China-Burma-India theater of war, or some other inaccessible place. Sure enough, he's got a leave coming too and planned to go from Guadalcanal to his home in Pasadena, then push right on up to the city to visit good old Rosie. Evidently I'm the chief correspondent to the Armed Forces. Soooo, the Navy and the Marines voice dismay and disapproval. The Army hasn't checked in yet.

It's all so ridiculous—these are good friends, great dates, and I've treasured each friendship—and sat up far too late too many nights answering letters to prove it. But, and it's a very big but, I've been very careful not to commit myself. Nor did they, now that I think of it, before they raced off to the Pacific and so many unknowns. I know they've each been through a hell of a lot and suffered long periods of boredom in between. Think it's then that their devotion grows. I thought I'd handled it well by always mentioning how much I enjoy my work, and dropping in an extra word somewhere about how great Henry King sounded at the Fairmont and what fun it was to dance that new English craze the Lambeth Walk in such a setting. Or details of my weekly stint at the Stage Door Canteen—always something so they wouldn't assume I was sitting home nights making quilts for my hope chest pending their return. Obviously, it didn't work.

So today I tried to be tactful and hope I'm successful. Expressed my disappointment at missing them and said how much I hope to be assigned to the Pacific area where we might run into each other. Emphasized how busy I expect to be and that my one big commitment is to write home often so the family doesn't worry, but will keep in touch with them whenever there's time. Wanted to say, "Look guys, I have no intention of marrying anyone in wartime, it's too easy to confuse a handsome uniform in a San Francisco wartime atmosphere with deep emotion." Instead mentioned, I hope pointedly enough, that so far all I have in my footlocker, which I shipped ahead to Washington, is extra soap, rolls of soft toilet paper (the Red Cross recommended extras on my list), and several favorite books—Mann's The Magic Mountain, Tolstoy's War and Peace, which I've already read twice, and two volumes of Marcel Proust's Remembrance of Things Past.

Hastened to add that Proust isn't a favorite, but the Book of the Month Club edition has been gathering dust on the shelf and I've never been able to get past his first problems with asthma, but plan to tackle it again soon. So may they conjure up a picture of me working hard in my Red Cross uniform and whiling away lonesome nights reading good books—which may be exactly what I'll end up doing and you can't say I'm not prepared. I do hope this war is over before I have time to reread the Bible

in its entirety. The begats in Genesis are even duller than Proust's asthma. Anyway,
I've done my duty to the troops and now can let them worry about me being overseas.
That's a nice switch!

∞∞∞

Saturday, 9:10 pm
June 10, 1944—almost to Omaha

Dearest ones,

Aunt Ida and Uncle Zina met the train in Cheyenne this morning, Dad. They
looked fine, were most cordial, and gave me a box of candy (that makes three I
haven't touched). They thought it wonderful you were working at Cutter Labs
to help the war effort, Mom, and when I showed them the latest pictures of you
Ida said, "Why, Bess doesn't have a gray hair in her head!" Also said how
worried Aunt Tessie is about Billy as he's on Anzio and she hasn't heard from
him since early May.

Joan and Marge and I are sitting in the crowded club car listening to the
Hit Parade. Radio reception so far is full of static but plenty loud so I *think*
they're playing a Lucky Strike extra—*Stormy Weather*. You should see this car.
It's full of military men and pregnant wives returning home sans husbands. The
guys are plastered with campaign ribbons and purple hearts and citations and
mostly returning home on leave. The race issue seems to have solved itself on
this train as there's a Chinese girl, a colored Navy officer, colored and Filipino
and white GIs as well as gentiles and Jews and whatever-we-ares mixed throughout the train, all getting along fine. Good idea, no?

Much love,
Roses

∞∞∞

Journal   *June 10, 1944—late*

*What is there about a train? As it rushes forward towards my future, my mind insists
on drifting back—to my early days in the Berkeley grammar school where I was
captain of the football team which met late afternoons in the fields behind our house,
being the only girl in the Garfield Junior High Band since the band was short on
clarinets and that's what I played, to my stint with the Fairmont Hotel swim team.
And the huge contrast between Marty who was a beauty at sixteen while I was still her
nuisance kid sister, flitting around with a butterfly net in dirty overalls as she tried to
entertain a new boyfriend.*

*Then my college days starting in the Cal class of '40. How strange the way things
turn out: by volunteering to work on the staff of Cal's yearbook, I discovered how
much I loved everything about publications—the writing, editing, printing, even the dead-
lines. My position as woman's editor, which led me to the world of elegance and perfection and a job in the city's finest store, Ransohoffs. Of course, it was the spreading*

Japanese aggression in the Far East, the war in Europe, and growing effects of the 1940 draft that played a part in my getting the chance to become their personnel manager in late 1941. And what a great send-off my professional "family" gave me both at the store and the station. I hope I can live up to this new challenge—whatever, wherever it turns out to be.

◈

The Capitol Limited
Sunday, June 11, 1944, 8:15 PM

Dearest ones,

Joan and I are sitting in the club car with an oversupply of majors and colonels and Navy commanders scattered around—the gold braid in evidence is overwhelming. And how do you like this fancy *Capitol Limited* stationery? This train is wonderful and strictly deluxe. I thought the other train okay considering it's wartime, but this one is so classy it makes our ride to Chicago seem rugged.

We left Chicago at 3:30 PM, and the country's simply beautiful now—Pennsylvania-style countryside and as green as can be. The Army sitting on my right says to tell you we just passed a cow. He's been slowing down my writing efforts for the last ten minutes (the Army, not the cow!).

Dad, this diner is the best I've seen in ages, war or peace. Waiters completely on their toes, service fast, and food really fine. So far I've written twenty thank you notes and a few letters. I can see it's going to be a long task to finish the list. Mom, I sent Aunt Stella a night letter from Omaha telling them not to meet me when the train stops in Pittsburgh and that I'd try to come down next weekend. Think I'll have the porter awaken me anyway just in case they don't get my wire.

Goodnight. Wish you all were here to enjoy this wonderful train.

Love,
Roses

◈

Chapter Two

WESTERN UNION

JUNE 12 PM 7:00

WASHINGTON D.C.
H.B. LANGHELDT
SACRAMENTO ST.
BERKELEY CALIFORNIA

ARRIVED SAFELY THIS MORNING   CANNOT FIND WAY
AROUND BUT LOVE IT ALREADY   ROSEMARY

Washington, D.C.
Monday, June 12, 1944, 11:05 PM

Dearest Folks,

Just to say hello—it's been a very busy day. The ride this morning on the B&O up the Potomac was beautiful. Joan and I were having breakfast in the diner when we passed Harper's Ferry, set in such lovely countryside, all green-trimmed with honeysuckle, and especially exciting for me as it's country I've only known before from books.

Washington is *beautiful*, if hectic and confusing. On the way to the campus the taxi driver drove us past most of the embassies. Our day at American University was spent mainly in filling out blanks and hearing introductory speeches. Marjorie is going into Red Cross domestic service so reported to another building. Joan and I were separated in the first five minutes of checking into a very large classroom full of milling girls. Sure was impressed with their attractiveness and high caliber generally. They come from all over the country judging from the variety of accents and some are surely *Southern*. They "you-alled" the rest of us all over the place.

We are free from Saturday noon to Monday morning but were informed we can't go over four hours away from Washington. So tomorrow I'll see if I can get special permission as I'd love to visit Aunt Stella and the family in Pittsburgh.

11

Rosemary, ready to go,
Washington, D.C.,
June 1944.

We will be allowed extra time to shop and sure will need it. Hadn't realized before there was so much shopping involved—at our expense. We're given one set of summer and winter Class A uniforms, paid for by the Red Cross, and must have them fitted. But we pay for a long list of required equipment. It specifies exactly how many white blouses, socks, cotton underpants, and cotton gloves we need, plus odd items like canteen, web belt, musette bag (what the heck are those?) boots, duffle bag, and footlocker. I'm realizing now that any sightseeing I manage will be side glances at monuments while scurrying all over town to track down every item on the list.

I'm staying at a little hotel on G Street N.W. It has the smell of an old Eastern house and it's picturesque—with shutter type doors here and there—if not spotless. I've already made acquaintance with a few cockroaches—another new experience. My roommate is a girl from Phoenix and she's a little bit scared now that she's actually here in training. Don't think she knew what she was getting into and she's starting to worry about overseas.

Big day tomorrow—classes and tackling the shopping list.

Love to you all,
Roses
A.R.C.—S.A.F. (Services to Armed Forces)
930 H Street N.W.
Washington, D.C.

Tuesday night—12:35 AM
June 13, 1944

Dearest Folks,

Your letter of last Friday came today, Mom—so glad we're back in touch. Also one from Larry from Annapolis, surprise! I've been wondering if he's still speaking to me after I turned him down last December and he sent me that silver eight ball for my charm bracelet, but it turns out he's planning a weekend here to see me. If I get clearance to go to Pittsburgh I'll contact him and ask him to come the following week. We've known each other so long it would be nice to be friends again.

Courses are most interesting—girls, too. A very attractive blond girl sat down beside me yesterday and we started talking when she admired my watch. I mentioned the Navy insignia and submarine pin she was wearing and found out her husband (a Navy j.g.) is missing in action, so she joined the Red Cross and is also hoping to go to the Pacific. Her name's Caroline, she is a Wellesley grad, but I'm not sure if her accent is Southern or New England. Was glad to find out she's staying at this hotel.

Oh! Guess what else I discovered today? I live one and a half blocks from the White House. We passed it this morning walking over to have breakfast before catching a bus to class. Unfortunately neither Franklin nor Eleanor were about. What a confusing city!

In a rush to get some sleep. Will write more when there's time.

Much love,
Roses

Wednesday night
June 14, 1944, 12:30 AM

Dearest Folks,

It's very late as they keep us busy. Five letters today including your nice one of Sunday. Dad, could you rush me my stencil by airmail? I have to stencil my footlocker on all six sides. If you can find any Kodak film or more movie film I'd love it as it's real hard to find here.

This is a wonderful experience. The classes are more informative than challenging, but fascinating. Sessions scheduled on Red Cross first aid technique review, one on military rank and insignias (guess so we don't insult a general or an admiral), and many on different aspects of Red Cross work and what is expected of us. A lot, I gather. Once in uniform we *are* the Red Cross to anyone we run into, so we've got to be nice to everyone we meet or they cancel their donations to the Red Cross forever. There are explanations of the varied type of work we might do overseas and of the problems faced by the Red Cross in the many areas they serve. For example, the British Command demanded that the

Red Cross charge for the food served in their clubs, because British troops have to pay for all food served in British service clubs, and our soldiers earn so much more than British servicemen. So there is a nominal charge and our GIs don't like it a bit and some blame the Red Cross.

Finally got the weekend planned—a round trip to Pittsburgh Saturday at 5:50 PM, arriving after midnight. Called Crafton tonight, Mom, and they're thrilled I'm coming. Night-lettered Larry and suggested the following weekend.

Goodnight now. Love,
Roses

Thursday, 12:15 AM
June 15, 1944

Dearest Family,

Another quickie as we have exams at 8 AM, which means we get up at 6. I'm dropping you a line every day, as once I get orders I'm incommunicado until arrival at my destination. Some girls have been as long as three months en route (India, no doubt), others just a few days. I don't expect to leave until after we finish the second week of training, maybe as long as two months after, but if you don't hear for a while keep writing and, who knows? I may turn up in San Francisco.

Caroline and I have dubbed one instructor Theda Bara. She's a thin older woman, her dark hair drawn severely back from her face, who served in France during "the last show" (as she calls the Great War). It was her duty to warn us of the pitfalls and perils women face in situations where they are sometimes outnumbered hundreds to one by men in uniform. And she certainly did, with relish. As Red Cross staff assistants, she emphasized, we are considered officers if captured, the equivalent of second lieutenants, and are covered by the international rules of war. We're supposed to date only officers and even then we must be careful not to let our heads be turned by all the attention.

"The uniform," she intoned, "does not make the man." She paused dramatically to let this revelation sink in. Then she cited examples of girls who did everything right before going on to a few who fell by the wayside in various sad ways. She saved her clincher for last, pausing dramatically to fix us with her piercing eyes. "Girls, *don't* think you're Theda Bara just because of all the attention you get!" Caroline and I had real trouble suppressing giggles as I doubt half the girls had a clue as to who Theda Bara was, but *we* knew and are glad we left our leopards at home. Caroline and I have such fun together as we laugh at the same things.

Had my hair done today—may have a three-inch cut before going. It would be more practical.

Write often. My love to the boys and especially to all of you,

Roses

Friday, 12:25 AM
June 16, 1944

Dearest Family,

Another quickie. Had uniform fitting today—was issued summer and winter uniforms, trench coat type raincoat, heavy topcoat with removable red lining. We all love the summer uniform as it's real good-looking, of light slate blue Palm Beach material—classy! Worn with an overseas cap with red ARC cross, white blouse closed at neck with red ARC cross, and on our uniforms a bronze ARC insignia on each lapel and an American Red Cross shoulder patch on our left shoulder. The uniform makes us feel jaunty!

The winter uniforms are more sober-looking, of dark gray, almost black wool with light blue inserts on upper lapels to show off the Red Cross insignia, much too heavy and hot for this climate.

I tested my Palm Beach uniform tonight. As it was a lovely evening, some of us went out to the Lincoln Memorial. There was a concert beside the Potomac—Percy Grainger was playing his concerto. We got caught in a sudden rainstorm and took refuge with Lincoln, and a few hundred others. My uniform drip-dried on me just great on the walk back.

Got your letter today, Mom. Am sorry to have just missed Bob L., and I hope you asked him to contact me pronto. It's all fate now anyway. I haven't the remotest idea where I'll be sent. Had an interview today with the personnel head. She said with my ability in Spanish and French, North Africa or England should be the first destination for me, but if they happen to need more girls in India when I'm through, I'd likely go there, or anywhere I'm most needed. Tried to tout the Pacific a little but said I really had no preference, just send me to a place where there'd be work to be done.

Mom, did I leave my new white fabric gloves at home? I think I forgot to pack them. Please send them as we wear them with our uniforms.

Much love to all of you . . . so tired tonight,

Roses.

But fun tired.
P.S. Will wear uniform to Pittsburgh. I figure it might help me get a berth coming back and I can travel lighter.

Saturday night, 10 PM—en route Pittsburgh
June 17, 1944

Dearest Family,

Happy Father's Day, Dad! From the looks of things all of Washington is en route to Pittsburgh to celebrate Father's Day. The Union Station was a positive madhouse today. I had a reserved-chair car seat, but the gateman directed me to the wrong train (two leaving within 10 minutes of each other) and there was such a pushing, yelling mob I did as he told me, which is always a mistake. And in just a snap of the fingers instead of riding the deluxe-chair car on the *Capitol Limited* I was *standing* (only two hours before I got a seat) on the local milk train. Now that the worst of the dreadful heat is over and 750 people got off at Cumberland, I can say it isn't so bad. But I am certainly going to try and get a Pullman back. My only worry at the moment is that I will arrive 15 minutes late, so I hope the Hoges wait. Several people who run this rat race weekly say this is the worst weekend they've ever ridden, but I still like the B&O. Just returned from the diner, which they're keeping open until midnight because of the crowds.

We had a lecture this morning on the China-Burma-India theater and what the Red Cross girls are doing there. Some are flown in over the hump to China, where the average cost per pound of air freight is $9. The girls often leave their footlockers behind as they have no room and live pretty rugged lives.

Another possible location is Persia, where the temperature can range from 40 below to 140 above. The U.S. Army tries to get supplies into Russia and Red Cross girls run a "trainmobile" which stops everywhere there's a group of our boys to feed them, give them parties, hometown papers, records, and magazines and do any Red Cross work needed. When I thought of that, this train wasn't really hot. Next week I take up Christian Science.

My uniform still looks unwrinkled—remarkable. The first soldier on the train to see me immediately asked if I had an aspirin. The standing joke at National Headquarters is that everyone is sure all girls in Red Cross uniforms are nurses and all men are ambulance drivers. Wearing this uniform also means I've spent most of the trip chatting with GIs. Feel like I'm on duty already. When I sat down at a vacant table in the diner, a sergeant carried his plates and food over to join me and proceeded to tell me his life, loves, likes, and hates.

Had my first tetanus shot today at the Pentagon and it's certainly huge (the Pentagon, not the shot!). Can't say this tactfully but admit we girls were pleased to note, while lined up for the shots, that three of an Army group in a separate line fainted dead away, one before he reached the needle!

Received nice letters from Larry and Bob L. today. Bob is going to send me a picture and Larry suggested I come to Annapolis some evening next week.

Goodnight now, all my love,
Rosemary

❧❦❧

Pittsburgh—Sunday night, 12:20 PM
June 18, 1944

Dearest Family,

The train's about to pull out of Pittsburgh and before "retiring" (I'm using quotes advisedly) want to let you know that the weekend was well worth the effort. Had a marvelous time and, more important, know the Hoges did too. Couldn't get a Pullman back but am in an air-cooled day coach and tired enough to sleep on a rock if necessary. This train gets in about 7 AM, so I'll be able to shower and change before going to classes.

I arrived last night at 12:45 AM and managed to look fresh with the aid of the best efforts of Elizabeth Arden. They drew straws to see who got to meet me and five of them were waiting, with tears and cheers. They loved my uniform and I was so glad I wore it. Aunt Stella waited at home—and she always greets us with tears and that wonderful smile, so it was just as I dreamed it would be, and the big old stone house was as inviting as it's always been since my earliest memories. Cousin Martha's little Gretchen (*your* brown eyes, Mom) and Caroline (at the awkward age but cute as a button) were supposed to be asleep but of course managed to be in on the party and help share the last box of candy that I brought with me. We all talked and laughed at once, Stella insisted I sleep in her marvelous big old bedroom with her, and finally, after Martha Hoge came into the bathroom to sit on the john and talk while I bathed, I finally fell into bed at 4:30.

The day was grand. Stella was thrilled I said I'd like to go to church with her (I did want so to hear her play the old Baptist hymns on that little organ, and she wanted to show me off in my uniform), so we all went. Even dear old Aunt Tillie came. Frail as a reed yet strong as an ox, she is still the bane of Stella's life and only wears new clothes after they've been in her closet at least three years. Well, today she put on her best dress (Stella says she's only worn it three times) and her silk slip. Cousin Sara tells me that is a great event. I wouldn't be surprised if Tillie lives to be 150.

As you must have gathered from our phone call, we had a wonderful time at Sara and Gerry's new house in Greenfield, with dinner served on the back lawn. They all cried when I left and demanded I come again next weekend which I know, but didn't tell them, is impossible.

Tired. Goodnight now and fondest love,
Rosie

Monday, 11:20 PM
June 19, 1944

Dearest Family,

Heat wave yesterday! Now I know what hot and humid means. So much mail today—been very lucky so far and sure hope my luck holds. Dad, the film is wonderful and am getting together a good supply (both still and movie) to stash in my footlocker. Mom and Sis, your letters make me feel as though you're with me.

Talked with Larry tonight and am going down to Annapolis Thursday for dinner. Have a hunch he's found the right girl as he sure wants us to get together. Am truly sorry I couldn't love him as he's a fine person and certainly the best prospect on any block. But it can't be me—my eyes always glazed over when he tried to explain the wonders of his slide rule way back in college. Anything mathematical or electrical does that.

Caught a couple snatches of sleep last night returning from Pittsburgh, and have coal dust liberally sprinkled in my hair, a stiff neck, and popped eyes from watching the goings on in a day coach during wartime. A plump girl got on in Pennsylvania. A Marine kissed her goodbye as she sat down next to a deaf-mute. A large group of them were in the car and when they were conversing and laughing the coach seemed full of flying hands and excitement—but absolutely silent. Long before Cumberland a sailor in front of me somehow conveyed the idea to a deaf boy next to him to trade places with the girl, who was riding facing backwards. For five minutes the sailor and the girl sat side by side in front of me; in twenty minutes they were so close together there was no space between them; from Cumberland on they were so tangled together I not only couldn't tell where one left off and the other began, they were involved in such close and noisy (how shall I put it?) interactions, I found it impossible to focus on anything else as the seat in front of me was really rocking. Gotta admit it sure made the ride go more quickly. Much better than a Class B movie—much!

Goodnight now and keep writing.
All my love,
Roses

June 20, 1944
To bed, 10:30 PM

Dearest ones,

Awfully tired tonight. Just finished vouchering expenses and that's a pain. Spent busy afternoon shopping, the list is interminable. Tonight is dedicated to catching up on some sleep.

All my love,
Rosie The Droop

P.S. Mom, would you ask the bank to transfer $75 from savings to checking for a list of supplemental equipment which we must buy (as in long underwear or tropical suits) when we get our starting orders?

P.P.S. Around the first of July, they tell us, I can start allotting half my pay ($37.50 twice a month) to you for deposit. Once I get overseas I probably shan't have a thing to spend money on and can easily repair my savings account.

Friday, 10:10 PM
June 23, 1944

Dearest ones,

Fell down on my writing schedule yesterday as it was after 3 AM when I returned from Annapolis. Larry and I had a simply wonderful time. When I arrived about 6 PM he was waiting to meet me in his dress whites, looking very handsome. He's lost weight and looks better than ever as he's been exercising and spending lots of time in the sun. I wore my uniform, which he loved.

We walked all over the Naval Academy grounds and it's far lovelier than I dreamed—all green and neat and beautifully laid out on the banks of the Severn. I took some movies but the camera jammed, so will have to have it checked before I leave.

The officers wear summer whites and Navy protocol is strictly observed, including very snappy salutes. Kept getting the feeling I ought to return the salutes as I too was in uniform! We had cocktails at the Officers Club then went across the Severn to an even swankier Officers Club for dinner. We took a cool drink out to a long cool porch, watched the river and the fireflies, and settled all the world's problems.

I have never felt as close to Larry before and yes, my hunch was right—he thinks he has found the right girl and wanted to get my advice before he proposes to her. He's told her all about us, including the eight ball. Was so glad I added it to my charm bracelet before I left home—and was wearing it. He dated her once two years ago when he was here on the East Coast with his subchaser but wrote her only a few times while he was at sea, telling her he was too busy writing to me. When my letters were so lukewarm he began to date her seriously and now, like the bright engineer he is, he wanted to go over his proposal plan so he'd do it right this time.

I told him I always will love him as a friend and that if I were so constituted that I could deliberately choose the right person to marry I would certainly have chosen him—but there was just something missing in any other relationship between us than as friends.

At which point we had another cool drink and he asked me about myself. I surprised myself and told him the truth. About both Bobs. That I was eager to see Bob L. after two years, and also Bob B., as I've always found him attractive in lots of ways—all the ramifications in fact. It was a beautiful sort of evening with a wistfully poignant note I'll never forget. We held hands and he seemed grateful I had come and he'll write as soon as he pops the question to let me know how it comes out.

In the morning we graduate and are usually given local assignments pending orders. Rumors are flying thick and fast and scuttlebutt has it none of us will be here long, that since the invasion lots of transportation to all parts of the world is opening up. Today everyone is sure the whole class is bound for the CBI

Caroline Drane and Rosemary
Langheldt, graduation day,
June 24, 1944.

theater but tomorrow we'll all be going to Africa. There's still a chance I'll go through San Francisco but might, or might not, be allowed to contact you. Only thing I'm sure of is that when we go to the POE (port of embarkation), wherever it turns out to be, we take our civilian clothes in a duffle bag and then send home any the CO (commanding officer) will not allow us to take. So you may be getting a package and can play guessing games. If my coat trimmed with nutria arrives, think tropics.

Best love to you all,
Roses

Chapter Three

Sunday, June 25, 1944
12:10 AM

Dearest Family,

Yesterday we graduated, which means we've finished our training and are now assigned to extension training, which, I believe, is short for various boondoggles we'll perform from now until our ship arrives. I've been assigned to National Headquarters Personnel Department with two others for a special project which I'll know more about in the morning.

I think I told you how nice Caroline is. She's the one from Boston whose husband is missing in action. We've had lots of fun together as we found we have a lot in common—including both playing clarinets when we were young (now *that's* a bond). Yesterday her mother came down from Boston to see our graduation and her father- and mother-in-law also attended the ceremony. They live right here in Washington, D.C. When they arrived at the hall Caroline's eyes filled with tears and I could see they were all teary-eyed at seeing her in uniform, looking terribly small and feminine, going off to war so soon after her husband had been reported missing. That's the moment when I missed your presence most. I so wished you could be here to see the impressive ceremony and me marching around in uniform with the class.

Caroline insisted I join her family afterwards and they invited me for lunch. They're lovely people. Caroline's mother-in-law is in charge of the famous Herb Cottage at the National Cathedral. En route to lunch we stopped to see the cathedral and the garden. Then they came to my room late in the afternoon to invite me to dinner and a concert but, worse luck, I had just gone out with some girls to eat. Caroline leaves tonight for her temporary duty at Sandston Air Base. We've got our fingers crossed that we'll end up going to the same place.

Had a lovely day today. Intended to get up early but forgot to leave a call and as my roommate went to New York for the weekend no one bothered me until 1:10 PM! Met Cal friends Winkie and Russ at 2:30 and we covered, with cameras, the Mall, Mellon Art Gallery, and Lincoln Memorial. Finally some sightseeing!

21

Goodnight now, I'm tired.

All my love,
Roses

P.S. Did I tell you, according to Larry, Bob B. is up for lieutenant commander and if he gets it, he'll be the youngest one in the Navy?

<hr>

Monday, 11:40 PM
June 26, 1944

Dearest Family,

A really short one as I'm exhausted, having walked all over Washington in the line of duty. Four of us from the entire class were chosen to take charge of setting up a lounge room at Headquarters for girls returning from overseas duty. We've been given some money and a week's time and told to go ahead. It's rather flattering, but what a job!

We decided how we want to do it and proceeded to tear the town apart to find the right maps for wall decorations, furniture, paint colors, etc. Tomorrow we start cleaning. The supervisor approved and liked our ideas. She says they've been wanting to do this for two years. It's fun being at Headquarters as we meet all sorts of interesting people.

Today a girl returned from sixteen months in the New Guinea jungle where she was club director. Her name's Phyllis. The GIs liked her so much they wrote, en masse, an article which first appeared in *Harper's Bazaar* and was reprinted in *Reader's Digest* about a year ago. She was injured in the line of duty—she can say no more—but is now sufficiently recovered to be given another assignment.

So sleepy I can't even write straight, so goodnight *and write*.

All my love,
Roses

<hr>

Journal   *June 26, 1944*

Another letter today from Albert, my Marine friend, back from Guadalcanal and still upset. He can't understand why I would leave the store. So I've written him a short note reminding him I'm only on leave from the store and have every intention of returning. Also mentioned the night after Pearl Harbor during San Francisco's first blackout when everyone in the city was wondering where the Japanese fleet was. We all worked late at the store helping install blackout curtains as fast as our custom workroom could turn them out—before I caught a very late bus home. Soldiers waving rifles stopped our bus right in the middle of the main caisson of the Bay Bridge yelling that an air raid alert was on.

It seemed logical to me during the 40 minutes we sat there in pitch blackness that if I were a Japanese admiral trying to hit S.F. I would try to hit one of the bridges first. The hysterical woman in the back of the bus evidently agreed with my logic. Ever since, I told Albert, I've wanted to do something and finally found the Red Cross. That should be clear enough, I hope.

⚓

Friday night, 12:10 AM
June 30, 1944

Dearest ones,

Today we finished our recreation lounge and everyone seemed delighted with it. Tomorrow we report back for a new assignment, probably to one of the local Army camps.

Have lunched the past three days with Phyllis, the girl who's waiting reassignment after sixteen months in Australia and New Guinea. Found out her injury in the line of duty was a severe head injury and she's had dengue fever twice. She's given us lots of useful information on what and what not to take to the tropics if we're sent there. As the rumors still say CBI theater we're soaking up her information. She also says she'd rather be in New Guinea at 135 degrees than in Washington at 95 degrees, so I won't worry about the tropics, as I don't seem to mind the heat here—perhaps because there are so many other matters to occupy my mind.

Last night I minded the heat a bit—at that point I minded everything because in the morning I had had a smallpox vaccination, typhus, and triple typhoid shots. Felt okay until I almost fainted off the counter stool at the corner store near our hotel where we were grabbing a bite to eat. Felt like my time had come—and gone. After a few hours flat in my room I not only found myself alive but feeling better so decided to go on until next Thursday when I have the whole thing to do over again, with cholera and yellow fever shots thrown in for good measure. At this rate I should be immune to all the diseases known to man.

Rumors say we'll all get orders somewhere, within next few days. Sure hope so.

All my love,
Rosemary

⚓

Monday, July 3, 1944
Hopewell, Virginia

Dearest Family,

At this point I feel like the original Rover Girl. Imagine spending the Fourth in Hopewell, Virginia, a first-class whistle stop of about 10,000 souls—five hours by Greyhound Bus and God's benevolence from Washington. Four of us have been sent here for our "extension training"—in plain English, to work in a Red Cross Club at nearby Camp Lee until we are shipped out. We're staying at the City Point Inn, which is complete with running water, summer doors (the kind Marlene Dietrich comes out from behind in movies set in Singapore—first cousins to barroom doors), faulty plumbing, and rocking chairs on the wide screened porch. Tomorrow we start our second week's extension training at the local USO, which is close to Camp Lee.

Today I came to grips with the South for the first time. After a hectic morning of packing, storing footlocker and duffle bag at the Union Station, and buying tickets, we managed to wangle seats on the bus. I headed towards the back as we always do at home but one of the girls grabbed my arm and sat us forward. That's when I realized only colored people were in the rear, and I didn't like the feeling. When we got off for a rest stop at Fredericksburg and rushed for the nearest rest room, two huge station signs said White Women and Colored Women. It was then I offered up thanks for my Western upbringing where we've never noticed who we sit beside in the bus or at the Opera House. Unless, of course, they wear exotic turbans and I wonder where on earth they come from and think about the interesting life they must lead.

As soon as we crossed over in the South everything got off schedule, including our luggage, which is probably still in Richmond. It was checked through from Washington and promised to arrive in Hopewell at 7, one hour after we did. With luck it will come sometime before Friday. In the meantime we'll sleep in slips—or out.

Our dinner here at the hotel was wonderful—fried chicken, biscuits, Southern gravy. The service was so terribly slow we were beginning to be impatient, when one of the girls who's been here a week explained that the charming old colored man who was serving us was also the cook and the busboy and the luggage carrier. So we relaxed and eventually had a fine meal.

After this long day think I could sleep on a rock, but the bed looks comfortable, and maybe our luggage will catch up before we report for work at the club.

Goodnight and so much love,
Roses

≈≋◎◎≋≈

July 4, 1944
Hopewell, Virginia, 3:30 PM

Dearest Family,

A grand and glorious Fourth to you all! I'm having one as my firecracker just exploded about an hour ago—a call from Washington ordering four of us back to clear!! And two of us just arrived last night for extension training at the Red Cross Club in Camp Lee. So within four days at most I should be en route to a

POE (port of embarkation). The fact that our bags only arrived this morning and we finished unpacking one hour before being called back increases our hilarity. We still work this evening and return to Washington on the early-morning bus. Surely have enjoyed my extended stay in the Old South.

I'll try to call you tonight so you'll know what's up as my lips may be sealed from tomorrow on. Rumor still points to the CBI theater. Passage to the ETO seems curtailed at the moment because they're pouring in troops to help the invasion forces. If so, I may get to see you again. However, we were told Saturday that twelve girls were flown to San Francisco to catch a ship last week. In a case like that they probably didn't even have a chance to see the city. So don't count on anything.

Gotta run—will write whenever I have a minute, even if I can't mail them for a while.

All my love,
Roses

Wed. night, 11:40 PM, July 5, 1944
Washington, D.C.

Dearest ones,

A hurried note as I have to be up at the crack of dawn to start clearing. I'm planning on phoning tomorrow night but if I'm not allowed to, just don't expect anything—and keep writing.

This morning on the way back from Hopewell ran into Caroline in the Richmond bus station and it was some reunion. You'd think we'd been friends for years. She's clearing too, as is a most attractive girl she roomed with at Sandston. Everyone calls her Ski—I don't know why yet but maybe it's because her proper name is Isabel and she's much too peppy to be called that. She's about my height and slender, with black hair, very fair skin, and dark eyes that sparkle at the least excuse. Her accent is New England—no *r*'s, or *r*'s in the wrong places—and she has a lovely low voice and laugh. Think she's from Connecticut.

So things are looking up for good company en route wherever—unless, of course, they send us off in opposite directions.

Caroline and Ski and I talked all the way back to Washington. Ski suggested we celebrate our impending clearance with dinner at a French restaurant she'd heard was exceptional. It was, but we weren't, as Ski accidentally spilled her French onion soup and most of it drenched Caroline. "Oh, *Horse!*" Ski shrieked and we dissolved in laughter as we'd spent the afternoon making sure our summer uniforms were clean and pressed. By the time we helped the waiter keep Caroline from drowning, we were a mess too. We stayed to enjoy the wonderful dinner then ended up the evening in one of those "Clean and Press While You Wait" places, giggling in our underwear in a sweat box of a dressing room while our uniforms were rehabilitated.

Larry called tonight while we were out but had left by the time I returned his call so have to drop him a note and get some sleep.

Write. All my love,
Roses

Washington, D.C., 6:30 AM
July 8, 1944

Dearest Family,

Last letter I can mail uncensored for a while. Am in great rush. Have had hair cut short and machineless permanent. Sending home keys to overnight bag via Railway Express this morning. Mom, can you possibly call Bob L. and perhaps Miss B. at the store or my secretary Elinore sometime to let them know I'm en route?

Gotta rush for more shots. Prepare for blackout for a while.

All my love,
Roses

P.S. Ended stay here in most exciting way last night—dinner at the Shoreham with Marge's ex, now a major on the General Staff. Mom, you remember our exquisite perfume buyer, Marge, the blond who fled from China carrying her family's Ming horse in a velvet-lined case? Seems she and Sid were married in big Shanghai wedding, but divorced soon after. Both too young to know what they were doing, but still good friends, so she had him call me and what a great evening! He's thirty-one, handsome, and a marvelous dancer. Surely was impressed with the Shoreham, the service majors on the General Staff get, and dancing on a tremendous terrace under a full moon beside a lighted pool to a darn good orchestra. Wanted to write Marjory to tell her she'd better review the bidding as he's certainly a charmer.

A.B. Have strong feeling that I'm about to try out my winter uniform, so most of my "civvies" are coming home. Will keep one or two outfits, but if I can get into a mobile unit I know my extensive (at this point) uniform collection will be more than adequate.

Chapter Four

Journal   St. George Hotel, Brooklyn, July 9, 1944

If there's one spot in the world I never expected to see, this is it! As the sum total of my acquaintanceship with Brooklyn is confined to the Dodgers and A Tree Grows In, the St. George is a far cry indeed. Very large hotel with tree-shaded streets around and lots of houses or apartments, a nice area. Can we be in Brooklyn Heights? Who knows?

The wonder is that Caroline and Ski are with me—hoorah! Our group assembled in the great concourse of Union Station this morning, sweating in our winter uniforms and struggling with all our gear. Way across the room we saw another large group of Red Cross girls, looking natty and cool in summer uniforms, obviously headed west. Felt really torn for a moment, one part rejoicing that I'm with Caroline and Ski, one part of me envying the westward-bound girls. So much for the can't-have-it-both-ways department. I can hear Dad's voice pointing that out.

Looks like we're about to tackle the Atlantic but wearing winter uniforms in a July heat wave, the rumors are already starting that our destination is Iceland—or is it Greenland? All we know so far is that a big bunch of us are on an upper floor of the hotel in a lot of large and small interconnecting rooms—wandering around in our slips. Already the card games and iron and curler borrowings have begun.

Am glad I didn't send this journal home with my excess clothes. See now it will be useful to remember where I was when. Security is so tight I can't write letters until we're aboard ship, and they will be censored on mailing when we reach wherever we're going. If censorship continues for the duration I'll have to use notepads as I'm already running out of space.

❧

Journal   *July 12, 1944*

So far, Brooklyn is full of surprises. Today it was the Brooklyn Navy Yard. Luckily it was a lovely sunny day with a brisk breeze off the water, so we didn't melt down in our uniforms during what they call Army processing. This was very serious business. Now we're all back at the hotel wandering around in our slips with newly acquired dog tags clanking around our necks. We're sworn to wearing them until we return home, unless

27

something befalls us and one is sent home as proof that we died trying. I am now officially No. 44244 on my dog tags, a number even I can remember, so am properly
grateful.

We also were issued battle helmets to be worn boarding ship, at drills on ship-
board, and while serving in combat areas. The one that finally fit me was obviously
secondhand as it had HORTON painted in big white letters across it. I couldn't help wondering what happened to good old Horton. And guess what Ski and Caroline started
calling me?

Then we had gas mask training after being fitted with the proper size mask. Mine
fits exceedingly well, everyone's does. The sergeant in charge saw to that, emphasizing
that the Axis powers are not known for following international war conventions and
now that the Allies are pressing them on all sides there's no telling what they'll try. He
drilled us on getting the masks out of their containers and fitted on, snugly and quickly,
then trooped us out to a Quonset hut that is the gas chamber. He gave us instructions
on entering the chamber at the signal, waiting inside until the doors are closed, then at
the signal again, donning the masks immediately as live gas is released. We were all
paying close attention at this point. When he finally ordered us to enter the chamber, a
cute girl from Fargo, North Dakota, standing nearest the entrance, called out, "Well,
I don't want to go back to Fargo now!" and led the way.

We piled in after her, the doors clanged shut, and another signal sounded as the
gas began to hiss. Our reactions were splendidly quick. The sergeant praised us all
when it was over, after he led us outside to remove our masks, then dismissed us for the
day. As we started to wander away lugging our new and unwieldy equipment, still feeling limp from the experience, he suddenly yelled, "Gas!" For one awful moment we
froze in place, then our reflexes took over and we had masks out and on in the next
split second.

How I wish I'd had my camera to capture our faces when he yelled—pure horror
on every face including, I'm sure, mine.

⚜

Journal   July 13, 1944

This waiting is beginning to get on everyone's nerves as we're all set to go, processing
all through yet we're confined to a few blocks of the hotel. There's so many of us wandering around this floor in our slips trying to beat the heat and taking turns in the showers, it's like being locked into a sorority chapter house. We've about worn out the card
decks and the magazines, everyone's hair is as clean as it's ever going to get, we're all
sick of hearts or bridge or double solitaire. We're ready.

Of course I don't really know what it's like to be locked into a sorority house as I
couldn't afford to join one in college. But this whole experience has been such fun
so far, almost like a paid vacation, that I've been feeling guilty at enjoying myself so
much. The biggest surprise to me has been the girls—almost without exception they're
outstanding, a cut above, and for some reason I hadn't expected that. There's not a
dull one in the bunch. They're educated and interesting and motivated and, of course,
because that's what the Red Cross seeks, generally outgoing and gregarious. Don't

think any of us signed up just to have a good time, we wanted to do something useful. The fun so far has been a wonderful bonus.

Phyllis, the gal from New Guinea duty, is our group leader and has scheduled a meeting tonight. Hope it means we're going somewhere soon.

Journal   2 AM(?), *July 14, 1944, New York Harbor*

Can't believe it, we're on our way! Or the next best thing, about to get under way.

Phyllis announced we were to sail tonight and our orders were to be in full winter uniform, all accessory equipment at hand, and ready to take off the minute the word came. From 6 PM until about midnight we waited in our rooms, packed and ready, sweating patiently. Finally the word passed and we geared up. I've never seen such a top-heavy bunch in my life—full winter uniform, musette bag (a canvas bag that's much more practical than a suitcase) hanging over one shoulder, gas mask over the other, our heavy black leather Red Cross shoulder purse jockeying for position between the two (no one's shoulders broad enough), a pistol belt around our waists to which is attached first aid kit and canteen. We carried one suitcase and our official raincoat, a Humphrey Bogart type trench coat we all agree is real classy. We had to wear helmets, so stuffed our ARC caps in our purses. The tiny girls, especially, looked like overloaded toadstools. It was hilarious.

Phyllis emphasized the need for absolute silence (to not advertise our departure, as ship sailings are classified top secret) and we filed through hotel corridors to the waiting transportation. This proved impossible as one after another we tried to pick up our suitcases and lost control of items draped on our shoulders. Finally we all got balanced enough to follow in single file through dark corridors and out onto a rusty fire escape, then down gritty, ladder-like stairs seven floors to a dark alley. At least three times we broke silence with colorful expressions as the person behind lost control and half fell into the person ahead. At first muffled chortles filled the air; the third time someone lost balance, a loud "Oh, Shit!" filled the night and we didn't bother to stifle our giggles.

When the fire escape steps stopped at alley level, there was about a four-foot jump off the bottom rung to the pavement, so more unloadings were inevitable before we piled into waiting buses. As the buses pulled out of the alley and turned into the street in front of the hotel, it was a real surprise to see a crowd of people gathered to watch us leave. They were waving, and one man called out, "God bless you girls!" I know we all appreciated it.

Once across the Brooklyn Bridge we headed for the docks, all of us staring hard through the blackness. Suddenly Ski, beside me, gasped, "Look, the Normandie!" as we passed a blackened ruin lying on her side at a pier. And then we all spotted the Queen Elizabeth looming up into the night sky just ahead and cheered when our bus turned into her dock. "Well," Caroline said, "no slow boat to China for us. Maybe we'll go first class!"

Sure enough, after we filed through thousands of troops marshaled and waiting in the shed area, we ended up in a first-class stateroom. Twelve of us to the cabin, which was chock full of standing bunks, three tiers of them. There was hardly room to move or turn or bend over, so we stowed some of our extra equipment in the lovely bathroom (complete with saltwater shower), just so we could maneuver at all.

I'm using my flashlight from my musette bag to scribble this from a prone position in my bunk—second tier. We are confined to quarters until the Queen sails and our portholes are blacked out. From the noises of chains rattling and shouts, I think it will be soon. Hope I can decipher this when the war's over. Know I'd better try to relax and sleep as it's way past midnight and we are to muster early.

⊗

Monday, July 17, 1944
Finally at sea!

Dearest Family,

Hello mates! Wish you could see my sea tan! Am permitted by the censors to say that I am aboard a luxury liner, and believe me this is no cattle boat. I am so grateful for my good luck and can't quite believe it. You would be proud of my sailing ability. We are several days out and you have no idea how fine my appetite is—unless you remember Dad's first tour to Alaska in 1939 and my seven meals daily then. There are no such trimmings now—two meals a day. We eat at 10:30 AM and 8:00 PM and the cuisine is excellent. Even to the extent of fish courses with both meals. I still am not crazy about corned beef cakes for breakfast but the fresh fruit after the meal I love. Linen tablecloths and napkins too!

Right now I'm on the sports deck—it's lovely and clear—the water the most gorgeous deep blue I've ever seen. This is where the Red Cross girls are allowed to gather and is known as the Bird Cage. Also all officers over the rank of major and there are lots of them. Today during battle station drill I sat in "my" porthole (only twelve others to share two portholes—this is the Army, Mr. Jones) and leaned out, wishing again I could use my cameras but they're prohibited. That wonderful blue water cut by the bow so that long trails of white foam sprayed out to the side and the GIs on the lower decks were leaning out and talking up at us and laughing, their faces tan against the ocean.

I think of you all daily. It was so hard not to write while we were waiting to go. Now that we're en route I feel as though my job has already started. We were told we'd be around men continually but it still comes as a surprise to be hiking to the dining salon and have twenty men trying to get you to say hello and talk. Most of our time is spent in the Officers Lounge (about two stories high), which obviously was the grand salon of the ship in peacetime. There the young officers, returning from leave or en route for the first time (and I keep thinking how soon so many of them will find themselves on battlefields) spend most of the hours between meals, as do all the women aboard. These guys are wonderful. Many Air Force and infantry officers, young and good-looking and fun—and all intent on enjoying every minute while they can.

Caroline and Ski and I have been trying for days to get a quiet bridge game started, but the minute we enter the lounge, guys gather around and we end up in a game (never more than twelve) of black jack, hearts, or rummy. With so many of us, mostly we sit in circles on the gorgeous carpet. The men play for money when they play alone but when even one girl plays with six or more guys, they're happy to play for strips of paper.

It's been fascinating for me to watch our Southern girls in action in this setting. Caroline, for instance. Reason I couldn't place her accent when we first met was that although she graduated from Wellesley, she spent most of her growing-up years in the South. Consider her as intelligent as any girl I've ever known—sharp and witty and funny. But when men are around, her accent and voice soften and utter femininity takes over. "Y'hear?" and "you-all" begin to pepper her conversation. In no time she has men practically standing on their heads. So do our other Southerners—they must be reared from birth to project sincere charm and admiration. Know Caroline is still grieving deeply for her husband, hoping against hope he'll turn up. We've had lots of teary times to talk about that. The last thing she wants at this point is another emotional attachment.

Late in the evening the singing begins. Somewhere in the great lounge a few start singing and the noise and laughter stop, cards are put down, and we all join in. First the nostalgic old favorites from home, and then the "retreads" (those servicemen returning to their units after leave) start English pub songs. "I've Got Sixpence" we all know, but soon the retreads started one I'd never heard, an outrageous one, *but* I had to smile even while my better self was censoring it, "Roll me over in the clover, roll me over, lay me down, and do it again. . . ." The first verse begins, "Oh, this is number one and the evening's just begun, roll me over, etc." The et ceteras only get worse.

Goosebump time for me started the night they began singing, "Bless 'em all . . . the long and the short and the tall . . . bless all the blondies and the brunettes . . . some we remember and some we forget . . . but nevertheless bless 'em all." For I looked around and there they "all" were. Last night my goosebumps broke out all over and my tear ducts got into action when an officer with a wonderful voice stood up and began, "God bless America, land that we love," the song Kate Smith has made into a cliché, sung so often lots of us supposedly sophisticated young adults tend to write it off as propaganda. But when he started singing, almost as though on command, every one of us in that great room rose and joined in. The huge ship zigged sharply and in a few seconds zagged, but on we sang, our veneer of sophistication wiped away as we joined in this reaffirmation of why we're all here. Moments like this make me more sure than ever that this is where I want to be. I am so glad to be a part of it all.

Days have passed and this letter is progressing by stolen snatches of time as every minute is taken. By now I have all games down pat and have learned to catch names rapidly, so when I enter the lounge I'm ready with a "Hi, Jack,

Dick, Cal, Pete, Texas, Raleigh. . . ." They all expect us to remember them and are doubly pleased if we associate them with their locales. Think I know at least sixty by name now.

Yesterday we were allowed below decks to visit the GIs, and were they ever appreciative, which surprised me. There are thousands of troops aboard, packed in to way below the water line and double- or triple-bunked. Each guy has a bunk to use for 8 hours then must vacate it for the next guy, so when it's his time to have the bunk he's supposed to sleep no matter what time it is. After an hour of close contact with the troops, talking and singing with them and having an occasional few minutes with a shy guy who proudly shows you pictures of his family, we were ordered back to our deck. I found myself with a foreign coin for luck and four bars of soap. Some of the retread GIs had been talking about the soap shortage overseas and were afraid I didn't have enough so they slipped the soap into my purse.

Tonight we went below again taking some records and a portable record player and oodles of GIs escorted us back to our deck. Caroline and I sat down with a circle of about fifteen men who had followed us to the "out-of-bounds" area limit, beyond which they can't pass. A few minutes later I glanced up and was amazed to see a huge number of guys crowding around our circle, enjoying the silly small talk and laughter as much as we were. The group grew so large an MP broke it up, but the guys were so happy it made me feel sad.

We assembled for muster this morning at the Bird Cage and it was so cold we had our trench coats on and the helmets and life preservers plus lots of other equipment. Wish you could have seen us, as we were a sight. It had suddenly turned so cold someone started us doing a Virginia Reel to keep warm.

Will mail this on landing and hope it passes the censor. Write often and soon.

All my love,
Roses

Journal   *July 19, 1944*

Almost sure we're close to landing. First few days we must have gone south away from regular shipping lanes, as suddenly warmth and my idea of Bermuda blue water was everywhere. For a short time flying fish leaped and at night phosphorescence sparkled the waters. The Queen is so fast she doesn't travel in convoy as she can outrun anything. To evade Nazi U-boats trying to angle in on her, she zigs then zags every so often as she speeds through the water. This huge, high ship going full throttle and heeling over just when you least expect it sometimes interrupts card games, meals, and quite a few stomachs. I feel great—maybe it's all in what you anticipate. One of our group turned pasty shortly after we got aboard and suffered premature mal de mer before the ship even sailed. We all had to reassure her that we were still in New York Harbor, but it was a blackout so we couldn't let her look out to prove it.

A ship's officer let it slip that U-boats have a real campaign on to zero in on the Queens (the Mary is also a troop carrier). Now that our Allied troops are pressing forward off the invasion beaches and the war gets more desperate for Hitler, it's crucial for his U-boats to hit these two ships that carry so many thousands of troops each crossing. And that's why we're taking an unusually circuitous route. Rumors pass around quickly and regularly when there's a submarine alert on. Yesterday it was so reassuring to spot, way off, the famous old Aquitania as we crossed paths in midocean, her four stacks silhouetted against the sky. And later to see a Navy patrol visible on the horizon. Eloise, a perky redhead from Westport, was particularly glad to spot the patrol as she found out while talking with another ship's officer that there are at least 14,000 troops aboard each trip, but only enough lifeboats and floats to take care of 5,000.

Know we're headed north these past days as it's much colder. Everyone is guessing Scotland. The cynics are reminding us we can still be sent back to Iceland after we land. I'm hoping for Scotland.

⚓︎

Journal   July 20, 1944

Word circulated earlier that the Queen had just passed the tip of Ireland and we were to land today. Ski and Caroline and I rushed on deck to check it out. Portia, a lovely girl we all enjoy, was smart enough to bring along a fine map. She seemed familiar with the area and even identified a giant rock (island?) as Ailsa Crag and said we were heading up the Firth of Clyde.

That set Ski off, her dark eyes sparkling. "Did I mention I'm related to Mary, Queen of Scots?"

"That's about the only part of your family we haven't explored in depth," I said, for the three of us had had nothing but time to talk together while waiting to sail. I think Caroline and I could walk through Ski's little hometown of Moosup in Connecticut and spot the family white colonial house, and probably recognize her mother and dad and two sisters and younger brother, she's told us so much about them. Not to mention the family business (which has something to do with J. P. Coates, makes thread, I think). But our kidding didn't faze her and she bubbled on about the wonderful Mary and her ancestors as we watched the brilliant green shores of Scotland pass in review. This started the rest of us, as we stood inhaling the damp and fresh air of the overcast morning, to recalling any Scottish connections we could dredge up. At which point I wished I'd paid more attention to our family stories about Grandpa Ankrom's ancestors leaving Holland to stay in Scotland a long while before sailing to the New World—well before the American Revolution. By the time we'd all added our two cents' worth we felt quite at home in our newly discovered ancestral land.

So we were all feeling very Scottish by the time the Liz, her camouflaged wavy gray paint job blending in perfectly with the morning, docked at Gourock, near Greenock (or vice versa?), which is near Glasgow. Before debarking we all assembled in the lounge to get orders. A handsome Royal Air Force major was the last official to speak to us and ended his graceful welcome by saying, almost as an afterthought,

"And oh, you'll find the buzz bombs a bit of a nuisance!" We all buzzed at this as we have no idea what he was talking about. We hope someone will enlighten us further.

Been jotting these notes down between many interruptions, all day and into the night. Right now we're crammed into a railway carriage on a troop train and pretty darn sure we're headed for London. Love these little compartments on the railroad cars, even with all our gear. We can just go out into the main aisle running along one side of the car to stand awhile, but at the longer stops we can open the outside compartment door and step right onto the station platform.

This long day seems to prove the GI theory that troop movements are a "hurry up and wait" proposition. Geared up and lined up, we waited a long time to offload from the Queen onto lighters—open barges—as the water's not deep enough here for the Queen to dock. Then waited in the train-loading area, then loaded onto the train and waited again before finally pulling out. A stop in Glasgow, then through tidy cultivated countryside—green fields dotted with whitewashed or stone houses, flaming red poppies, and black cows. There was a two-hour stop in Edinburgh, so some of us had a bite to eat in the railroad station dining room. (Ugh! Food terrible but atmosphere and tea great!) Afterwards we stood looking down Princes Street and up towards Edinburgh Castle, which was silhouetted against a murky lavender sky. The view was enchanting and we all have vowed to return when we can stay longer.

Night now and traveling south. There's scarcely elbow room to write. The light has gone, yet no one wants to pull down the blackout blinds so we can turn on a light. Phyllis just looked in to say we'll be stopping briefly somewhere in the Midlands so the British Red Cross ladies can serve us meat pies. She doesn't know what buzz bombs are either, or isn't saying.

Part Two

Somewhere in England

We landed in Britain knowing the D day Allied invasion forces under the command of General Dwight D. Eisenhower were off the beaches and pressing inland on the continent. This greatly raised morale in war-torn and war-worn England.

Our country had watched and applauded as England had stood alone against the German Blitzkrieg of May 1940. When Germany invaded Belgium, British forces were trapped at the seaport of Dunkirk. A magnificent rescue effort was mounted using all available craft from England, down to the smallest motorboat. Some 338,000 troops were safely evacuated, but all equipment and supplies were left behind.

Then Hitler ordered his Luftwaffe to start massive bombing of the beleaguered island in what came to be called the Battle of Britain. The Royal Air Force finally won back control of the skies over the English Channel, ending the firebombings and the threat of an immediate German invasion.

By July 1944 when we arrived, Britain faced Hitler's newest weapon, the V-1, a deadly unpiloted bomb, for which there was no early warning system to allow people to take cover. No one knew it would be followed within months by the V-2, a bigger rocket bomb that gave no warning at all. Nor did we know that the early advances by Allied Forces to liberate Paris and reach Germany would be challenged by a massive Nazi counterattack in December, the Battle of the Bulge.

Chapter Five

What a long haul the ride down was. Don't think any of us dozed more than a few minutes during the night, so we were pretty bleary-eyed when the train started through the outskirts of London past miles of closely packed brick houses with chimney pots all over the roofs. Just as we seemed to be approaching railroad yards and the sky began to lighten, the train suddenly jerked to a stop. We heard sirens and the British conductor poked his head into our compartment. "Put out all lights and cigarettes and draw your window blinds," he ordered. "We just got a buzz bomb alert."

Almost in unison we asked what that was. "It's the Nazi's latest weapon," he told us, pronouncing it "Nassi's." "A pilotless aircraft—mostly a bomb with wings and motor attached. Looks like a small airplane as it approaches. When the motor cuts off the bomb either falls straight down and explodes or drifts on awhile before falling to explode. You're all right as long as you can hear the motor. Get your helmets back on, girls, as the Nassi's send them over in swarms, any time of the day or night." And he rushed off to the next compartment.

As we buckled on our helmets we tried to joke about our timing in managing to arrive in England just when Hitler had decided to plaster it with his new weapon, but it didn't seem all that funny. Then we decided to open a window blind so we'd have a chance to see one if it came over. We sat waiting, listening hard in the darkness and silence. A girl in our compartment, a stranger to Caroline and Ski and me, couldn't stand the silence. She's been a pain since we boarded the train—the one in a hundred who makes me wonder how she ever got into the Red Cross as she's a know-it-all and generally obnoxious. After about three minutes of nothing happening, she huffed, "This is simply ridiculous! Just another example of British propaganda. Everyone knows the Blitz has been over for almost two . . ."

In mid-diatribe she, too, heard the unmistakable sound of a single motor, like a little airplane, and abruptly stopped talking. The motor sound grew louder. We were all staring out the window when the steady putt-putt materialized into the dark form of a little plane in the sky, headed right over the train, trailing a smoky, fiery tail. The sound seemed directly overhead when the motor abruptly cut off.

Waiting for the explosion was the longest few seconds of my life. For some dumb reason I started to count seconds, getting to about ten before a terrific explosion rocked our car. The bomb evidently landed well beyond the train but our ears rang from the force of the explosion as we sat numbly absorbing the shock. Our cynic didn't say another word as we all listened intently to the sounds of other motors in the distance, none of which, thank God, came as close as the first one. While we waited out the long alert I kept thinking about the big part luck plays when bombs are falling. It's a helpless feeling.

What a first day in London! At this point can't remember when I last slept. British army trucks were waiting outside Charing Cross Station to take us to our billets (my new word for the day!). The "Tommies" (that's what British soldiers are called) helped hoist us and our gear up into the open backs of the trucks and we bounced through London, by turns thrilled with glimpses of famous landmarks looking like postcards and appalled at the evidence of bomb damage everywhere. The rubble of the Blitz seems pretty well cleaned up, at least the rubble is stacked neatly even where gaping holes remain. But we passed some blocked-off areas where they were digging out fresh damage. And couldn't help noticing how shabby and worn the buildings—and the Londoners hurrying along—looked. Cracked and broken or shattered windows in all directions, no fresh paint or sparkle anywhere.

When our lorry (that's British for truck) pulled into Princes Gate, it was instantly reassuring as it's a residential area of picturesque Georgian town houses—a scene from an English novel. Our town house, taken over by the Red Cross as a billet for personnel, looked so proper and charming when we unloaded that it was a wonderful lift for all of us. Portia, the girl with the maps and obvious familiarity with England, says we're in Kensington, in London's posh West End area, so we're close to Hyde Park and Buckingham Palace. Some of us have ended up on the top floor on beds, or should I say, cots. The linen was laid out and we made up our own beds immediately. We're evidently in what was originally the conservatory as the ceiling is composed entirely of glass panes. This not only makes it draughty but we can hear—and probably see—the buzzers as they come over.

We've been told we have the weekend free to rest up before reporting in to Red Cross Headquarters on Grosvenor Square Monday morning. So I started to jot down details of the trip when Caroline and Ski and a few others interrupted me, insisting we take a look around and get our bearings.

It's very late now and Caroline and Ski and I have finally managed to grope our way back to Princes Gate, quite an achievement in the blackout. We got separated from the others and sat out another buzz bomb alert in a quiet cemetery nearby. We giggled at the appropriateness of our position as we perched on an old stone bench and discussed luck and fate, unable to turn on our flashlights. Oops! Excuse me, they're called torches here, which we discovered when we tried unsuccessfully to get new batteries for them at a little store.

Very cold in the conservatory now, have just put on my red wool topcoat liner over my pj's and intend to sleep well, despite the random intruders that seem to be coming over like arriving trains.

✦

Journal   *July 23, 1944*

Days and nights are starting to run together with no time to jot down impressions, which change so fast it's like looking into a kaleidoscope—they're exciting and terrifying and sad and inspiring and jumbled.

Sleep is something we mostly remember. That first night in London we were so tired we thought we'd sleep through anything. Buzz bombs were coming over, some too loud and low, but after checking to be sure my dog tags were in place and reasoning that there wasn't much point in taking cover under an Army cot, decided to leave my fate in the laps of the gods. I drifted off quickly only to be brought back to awareness by a few "Oh, my Gawds!" when a buzzer came over horribly close. Way after midnight one cut off right above us and we were all instantly awake. It exploded so nearby some of the glass panes in the conservatory roof shattered and pieces crashed down as the floor shook. So much for sleep. We tried to clean up the fragments—and Eloise took refuge behind a sofa in the corner of the room, using pillows as a buttress. With the first sign of daylight we went down to the kitchen to drink hot tea.

The British personnel told us Princes Gate is right in the middle of "Buzz Bomb Alley," the route the bombs aim for trying to hit the Palace and the West End, where most of government is located. The staff refuses to make up the beds on the top floor, just leaving fresh bedding piled on the beds when new people check in. Evidently a buzzer had landed during the night in the gardens behind Buckingham Palace and another has caused terrible damage and loss of life at the Horse Guards headquarters near the Palace.

So that morning they evacuated us to quarters on Baker Street. Couldn't remember Sherlock Holmes's address but was positive at first sight it can't be near where we are—a very bare and large room filled with tiers of bunks. Thought I was lucky to grab a lower one, with Ski and Caroline in the ones above me. The building superintendent told us a spotter on the roof sounds a bell if a V bomb (that's the buzz bomb's official name) is headed right at the building and that's our signal to take cover. This was reassuring and we all were so exhausted I think we fell asleep immediately.

When the warning bell rang late in the night, I only vaguely remember half falling out of my bunk. Think I intended to crawl under it. I got flat on the floor all right but wasn't quick enough to slide under the bunk before Caroline and Ski jumped down in the complete blackness, right on top of me. It was funny—but hurt so much I was laughing through tears. For a time we debated whether this would qualify me for a purple heart. Thank goodness they're both slender, but even so one hip is black and blue and I'm still sore in several places.

Tomorrow we go to a big Monday meeting and check into Headquarters, so maybe we'll find out where our assignments will be, whether we three will go into Clubmobile work together—the duty we'd prefer—how much we can write home, and all that. Hope we get more sleep tonight. So far, so good—the doodlebug noises are all in the distance.

～⚬⚭⚬～

July 24, 1944
8:45 PM

Dearest Family,

Greetings from London! Yes, it's all right for me to tell you where I am and it's lucky as otherwise I think I'd die if I couldn't let you know what a wonderful city this is. Despite the highly visible Blitz and bomb damage, it's almost past description. Caroline and Ski and I hope to swing a Clubmobile assignment together, which would be perfect. We enjoy each other's company so much we're sure we can laugh our way through almost any difficult situation. In fact we already have, through several. Phyllis, our group leader, has recommended us as a good working unit, so chances seem excellent.

Arriving on a weekend has given us a chance to squeeze in some sightseeing. First day started off with me taking movies of the changing of the guards at Buckingham Palace—wonderful, even if of course they weren't in dress uniform. Yesterday the three of us hired a cabbie to drive us around the city. In three hours I saw more famous places and enriched my experience probably more quickly than at any other time in my life. The cabbie was priceless—a little old and almost toothless, blue-eyed, white-haired Englishman who, with the help of American cigarettes and candy, proved to be most interested in our really seeing London. We all wished our families could have glimpsed us hanging out the windows of the tiny cab, gawking as it scooted down the left sides of streets past all the famous landmarks—even by Dickens's Old Curiosity Shop. Finally he took us to St. Paul's Cathedral, right in the middle of the area so badly Blitzed. It stands in a sea of devastation, the only building left in a wide swath—just like those pictures in *LIFE*. St. Paul's had just closed so the cabbie suggested we walk around the Blitzed area a bit while he had a cigarette.

As we were exploring, horrified at the implications of the rubble and ruin, the dearest little old man walked towards us from the cathedral steps and greeted us. He wore black leggings, a black frock coat, and a black rolled-brim, flat-crowned hat with a black rosette in front. He was delightful and so sweet and kind we wanted to hug him. Maybe it was his cherubic face with those rosy cheeks or his fatherly air. He inquired where we were from, then described in detail the miracle of St. Paul's survival during the terrible firestorms and bombing during the Blitz and his experiences during those awful hours. He said his house, a block away, is the only one in the area still standing.

Then he led us over to Amen Corner and into a tiny and wonderful group of houses built by Christopher Wren, where the young ministers live. We walked into the courtyard and he picked mulberries from the tree for us to eat and let us play with the big black cat who came over to greet us. After a simply lovely half hour he shook our hands and said, "I guess you're wondering who I am." We all certainly had been wondering as he had such a wonderful presence, but when he said, "I'm the Archdeacon of London," you can imagine how far open our mouths dropped. Then he added, "God bless you" with such sincerity we had tears in our eyes as we returned to the cab. Ski says he's about the third highest ranking member of the clergy in the Church of England, just under the Bishop and Archbishop of Canterbury. Whatever rank he holds, he was gracious and dear to us. Maybe I'm on my way to becoming a confirmed Episcopalian.

Our cabbie had a marvelous sense of humor. We were discussing the buzz bombs. They're called doodlebugs by Londoners and Bob Hope bombs by some, the cabbie explained, as in you just "Bob" down and "Hope" for the best.

The cabbie said Londoners preferred the Blitz if they had to be bombed, because when the sirens sounded everyone went to shelters and took cover until the raid was over and the all clear sounded. But these V bombs come any time of day or night, so everyone has to "carry on," as he put it, with work and duties. Each day here only increases my admiration for Londoners, as that's exactly what they're doing.

"The bombs are really not so bad some days," he added. "For instance, if you see one coming now overhead and hear the motor, you're all right." He paused (his timing was polished), "*And* if you see one overhead and don't hear the motor, you're all wrong!" Of course he laughed as hard as we did and probably more sincerely as one had just passed over.

We had a terribly funny [two-thirds of a page of the letter scissored off by the censor].

Tonight we're resting so think we'll have a spot of tea as it were and carry on to bed. (This English jargon is sure catching, no?) I love you all, I miss you all, but I'm completely happy, as I feel I'm where I should be. The only hard part is not being able to tell you everything, but censorship is fierce. Am trying desperately to get it all down, uncensored, in my journal—at least the important facts—and already imagine us sitting around the fire when I'm back home and filling you in on all the things I can't write now. But even making notes is hard—the girls keep saying, "Come on, Rosie, we've got to go." And you know me, I go, for I don't want to miss a single experience.

I love you all, I miss you all. Write soon and often—some of our mail should catch up with us soon.

Goodnight and best love from London,
Rosemary

P.S. London is full of adorable cats, dignified cats, playful cats, scroungy cats—all kinds of cats!

WESTERN UNION

JULY 25 PM 4:08

H.B. LANGHELDT
SACRAMENTO STREET
BERKELEY CALIFORNIA

HAPPY TO REPORT SAFE ARRIVAL ROSEMARY LANGHELDT
IN GREAT BRITAIN

NUTTAL ARC

Journal   *July 25, 1944*

Now we're getting down to brass tacks, as Mom says. Yesterday morning we reported in to American Red Cross Headquarters at 12 Grosvenor Square. The square has great dignity—a green park squared with rows of impressive buildings. Number 12 shares one side of the square with the big State Department building and U.S. Navy Headquarters. Number 12 is small by comparison, a very narrow converted town house, about six floors high, its stone facade and narrow front steps almost flush with the sidewalk. Our group is so large we couldn't all enter at once, so stood around outside rubbernecking while we waited our turns to report in.

Directly across the square, U.S. Army United Kingdom Headquarters takes up the whole block and a steady stream of Army vehicles and Army sedans painted olive drab, some flying little flags on their hoods, come and go. People in uniform outnumber by far the few diplomatic types in civilian clothes near the State Department doors. Right down the block from Red Cross Headquarters, the blackened ugly remains of a house half blown away by bombs is a stark interruption in the general neatness and order of the square. Most of the front of the house has been destroyed, but you can't help seeing remaining parts of each floor with remnants of wallpaper, furniture, and fireplaces (andirons still in place), even a tilted light fixture hanging crazily from a back wall. It's a jarring reminder of the way war shatters lives and an explanation of the urgency with which everyone rushes about.

As three Red Cross girls emerged from Headquarters, Caroline nudged me and whispered that the classy, smiling one was Kathleen Kennedy, Ambassador Joseph Kennedy's daughter. We all tried to gawk discreetly as the New Englanders among us, who are up on such things, reported that she is rumored to be engaged to a titled British officer. She looked great in her uniform.

The meeting of new arrivals yesterday afternoon answered lots of questions. It was held in a building somewhere in Kensington. An alert was on and we could hear buzz bombs coming over, so we weren't strolling through the parklike setting towards our meeting place—we were rushing. Suddenly an explosion literally rocked us and flames and smoke shot up into the air a few blocks away.

The meeting was held in a huge ballroom with hardwood floors and large-paned glass windows looking out on a park. We sat on folding chairs while we filled out official forms to be cabled home so our families will know their loved ones have arrived safely. The sound of doodlebugs and sirens was loud in the distance. Think we must be acquiring the proper British attitude and accepting the part luck plays. Why worry about events we can't possibly control?

Red Cross officials took turns briefing us, first our American Red Cross commissioner for Great Britain and Europe, Harvey Gibson. He's the one who dreamed up the idea of providing a mobile service—Red Cross girls driving buses or trucks converted into mobile clubs, to bring a touch of home and hot coffee and doughnuts, gum, records, and conversation to troops in isolated training spots. Or small villages, anywhere in the war zone for troops on duty yet not on leave or free to go to the cities where Red Cross Clubs are already well established. So he started the Clubmobile service, which has proved a great success with the troops and the most sought-out duty by the girls.

Then a lovely British lady, looking positively smashing in her uniform, welcomed us in a veddy top-drawer British accent. (I've already discovered there are many different accents here, and the accent determines which drawer you're put into.) She talked of the V bombs and assured us that many are shot down by ack-ack fire long before they reach London. The ones that make it through come at all hours, but, she reassured us, most buildings have a spotter on the roof during alerts ready to sound a bell if a bomb heads directly for the building. That is the only time it's necessary to take cover. If a bell should ring, we simply take cover under anything handy—get flat under a sturdy table, in a stairwell or whatever's nearby, as there's not time to go to a shelter. Otherwise, everyone carries on normally during alerts.

She paused to consult her notes a moment and a loud bell sounded. For the briefest instant we all froze in horror, then tried to get down to put our heads under our chairs—the only halfway solid objects around—and in the process upset most of the folding chairs. The bell rang loudly again. I've never seen a roomful of girls turn red quicker when we realized it was the phone on the official's desk ringing. Don't think any of us had heard an English phone ring, but we'll never forget the sound now. The room rocked with embarrassed laughter as we turned our chairs back up and scrambled around to gather up our instruction papers which had skidded every which way on the hardwood floors as we dove for cover. When the speaker had finished with her phone call, she turned and complimented us on our quick reactions, in the calmest of voices and with the briefest of smiles. Talk about aplomb, the British have it.

July 1, 1944

CLUBMOBILE DEPARTMENT
Room 31
12, Grosvenor Square, W.1.

INFORMATION FOR NEW CLUBMOBILE PERSONNEL

Driving Licence   British driving licence must be obtained from the Royal Automobile Club, Pall Mall, off Lower Regent Street, W.1. The price is 5£ and can be vouchered.

Battledress   Each girl should immediately order a battledress from Debenham and Freebody's, Wigmore Street, W.1. An authorisation for this must be obtained from Room 33, 13 Grosvenor Square.

Clubmobile Insignia   May be obtained from this office.

Rail Travel   All rail travel in this country is taken care of by a travel warrant. Authorisation for this is obtained at Headquarters, Room 41. This authorisation is changed at Headquarters for a warrant if there is time; if not, it is changed at the R.T.O. Office, at whichever station you commence your journey.

Cash Advance   When checking your financial status at the Paymaster's Office, Princes Gate, please mention if you need an advance to cover your expenses for the time being, as this can be handled on the spot.

Vouchers   Receipts for laundry and lodging should be attached to your vouchers; otherwise these items will not be reimbursed. If you are staying at a Red Cross Staff House no receipts are necessary.

Fleece-Lined Boots   These boots can be obtained from the Q. M. Stores, and vouchered in if accompanied by a receipt. An authorisation slip to purchase these boots is obtained from this office.

Immunisation Slip   Please have copy of your immunisation slip made and hand to the Department. This can be copied at the Dispensary, Mount Street, W.1.

Cheques   Cheques can be cashed to Barclay's Bank (American Branch) North Audley Street, corner of Oxford Street, W.1.

Ration Books   Be sure you have both ration book and PX card.

❧❧❧

July 29, 1944

V-MAIL

(Form letter)

Dear _____ Family,

   <u>PLEASE ADDRESS ME AS SHOWN BELOW UNTIL OTHERWISE</u>
<u>ADVISED</u>

<u>Rosemary   Langheldt   ARC #44244</u>

CLUBMOBILE　　　　AMERICAN RED CROSS

A.P.O NO.　　887,　%POSTMASTER, NEW YORK, NEW YORK

THE above COMPLETE ADDRESS should be placed on ALL MAIL sent to me. MY CODE CABLE ADDRESS IS　AMCROSS　AM

Normal signature　*Rosemary Langheldt*

SPACE BELOW FOR MESSAGE

Letter follows—really! Well and happy—Best love, Roses

July 28, 1944

Dearest ones,

Hectic these past few days—no time to write as Ski, Caroline, and I were accepted for Clubmobile Monday and have been scrambling around London picking up all the extra equipment we need. It's a wonderful way to learn our way about this city. To Debenham and Freebodys, my deahs, to order our battle dress (English for working clothes). On Wigmore Street no less—somehow Dickens and Thackeray keep popping into my head as we tootle about London. We all love the outfits—Eisenhower type battle jackets (short and belted at waist with deep pockets on the front of the jacket) with slacks in the same shade of RAF blue and a jaunty billed cap. The car coat is also RAF blue, of even heavier wool, three-quarter length and lined with bright red. Should keep us warm in the worst conditions.

They seem to be rushing us through fast. Lots of the early Clubmobile girls who came over in '42 and worked with our first troops in Ireland are slated to go to Zone 5 as conditions allow. Zone 5 is the official term for cross channel to France and beyond. So replacements are needed in Great Britain. Scads of details to attend to quickly—British driving licenses, immunization slips, fleece-lined boots, rail travel warrants (which allow us to board any train) and (Ugh!) a supply of vouchers so we can report our out-of-pocket expenses for reimbursement. Filling in a voucher in pounds, shillings, and pence (a three-column deal) takes five times as long as it would to do in dollars and cents. Stray thought for the day: Did you know a guinea equals 1 pound plus 1 shilling? Imagine how that complicates totaling the columns!

We've moved several times since arriving. As soon as we were assigned to Clubmobile we gathered our gear again and went to a special club run by a British Mrs. Belville, who is most charming and (scuttlebutt has it) spends oodles of her money on Clubmobilers, her special project. This residence is her town house and she's getting ready one of her country homes for Clubmobilers to recuperate in during time off as she thinks Clubmobilers work much harder, at least physically, than other workers. She sure impressed us, the night we moved in, with a dinner of *partridge*, vegetables, and ice cream filled with fresh strawberries (unheard of in England these days). Her town house has the only electric freezer around and, most wonderful, all the rooms are warm enough to be comfortable. Most buildings here, we're discovering fast, are warmed solely with little coal fireplaces, or gas-metered ones, and don't begin to remove the chill and dampness of London nights.

Every moment is exciting, sometimes marvelous, and I wish censorship didn't forbid writing about important happenings. I can tell you about the fun side though. One afternoon Phyllis, our group leader, took the three of us to tea at Claridges—high tea as it were, pip! pip! We returned for dinner one night it was so elegant. Yes, even in wartime the doormen wear livery and top hats. Food at top-drawer places like Claridges is served with such style and service it's a delightful experience no matter how limited the menu. Generally, food so far has been fair to dreadful. At the Grosvenor House Officers Mess, close to Red Cross HQ, we eat filling meals for two shillings (40 cents). The mess takes up the entire lower floor of the hotel and is always crowded. So many are served daily it's called "Willow Run" as service is cafeteria style and almost like an assembly line. You get a well-balanced meal, but I'd give a month's pay for a quart of real milk and a real egg instead of powdered ones. Which shows how important food becomes when the usual bite we grab is mediocre to terrible.

Then there's our adventures in London at night. Very early in our stay here, Caroline and Ski and I were groping our way in the blackout along Park Lane after dinner at the Grosvenor House—wondering how to find our way back to our billet. Suddenly we almost bumped into three Air Force officers coming towards us through the murk and Caroline shrieked, "Frosty!" and threw her arms around the tall blond one. Talk about old home week! Hadn't seen each other since college days in North Carolina and they were delighted. Nothing would do but that we join them to celebrate their three-day pass from the air-field.

First we had to go back to their rooms near Hyde Park Gate to see if their other buddy wanted to join us. Gear was strewn all over the little sitting room and we started to clear places to sit down while Frosty went into a bedroom to check on old buddy No. 4. He was out again before we could sit down. "He's catching up on sack time," Frosty said. "We'll go on."

At which point a very disheveled and bleary-eyed buddy emerged from the bedroom, followed by a woman—not dressed either and also in general disarray. Dad, she reminded me of those flashy women who waited on the pier in San Francisco for the Navy ships to dock, when I was small and you took us to go aboard a battleship. Remember, you called them sea gulls, which made Mother mad. She said, "Harry!" in that certain tone and you changed the subject abruptly.

So will I. The three of us who think we're so sophisticated suddenly felt like innocents abroad and gratefully followed Frosty out of the room to let the Air Force, minus Buddy No. 4 and his friend, show us the wonders of wartime London at night. The boys knew two spots very well—Manetta's and The Paradise.

Think smoky, crowded, small band–type clubs in San Francisco with everyone shouting to be heard and you have the idea. Add frequent sirens piercing the din and everyone ignoring them completely. There's almost a desperate sense of urgency in the gaiety, but somehow the smoky air's electric with a vibrant sense of the joy of being alive.

Caroline and Frosty were having a wonderful time catching up on the years since college, while Ski and I had our hands full trying to keep the two buddies in line. It was the second day of a three-day pass—in their case, binge—and the politest way I can put it is that they were completely uninhibited in their efforts to sample all the brews, spirits, and pleasures of London in the hours they had left. Ski and I slowly sipped our mild Pimms Cups (an English drink that is mostly fruit and cucumbers and punch with a touch of gin), but it was soon obvious they didn't think we had a properly festive attitude. We finally managed to get them on the postage stamp dance floor, but it was hard to dance with them hanging all over us and moving with the agility of wet cement. It took a major effort just to weave them back to our table.

Ski was signaling me frantically with those dark snapping eyes and nodding her head towards the door. The obvious question in our minds was how we could slip away without spoiling Caroline's fun. Suddenly someone came up behind our table and pulled my cap off my head. "Aren't you *Rosemary?*" he asked.

I turned and there stood a grinning and good-looking Navy j.g. Despite the smoky atmosphere and dim lights I recognized Johnny E., a guy I had a blind date with my senior year at Cal. Johnny and I had a lousy time, so dismal I recall we switched partners while dancing and hadn't seen each other since, nor wanted to. But I've never been happier to see someone from home in my life. Know he was too, for he brought over two other Navy officers who serve with him on the landing ships (LSTs and LCIs) that work the Normandy beaches. We all had a great time. Bonus of the evening was that Johnny's really learned to dance since our blind date. He's called several times since and I'm sorry I've always missed his calls. Oh! Last time Ski and I noticed the two Air Force types they were headed for Piccadilly Circus and some real action.

Gotta close or it will be time to get up. Don't worry, I feel wonderful despite the short nights as our pace helps us sleep twice as hard in the hours available. No mail has caught up with us yet—we long for the day.

All my love,
Roses

P.S. Forgot to mention we took the London Underground home from the night-club as there were no cabs available. I wish you could have seen the entire families trying to sleep down in that hot, smelly, noisy Tube as the trains rolled through. I felt especially sorry for the children crowded into the tiered bunks. Will never forget the smudged face of one little girl, her arms around a shabby teddy bear. Her father's arm was all that kept her from falling off the edge of the bunk. But she was sound asleep.

Caroline ready to be evacuated from Princes Gate, Kensington, July 1944.

July 30, 1944

Dearest ones,

Ski and I have had a marvelous Sunday together. We were sad that Caroline has been sent off on her first assignment, so decided to do the Tower of London. Two British lieutenants (as they say, "leftenants") trailed along with us through the chapel where royalty was beheaded, to the executioner's block, up in the Bloody Tower and St. John's Chapel and all the historic spots we've read about all our lives. A doodlebug just missed the Tower area twenty minutes earlier and knocked out much of the old leaded panes of glass from a window, so I have a tiny one as a souvenir.

The lieutenants suggested we might like to walk with them to St. Paul's, and of course ended up spending the afternoon with us. After studying St. Paul's they suggested they accompany us to Westminster Abbey, where Ski and I planned to attend evening services. "It's just a nice stroll," the blond one assured us, for by then our feet were beginning to hurt. Didn't feel a bit over eight miles as we wandered along the Victoria Embankment beside the Thames and past the famous bridges. It was not the safest walk we've ever taken, but we were determined to see more of London before leaving.

We arrived a little early for the services and managed to shake the lieutenants, grateful that we could sit down awhile. We had about forty minutes alone savoring the beauty of the Abbey and the souls of England's great departed buried there. Two close buzz bombs went over, the second actually rattled the windows (and incidentally our teeth), but as I reminded Ski, we were in awfully good company even if the Abbey fell in. It's not everyone can be buried with Shakespeare, Thomas Hardy, and the rulers of England. (I'm labeling this "joke" for Mother!) And yes, Mom, the organ was magnificent and the service simple and lovely.

Goodnight everyone.

All my love,
Roses

Journal   *July 30, 1944*

Just got word that I am to go off on my first assignment tomorrow—alone. Ski's supposed to follow in a few days, Headquarters says, but Caroline's already working in Liverpool so who knows what will happen. Must keep reminding myself not to count on continuing relationships in wartime, as hard as that is proving to be. Common sense tells me I shouldn't expect the Red Cross to make special arrangements for each of us, but a congenial pal or two around sure is a morale booster. Especially when we can share so little with our families because of censorship.

On the bright side we've found the Red Cross gives us credit for intelligence and being able to cope. So tomorrow I venture forth on my own and am expected to make my way and handle any situation that arises as I judge best. This I look forward to. After all, they didn't allow us to join until we were old enough to be deemed mature. Of all the hundreds of Red Cross personnel I've gotten to know so far, only a few seem to have slipped through the cracks of the qualifications. So I guess it's "¡siempre adelante!" as Don Quixote said bravely—always onward, Rosie!

July 31, 1944

Dearest Family,

Riding the rails again, Dad, finally en route to my first assignment—hoorah! Ski is supposed to join me in a few days and Caroline to be transferred to our group from the other side of England soon. We're sure hoping it works out that way.

Feeling very cosmopolitan these past hours as I've just left London in full battle dress complete with helmet and gear. When my cab pulled up to Waterloo Station I managed to tip the cabbie and the baggage porter the correct amounts in English money without fumbling or hesitation. What a difference a week or so makes! As I passed the great steaming engine I even remembered to have my travel warrant in hand and find a first-class carriage. Warrants are good for any seat in any class available and I selected a window seat. A British colonel opposite jumped up to put my Val-Pak away and a tweedy type gentleman (resembling a tired Anthony Eden) just loaned me his newspaper and this lovely train is rolling through lovely green pastoral countryside. *How* I wish you were with me. You really are, I know, in spirit, so I'm enjoying everything fivefold, for all of us.

Must at least scan the newspaper which headlines that the Allies are advancing well. Sure hope so. Keep writing, mail's bound to catch up with me eventually.

All my love,
Rosie (going to work in her new working clothes).

P.S. Train just stopped and a tiny child getting off with her mother at this first station peeked into our compartment and trebled, "Cheerio!" Her first words, no doubt.

✦

Chapter Six

Monday, August 7, 1944
10:15 PM

Dearest Family,

It's lucky you're understanding as I realize it's been a week since I've written. Excuse the Baltimore & Ohio stationery—I'll probably be using toilet paper before I finish as I made a serious calculation error in packing. Sis asked me in a letter (*Yes!* Mail is finally beginning to catch up with me) how I liked living out of a footlocker. Marty, I'd feel positively luxurious if I had my footlocker to live out of. Came across with musette bag and the Val-Pak—"lightly enough packed to be carried by owner" when the owner is also lugging all the rest of the gear I've told you about. I have no idea when my footlocker and duffle bag will arrive. When they do I will have some stationery and more than three blouses.

Several letters have gotten through, from the Bobs, Albert, other friends, and one from Mom and Dad and two from Sis. It's like a lifeline from home.

I'm not allowed to say where I am but it's what Clubmobilers call ranging— working with troops de- or embarking for the continent. I love it here and the work is wonderful as I feel useful. The hours are long and irregular—when the troops are on the docks we are there, day or night. On night of arrival and after settling into Room 15 of an old High Street hotel (originally a coaching house in the sixteenth century), I had a superb twelve hours of uninterrupted sleep. Blissfully calm. No buzz bombs or sirens. Peace, on a good, firm mattress. Have been working almost round the clock much of the time since.

Ski has arrived to fill the other bed in Room 15 and we've mastered driving on the left side of the street in a British Hillman, a tiny pickup not big enough to be called a station wagon. I confess, though, that the first corner I turned I veered to the right side but luckily didn't get clobbered. The Hillman has four gears and no energy and now we're driving British Bedfords, which are the large Clubmobiles. They are high, squarish, two-ton jobs, (like a big old moving van) and have side panels that lift up while we serve hot coffee and fresh hot dough- nuts to the troops.

Ski and I thought that once we mastered the right-hand drive everything would be easy but had not figured on a few other factors: the wonderful if undecipherable hand signals of a Bobby directing traffic, the cyclists, or the pedestrians. Most people cycle to work and cyclists are everywhere, that is everywhere but on the sidewalk. Clusters of them pedal blithely down the right or wrong side or, preferably, the center of the road paying no attention at all to vehicles. Learning to dodge them while weaving in and out of docks, sheds, equipment, cranes, and piers to locate the correct "Hard" (a cemented or bricked strip of beachfront used for loading LSTs, which are landing ships that pull right up on the beaches) is really an adventure. Learning to do this while managing to smile and wave back to all the GIs and tankmen and infantry and Navy (and believe me, there are thousands) is a fine art we're still working on. Give us a week or two.

Besides the dock area work, we are often called out into this beautiful and historic countryside to nearby hospitals, as well as servicing the hospital ships when they pull in and working the hospital trains. One day a Marine photographer making documentary movies took several shots of me—so keep an eye out when you're watching newsreels at the movies.

I steeled myself the first time we served the wounded as they're just one to three days from the battlefield. They're brought cross-channel as quickly as possible to be washed, shaved, wounds cleaned, then sent on for long-term care. So they arrive in field dressings sometimes three days old. It amazed me that they're generally so good-natured, appreciative, and hungry. Still, it's terrible to glance down and see a boy with two stumps instead of legs, or a horribly burned face or blood seeping through heavy field bandages, while you're also inhaling nauseous whiffs of gangrene. You want to stop breathing—it's an odor I'll never forget—but of course you don't, you keep smiling.

Maybe that's why it was so wonderful to hear jokes coming from a boy with his head in my lap (this was on a hospital train) as I helped him drink coffee through a straw and kidded him about his curly hair, especially as his whole body was in a temporary cast and his head bandaged. It's a real joy to serve the ambulatory cases, the walking wounded. They keep us busy with wisecracks and autographing their casts. The hospital trains are great—tiered bunks and a radio broadcasting popular music through the cars.

Our hours get longer as we work when needed, which is certain to be all day and some nights. But the payoff for us is to see the change in a horde of troops, crowded into loading sheds larger than a football field or massed on a cold pier, when we pull in the Clubmobile, music blaring from our record player. Already I know Tommy Dorsey's "Marie" and Glenn Miller's "In the Mood" forward, backward, and sideways. The guys cheer and come running and for however long it takes to serve them before they're ordered to board ship, they can forget they're on the way to fight. First they stuff themselves, then they laugh and talk and argue about the weather in California versus Illinois or Keokuk or wherever. They try to give us everything imaginable: the boys leaving—lipsticks, division patches, chewing gum, even field jackets; the returning wounded—francs, rings made from francs, perfume. It's hard to refuse, but we try to, gracefully.

We keep a stack of records playing in the Clubmobile and before they embark they dance and jitterbug with each other and with us, if we're through serving and aren't off talking with the shy ones. Often a GI will pull me aside to show snaps of his new wife or baby and talk about his home town. When the order comes to load ship, we put marches on the record player and, if we don't have to rush off, line up on the pier to cheer them off. Then it's on to the next loading or marshaling area.

Today, driving back through the countryside from a hospital, we stopped to feed a long line of armored troops, their tanks and equipment almost blocking the road as they waited to come into the port to load. They'd been there for hours with no chance even to use the powdered coffee in their K rations. K rations are field rations that come in a box that looks like a pound box of butter. They contain a small can of Spam or cheese, a few crackers, cookies or a candy, a few cigarettes, and a powdered beverage. Ski and I stopped to use up the rest of our supplies and our coffee. The doughnuts were a big hit. As we were climbing back into the Clubmobile to drive off, a GI who had just shown me through his tank stuck out a closed fist and dropped something into my hand, warning me not to tell the other guys, as they'd kid him. It was a cheap lipstick he's brought from Georgia, undoubtedly intended for a French girl, but I considered the gift a compliment anyway—whether to the Red Cross or to me, I'm not sure.

The other morning I had to serve about 3,000 men on my own. We have to split up when too many loadings are going on at once. It was about 10:30 and they'd eaten no breakfast although they had been at the marshaling area since 5:30 AM. A GI with his mouth loaded with doughnuts said, "Florence Nightingale had nothing on you, California!"

"Except she's dead!" I retorted, and the guys loved it.

There's an art to avoiding a date and Ski and I are having to work at it. After socializing with literally thousands of men on duty, we anticipate returning to our room to rest and recharge our batteries. But a few nights ago when we were leaving the old dock area around midnight following a big troopship loading, a Navy jeep cut in front of us and flagged us down.

"What now!" Ski groaned, but it was only two Navy lieutenants wanting us to come aboard their LST for something to eat. Their timing was perfect as we had missed dinner completely, skipped lunch, *and* as great as hot doughnuts are to the troops, we have reached the stage of not being able to look one in the face.

We told them we were exhausted and didn't want to party and, bless them, they said they just wanted to feed us and talk awhile. The mention of steak and ice cream did it and we followed them over to the LST. They kept their word and it was wonderful. A mess steward served us in the quiet wardroom, and Ski and I not only wolfed down *T-bones* and fudge sundaes, we loved the quiet chat with the two officers. Always have been partial to the Navy—but how they manage to get this kind of food when everyone else eats so poorly is a mystery.

The pleasure of sitting, the four of us, and quietly sharing our experiences was a real tonic.

We dodge almost all social invitations, but last Saturday night Polly, our Red Cross captain here (about to go to the continent so she had lots of things to do before leaving), asked Ski and me to represent the Red Cross at a dinner the Navy staff was giving. We had no choice. We wore our Class A uniforms and heels and two Navy lieutenants picked us up to escort us to the party at the Navy hotel, very near ours. At the big table were four lieutenants and j.g.s, a full captain and a Commander Aldrich, Navy Commandant of the Port. There were also several attractive British WAAFs or WRENs (I haven't quite sorted out the uniforms of the British women's service groups yet) as dates for the other officers. I was seated on the left of the Navy commander and my escort, a quiet lieutenant nicknamed Hug, was on my left.

The Navy commander was a tall, handsome knockout of a man—chiseled features and urbane manners and bearing. Most attractive. On his right was a very young and lovely WREN, probably all of nineteen, who started to bemoan the fact that she would be old before her service was over and that the war was ruining her life. I opened my big mouth to disagree and say her life was just beginning and her war experiences would make her a more interesting woman. Threw in, I'm afraid, that I agreed with the French who say a woman doesn't start to peak until forty—or at least that was what I was hoping for.

"Look at all the great actresses!" I added, to clinch it.

At this point the Navy commander jumped in to agree and started talking of his wife. Said he'd only seen her twice in the past ten months but hoped to soon as she was going to France to entertain the troops. In a sudden flash I realized he must be the New York Richard Aldrich married to my favorite (as you well know) stage actress, Gertrude Lawrence. I was about to ask him when Hug grabbed me and said it was our dance. He warned me that the Navy personnel never discuss the commander's wife as they don't think he wants it to be known. But the minute we returned to the table the commander asked me if by any chance I had seen his wife, Gertrude Lawrence, in the San Francisco Light Opera series last season. What a pleasure it was to report that I had seen three performances of *Lady in the Dark* and I'd had the privilege of meeting her when she'd been shopping in the store. This so delighted him that he talked of Gertie and other great actresses for most of the evening. Hug was impressed.

Think I did well by the Red Cross, as before we were through, the commander had opened his Navy Officers Mess to all ARC personnel from this time forward. A great blessing since our hours are so irregular we have trouble making meals during our hotel's service hours or even the Army mess hours.

Coincidence of the week—seeing Dinah Shore in *Up in Arms* and then embarking for France within four hours of each other. Ski and I had been to a matinee at the movie theater on High Street, between ship loadings, then rushed down to serve the next ship only to find Dinah Shore among the "loadees," looking great in army fatigues, complete with helmet.

I'm tired—so goodnight now. I love you all very much,

Roses

P.S. Most prevalent saying in England comes after an Englishman gives you long and completely confusing instructions on how to get somewhere, then adds, "You cawn't miss it, rawly!"

P.P.S. Ski and I have hung an artist's map of London over our little mantel. We have a gas fireplace we drop sixpences into to take the chill off. We're still working on getting Caroline here—hope to soon.

⚜

Journal   *August 9, 1944*

Have discovered these past days that this is without doubt the simplest work I've ever done, yet the most demanding physically. And the most satisfying. Am so happy to find this out, feel like shouting. Any doubts I had about leaving a career job to drive trucks and give out doughnuts and coffee and conversation disappeared the first twenty-four hours here. I'm finding I love every part of it—the physical exercise and effort (the old Girl Scout in me?), handling the big trucks, heaving the huge coffee urns around and the stacked trays of doughnuts, scrubbing the Clubmobiles out when we're finally through for the day, or night, and arriving back in the room grease-soaked and smelling of doughnuts and coffee. Tired to the bone—but satisfied.

Just finished at least notes to all the friends who have been so good about writing and my conscience feels a little better. The ones bored on patrol duty in the Pacific, especially, are worried about the wolves in the ETO and don't understand why they haven't heard. I told everyone not to worry, I'm well and happy but there aren't enough hours in the day to get our work done, grab a bite to eat and a few hours of sleep—let alone date. So I plan to concentrate on work, keep in touch with my family in what time I can find, and we'll probably have to wait until the war's over to catch up. And that's the truth. I have absolutely no intention of getting emotionally involved overseas where everything's in a constant state of flux. Sure, we meet and work with hundreds, no thousands, of attractive men, but only for a few hours, a few days at most. Didn't add that by the time we've spent sixteen hours feeding thousands of men, they all begin to look and sound alike and our big desire is a bit of solitude.

Polly just poked her head in our room—there's a loading of replacement troops she just discovered. So it's back to the docks. . . .

⚜

August 14, 1944
9:15 PM

Dearest Family,

Not writing on toilet paper yet, but the next best thing. Excuse it please!

The mail is picking up as I've heard from both branches of the family and am glad you got my safe-arrival cable. Sorry my letters aren't coming through well but at least now you know I'm in England.

Marty, your letters are getting through and I can't tell you how much they mean. We Red Crossers have British ration cards so can eat at the hotel. The few times a week we're free to breakfast here we do so as the tables are set with white cloths, the waitresses wear black with white aprons and caps, and wonderful tea is brewed in a proper pot, with tea cosy to keep it warm. The toast comes in a silver toast rack accompanied by a small pot of marmalade. Thick old-fashioned porridge is also available. Breakfast is the one British meal not ruined by war shortages, although we only ordered sausages once as they taste as though they're 90 percent sawdust or pencil shavings and 10 percent sausage. We're allotted two eggs a month on our ration cards but so far haven't seen one. The real reason we enjoy breakfasting here is because the night mail from London has just arrived, and mail from home makes anything taste marvelous.

Don't think I've told you about our hotel. It's so typically English am sure the censor can't object. (Censor, please note.) It's two blocks up from the docks on High Street (and there are High Streets in every English town or city, Mr. Censor). One side of the street was bombed out during Hitler's Baedeker air raids when he was trying to obliterate all the historic sites of England, and is rubble. But our side is fairly intact, although the church on the water side of the hotel is a stone skeleton—a few arches, half the tower, and only heaps of debris remaining. Our hotel began as a coaching house centuries ago. Tall, thick, wooden coach doors dominate the middle of the stone, brick, and bay-windowed facade. And yes, a little man opens the tall coach doors early each morning and closes them promptly at midnight, after which time you have to ring an ancient bell so he can admit you into the cobbled mews (a stabling-coaching area now used for a parking area). Our Clubmobiles barely clear the entry.

To the right of the entry is a door to the public bar. That's where sailors of all nations drop in to drink as they wander up from the docks, and then sing bawdy songs loudly late at night on their way back to their ships. The day I arrived a little boy was scrubbing the hotel entrance doormat and, just inside, a gray-haired old woman on hands and knees was polishing the brass rods that hold down the carpeted stairway to the second floor. I again marveled at the British keeping up appearances no matter what. At first glance the hotel is "olde Englande," with flowered carpets, polished brass, dark paneling, Victorian wallpaper, and fireplaces in the lobby and side lounges. Opposite the stairway is a small-paned glass enclosure where another old lady checked me in and gave me a key to Room 15.

During the day British women come to take tea near the bay windows looking out on High Street, but at night, we've already discovered, the hotel is a favorite lodging and watering spot of old merchant mariners. Sitting on the worn leather sofas or standing backed up to the fireplace, whiskey in hand, ruddy or leathery and bearded faces beaming, tarnished gold braid reflecting in the firelight, they ogle every female entering the lobby. So it's not easy for us to make it past the stares and sometimes shouted invitations of the old sea dogs.

Once safely up the stairs, we head for our room on the second floor, past the dining room, sharp turn right and halfway down the narrow hall. As this inn-become-hotel has evolved over many centuries, the floors are all slightly out of plumb—up three steps or down two. Our room overlooking the mews contains two single beds, two wardrobes for our clothes, and a shared dresser. A washbowl on legs stands in one corner, the most important fixture in the room, as we are permitted a tub bath only every five days, using no more than five inches of water. Other days we strip down on returning from duty to do complete bowl baths (didn't you used to call them French baths, Mom?), sometimes going through three bowlsful trying to get the greasy doughnut-coffee odor off our bodies. Ski uses a heavy fragrance I was given, Tabu, to finish up. I still have plenty of Elizabeth Arden.

The toilets, complete with pull chains, are a row of separate cubicles and a big claw-footed bathtub occupies a cold linoleum-floored room just past the row of toilets. These essentials to our well-being are back up the hall, turn left, down two steps, and straight ahead. This is where we bathe every fifth day—*if* we count the days correctly and *if* there's any hot water left when we get through working. Our first two tries at a bath yielded one tub of tepid water and one of ice cold. Talk about a disappointment—evidently the sea captains beat us to the hot water.

When our footlockers come we'll be able to put one at the foot of each bed to lean against while we drop sixpences into the gas fireplace meter to enjoy 30 minutes of heat and take the chill off our room at night.

Am enclosing snapshots of Ski and me in battle dress so you can see how we look while working. Ski and I usually crew the *Wyoming*, Dad (your home state!) although some days it's the *Arizona*. Sitting at the wheel in the front cab gives us a nice feeling of power, as the Bedford completely dominates most of the narrow streets and roads we travel on daily. The light gray paint on the Clubmobiles is emblazoned with American Red Cross painted in red on the sides. You'll notice too the side panel which swings up, through which we serve the troops, and see how the back end has an entrance so the guys can come in and help us. We both love the Bedfords even if they are supposed to be the hardest trucks to handle. They remind me of a Bekins moving van jazzed up for war duty.

The big plus in working in such a big loading area is that we don't have to make our own doughnuts, as the girls working airfields and small troop detachments do. We serve so many thousands the Red Cross set up a doughnut kitchen run by a British couple who were bombed out of their London home. A Mr. and Mrs. Harris—or as they say cheerfully, "We're the 'arrises!" We back up to the kitchen behind the Army mess (a converted restaurant just up High Street), cram our truck with trays of hot doughnuts and racks of extra cups, drive to one dock where the Red Cross has set up a coffee kitchen manned by an Army detail, cram in 40-gallon containers of coffee, and rush off to our dates with the troops.

Rosie and Ski with
Clubmobile *Arizona*,
Southampton, August 1944.

Still working on getting Caroline here. Have called her several times and Headquarters says she may be coming soon.

Have to catch up on sleep tonight. All my love from Room 15,

Roses

P.S. Hope you can read my writing. I'm squinting from the effort of writing on this terrible paper with a 20-watt globe. We have a total of three lights in the room, all dim.

⚜

Journal   *August 27, 1944*

Having a roommate for the first time in my life is turning out to be a remarkable expe-rience—fun, and fascinating in the oddest ways. Ski and I couldn't be more different. She gets her tea hot over everything, I come to a boil rarely, yet we enjoy each other's company immensely. Perhaps because we are so different?

Intense is the word for her. Intense about everything with firm convictions on any subject—the war, politics, the weather, her hair, my hair, the crew, you name it. She fumes on spotting three white hairs in her head with the same fervor with which she fumes about Hitler. (Or Roosevelt—she doesn't much like him either.) "To be turning white at twenty-five!" she moans, her throaty voice frantic with worry. "But Ski," say

I, *"you've told me your Mother turned white early and is a very handsome woman. A white streak through your black hair would be attractive anyway, and at the rate of three hairs a year it's not likely to happen soon."* And so we laugh and go on to the next crisis.

She even drives intensely and attacks any problem or relationship the same way. There's simply no halfway about her, she doesn't know the meaning of the phrase. Her dark eyes seem larger than they actually are as they telegraph whatever message she's delivering at the moment—they twinkle with delight as easily as they snap with fury or burn with anger. The energy she creates ensures that it's never dull in Room 15, and is probably why my favorite books are still reposing in the bottom of my footlocker.

It's easy, even for me, to see at a glance that two very different people share the top of the dresser. Granted I've never been a model of tidiness—unless you compare me to my roommate. Her side is littered with wadded-up gum wrappers, crumpled cigarette packages, bobby pins, anything she pulls out of her pockets before she tosses her dirty clothes in the bottom of the wardrobe. Which creates another crisis when it's time to prepare our weekly laundry lists, because she knows precisely what's due to be laundered but hasn't a clue as to where the missing items might be.

And here I always thought New Englanders were quiet and conservative. What an altogether new experience for this generally (I'm just realizing) laid-back Westerner. The wonder is, I'm enjoying every minute of it.

⁂

Sunday, August 27, 1944

Dearest Family,

Can't believe it's two weeks since I've written, just as I can't believe we only seem to get busier every day. You're the only ones I've really written to and somehow I'm going to have to make time to write friends—how I don't quite know. Your letters are marvelous, I just love them and today I have time to savor them again. Have already put the picture of Marliss on our mantel, Sis. My darling little niece is sitting between photos of Bob B. and Bob L. and a few other military friends Ski pulled from the bottom of my footlocker to adorn our mantel.

For yes, hallelujah! our footlockers have arrived (as you can tell from the paper I'm writing on) complete with stationery supply, ink, toilet paper that doesn't feel waxed, and various essential sundries we've been making do without. Oh, happy day!

More wonderful still, Caroline has joined us, along with her working buddy in Liverpool, Ann, a beauty from Los Angeles. Ann has lovely long blond hair, the bluest of eyes, classic features. Ski mentioned to me that she must be pushing thirty, but then Ski tends to notice all physical details—especially if the girl is beautiful. Whatever age, Ann's lovely and a real addition to our crew. Her husband is a Navy lieutenant serving in the Pacific for the past two years and she had the bright idea of joining the Red Cross to go to his general area.

So much for personal plans in wartime. She and Caroline are a good team as they're both married to Navy men—or at least Caroline was, for it becomes clearer to Caroline every day that her husband's submarine was lost.

We rushed to their room to greet Caroline as soon as we finished on the docks. They're back down the hall, veer sharp right, and we were still bubbling over with Caroline when Ann, in a lovely robe, walked in from the bath. She doesn't just walk in, she makes an entrance—somehow I sense she's had stage experience—pausing at the door until you're aware she's there, then radiating charm and cordiality with her lovely smile and sparkling eyes. Now, if we can only manage to stay together. It makes so much difference having compatible people around when the hours are long and the work is tiring and often emotionally draining. We find ourselves laughing all the time. With the wrong people around, it would be easy to cry instead.

The other day Ski and I were snowed under on the docks, both ways, by two or three thousand hungry men who'd been on C rations for some time (C rations are cans of stuff like beef stew—you open the can and heat it in whatever's available). Several handsome *young* colonels ran up to us as we drove in, begging for food—if you can imagine colonels doing that—and we rushed to open up and start serving. GIs are always eager to help us and I was right in the middle of a "Put the coffee urn over there" when I noticed the eagle on the man's collar and added, "sir, please." I looked around and four colonels were aboard our Clubmobile. They were good sports and the GIs loved it. One sergeant getting his coffee and watching a colonel pushing a tray of doughnuts through the side window said, "How about that for duty, sir!" The colonel said, "I haven't done KP for a long time and I love it." It's easy to see why this is a crack fighting outfit.

I can't tell you how lovely the country is around here. Last week for the first time Ski and I had a whole day off and drove the little Hillman to Winchester. We spent hours in the gorgeous cathedral. The sense of age and history is almost overwhelming. The guide kept referring to the old part and the new part. The new part is only 500 years old and the old part dates from 1070. Facts like these really make us realize what a young country the United States is. Canute and Hardicanute are buried in the cathedral, and Rufus the Red Beard. More recently, Sir Isaac Walton and Jane Austen. Egbert, the first king of all England is there, also Saint Swithin. Bloody Mary married the King of Spain there in a four-hour service—the 3,000 invited guests wore white velvet, she wore black velvet (and velvet was then $6 a yard) with red shoes. Her hair was red, too. Henry VIII gave parties in the Deanery next door and Nell Gwyn's house is close by. *Great* guide who made English history really come alive.

As we clambered after the guide up hundreds of stairs to the roof and the bells, two GIs joined us and ended up showing us the rest of the town, as they're stationed nearby. We lunched at a quaint inn, then shopped at antique and book shops (me looking for histories to recount who the heck Saint Swithin *really* was), and ended up touring Winchester College. It was a cold damp day and the great dining hall was clammy. The square wooden "plates" the boys eat from, cracked and worn from hundreds of years of use, and the chill of the great room made me think that perhaps the English have such rosy cheeks because half the time their faces are frostbitten. It was a lovely way to spend our day off.

Not long ago Ski and I were out in a pouring rain serving an evacuation hospital train and the guys were so glad to see us we didn't mind missing an LST dinner invitation (from the Navy friends who had dined us at midnight on their landing ship), although we'd looked forward all day to some more wonderful Navy food. Many of the injured were badly wounded, but so glad to be headed home it made us want to cry.

One of them started a routine snow job on us. "There's nothing I'd rather see than a Red Cross girl," he began. As I offered him doughnuts he added, "You know what goes with a Red Cross girl, don't you?" His buddies laughed in anticipation and he said, "Doughnuts!"

"That's right," I said. "That's all Red Cross girls have time to go with." The guys loved it but they'll laugh at anything, which makes our job easy.

Most wonderful kind of dock work is serving returning troops. When Ski and I were sent down to meet some D day troops coming back, we expected worn-out, beat-up troops. Instead they were all polished up, boots shining, and yelling appreciatively as we pulled in, our music blaring. A couple of them started jitterbugging together really well—and they were typical all-American types. Their captain told me proudly those two were the toughest snipers of the outfit and sometimes only brought teeth back as trophies. He was bragging, of course, but I was appalled. I suppose that's the contradiction of war—where is the truth about a person? You see a fighting outfit, mechanized and looking hard as nails and ready to play Attila the Hun. When you look closer, one guy will have a kitten in his jacket pocket, another a dog on a leash. Which, incidentally, is probably why I've cuddled and hugged more animals since being here than in a lifetime.

The worst kind of dock operations is when we see boys off one day and returning a few days later—minus most of their uniforms and equipment and some of their pets, looking gaunt and exhausted, all because of enemy mines and torpedoes. This war in the ETO may be considered over by some experts because our armies are advancing, but it's hard to believe when ships are still being sunk, bombs are falling, and our daily influx of wounded continues.

> All my love to all of you,
> Roses

⚬⚬⚬

Journal   *September 10, 1944*

If only I could take movies of the armies moving through this port. That's a lost cause, of course—the films would be destroyed and I'd probably be sent home in disgrace. But what sights we see each day, things I'll never forget.

One morning as Ski and I were easing our Clubmobile out through the coach gate of the hotel, we had to stop while a famous British fighting force moved past us towards the docks. Pennants flying, bugles blowing, they marched by in perfect cadence, uniforms buttoned to perfection, boots polished, caps all at the precise angle, every column in perfect alignment. Then the men broke into a famous British fighting song and sang that in perfect cadence too. Followed by whistling a march, column after column of men, still in perfect cadence. Ski had tears rolling down her face, I had goosebumps all over, for they looked absolutely invincible. I've teased Ski for being overly sentimental about the British—she's very proud she has so many Canadian cousins because a portion of her family moved to Canada during Revolutionary days out of loyalty to the king. But I was cheering as resolutely as all the Britishers who stopped to cheer and wave the troops on.

After that, our first sight of an American division descending on the loading area was almost unnerving. For they came sauntering along, en masse, in no distinguishable formations at all, helmet straps dangling, shirttails hanging out, combat boots partially unbuckled, no one in step, no lines visible. They called greetings to bystanders, whistled at women, and were escorted by town children running along beside them and calling out, "Any gum, chum?" Besides their packs and rifles, which sometimes they dragged, many had a musical instrument in hand and occasionally one strummed a guitar. And pets. Many had a cat or small dog stuffed in the front of their field jackets, larger dogs they led by a rope or leash. They all seemed to be laughing and joking. It didn't look like a parade, but a picnic, and Ski cried and I goosebumped just as hard as we had done for the British. For in their very special American casualness, our troops were equally impressive.

Since then, a few crack U.S. infantry outfits or paratroopers have marched through with spit and polish and we've discovered the British can really aggravate the Army Transportation Corps loading officers and snarl up and delay important ship loadings at crucial times. For precisely at teatime they stop their convoys and troops wherever they happen to be, no matter how many battalions are waiting to come in to load, no matter how urgent the loadings, and calmly unhook little teakettles that dangle from the backs of the lorries (that's British for trucks), and brew up a spot of tea.

Chapter Seven

September 13, 1944, 11:15 PM

Dearest Family,

Your wonderful letters keep arriving and I'm so glad you understand why I write so seldom. A new excuse for having so little time to write is I've been made captain in charge of all Clubmobile operations in this area. This is the largest Clubmobile operation in England at the present time, so I feel flattered they'd give a newcomer the responsibility. It's a big one, getting bigger. The Adjutant General of the Port called me in the other day to inform me that all troop field kitchens have been pulled out of our area and the Port wants the Red Cross to serve *all* troops going through. Otherwise they'll have only C and K rations while in the marshaling areas and en route. With a crew of seven girls to serve thousands daily, we're not only working round the clock but I'm pestering London for more equipment and girls.

Our coffee kitchen is down in the dock area and the Army staffs it for us with GIs, although we may switch to German prisoners soon. Our doughnut kitchen goes day and night to keep up, so besides my crew, there are about twenty other people to ride herd on. Not to mention ordering doughnut-making supplies, constant reports to Red Cross Headquarters, and getting at least twice daily reports from the Army Port Transportation offices on all troop movements to find out what time to send which crew where, with how many supplies. It's like doing a jigsaw puzzle, but by splitting up and running shuttles we've managed. We are getting the job done somehow with what we have and still managing to serve everyone and dance with the boys—in our penny loafers (nice days) or our combat boots (most days and cold nights) on the concrete and wooden planking of the dock area. Think we're proudest of being able to dance under those conditions.

We're also turning out to be fine scroungers. Ski is brilliant at it. She was the one who suggested we stop by the supply depot regularly ("It only takes a few minutes, Rosie") with hot coffee and doughnuts. Within a week they've become our best friends and we now have combat boots, heavy socks, insulated long johns, and GI jackets, which are lifesavers on those cold docks.

German prisoners are pouring in, which speaks well for the Allied advances. It's a strange feeling to see them file off the ships. They're tired and dirty, some with belligerent expressions, some sullen, some looking dazed. They all look around immediately, even the wounded ones, as they've been told this place has been bombed to rubble and they seem to be checking to see if anything is left. Have even seen a German general or two. Everyone along the Hards where the landing ships pull up stops whatever they're doing when the LSTs open their mouths and disgorge the bedraggled Germans. As they file down the street along the old Roman wall towards the prisoners' temporary camp, crowds gather to watch. The English observe with typical British reserve, but their expressions reveal their feelings. "Supermen are they?" or "They don't look like supermen now, do they?" are typical comments.

Terribly tired so will close. All my love, I'm always thinking of you, but you know that.

Roses

P.S. *Yes!* I'll send a Christmas list—hold your horses!

A.B. Been wanting to tell you for weeks what fun it was to serve the first Free French troops of de Gaulle as they left to liberate Paris (at least Paris was the goal *they* had in mind). Thank goodness lots of them had served in the Foreign Legion or North Africa and knew Spanish, so with my high school French and adequate Spanish and everyone's hand gestures, we got along swimmingly. *Bon soir!*

⚜

Journal   *September 23, 1944*

Hooray! Eloise has come down from Warminster to join us and is settled in and how we need her bright smile and capabilities. Am sure I mentioned her on the voyage over when we got to know her. She's a redhead from Westport. Not only has dimples and a radiant smile but naturally curly hair. Headquarters gave me the go-ahead last week, but it took two days to get the message through to her. Tried calling from hotel lobby public phone and it proved an ordeal. The British system—"Press button A and then button B after inserting coins and before talking" (or words to that effect)—is easier said than done for a green American. Got disconnected many times before getting through and Eloise was not there so left a message. While I was struggling with the phone system Ski had an exciting time guarding the phone booth, running back and forth to the desk for more shillings, and fending off the friendly sea captains and their proffered drinks.

The next day Eloise wired me, "Traveling down at own convenience," so when she finally showed up I couldn't resist teasing her. "Eloise," I said, "Your wire sounded as though you were too busy playing tennis or riding to the hounds to interrupt your crowded social schedule."

"But Rosie," she laughed, "I was told that 'traveling down at own convenience' is the officially correct term to use. I asked an official." And darn it, found out she's right. She's a wonderful addition to our crew, and how much we need her.

Teamed Eloise with Ski to break her in to routine and the first day, wouldn't you know, their schedule included a hospital ship. As captain, I simply must remember to give new girls a few days to adjust to our work—which can range from hilarious to tragic in minutes—before sending them onto a hospital ship loaded with wounded. Eloise admitted she was a little apprehensive when she learned where they were headed as, she told Ski, "I'm even a failure at putting on Band-Aids."

They went down into the sick bays packed with wounded, but when Eloise looked around and saw the bandages, many of them bloody field dressings, and smelled the smells, she had to race topside. She just made the rail before throwing up, then filled her lungs with fresh air for a few minutes before going back down to do her job.

Ski had a haunting experience yesterday. She and Eloise were standing on either side of a hospital ship gangway, serving the littered wounded as they were offloaded. Ski smiled at a GI and said cheerily, "Grab a couple of doughnuts, fellah!" He stared back at her before saying quietly, "But I don't have any hands." Eloise told me when she next glanced over, Ski had tears rolling down her cheeks. None of us will ever use that expression again.

◦◦◦◦◦

September 25, 1944

Dearest Family,

Enclosing a few of the many letters we're getting from the GIs we see so briefly as they go through—think you'll enjoy them. They expect us to remember them even when they're one of 3,000 plus on the docks at one time. Stranger yet, we sometimes do. Still recall the face of a boy who helped us weeks ago. He was standing beside Ski and me heaving urns and doughnut crates. A captain outside the Clubmobile having his cup filled looked up and said, "If you get tired, I'll be glad to come up and help those girls." The boy grinned and flashed back, "It isn't my good looks they like, sir, it's my winnin' ways."

The GIs write us on lined pads or any handy piece of paper, as you can see, and often in pencil, so the messages look like they're scrawled in a foxhole and carried around in a helmet liner before mailing. We try to drop a card or note back. So many are arriving, it's hard to find the time.

Enclosures

August 29, 1944

Dear Rosemary,

Arrived in France okay and in the best of health. This is the first chance I've had of writing you. We have been pretty busy so far, so hope you won't mind if this letter is a short one. I have a lot of letters

Rosie and Ski outside
Dolphin Hotel, fall 1944.

Girls waiting for Club-
mobiles to be loaded,
Southampton dock area,
fall 1944.

Rosie and Ski in the *Joker*, fall 1944.

to write. I haven't written home in over two weeks. Well, Rosemary, how is everything with you? And how is the coffee and doughnut business? I hope this letter finds you well. If you need a good phonograph man just let me know. I'll write Washington for permission to join the Red Cross. How do you like working in the Red Cross? Do you expect to come to France soon? I'd really enjoy a good cup of coffee and some doughnuts now. France is a pretty nice place. The people are very sociable and generous and the kids are very polite. I've run across only one "dead-end kid" so far. The people give us eggs, bread, and fruit, and of course something to drink. In exchange we give them gum, candy, and cigarettes. They all speak French, even the smallest of the kids speak it well. I'll have to learn to speak it. I know a few words but not enough to start a conversation. The weather hasn't been bad even tho' it's raining now. Well, Rosemary, that's all I can tell you about France for the present. I guess I'll have to close now. Give my regards to your girlfriend. I'll be expecting to hear from you soon. 'Til then—best of luck.

Eddie

France
12 Sept. 1944

Dear Rosy,

Guess maybe it's time I was droping [sic] a line. How are you doing by now. I too think it would be wise to let you in on the secret of who is writing this letter. Do you remember when we were leaving England and the three farmers crawled in the back of your truck and played the phonagraph [sic]? And discovered that you were from California—well this is Bill. The other two (Dick and Jimmie) are on gaurd [sic] so I thought it was time we finding out where you are. Did you get over here yet? You know we have a date when you get here—we haven't forgotten.

So how about getting hep and make with the pen and paper— (Throw in some ink) and jotting us off a few lines.

Hope you are okay—and we are still making plans. So here's hoping you are on this side of the channel. How would you like to be in California this weekend? Well 'til later I'll bring this to a close hoping to hear from you soon.

Bye Bye
Bill, Jim & Dick

P.S. We saw Dinah Shore yesterday—she can really sing. I could listen to her all afternoon.

P.S.S. Excuse the pencil I couldn't find my pen—okay?

Bye again
3 GIs (not a wolf in the crowd) ahem

Am also enclosing this note from a London official. We really keep them on the run when they come down to check up on our work as we don't stop long enough to take them to a lunch break—but they all seem pleased to grab coffee and doughnuts on the docks with the troops as they load.

Might as well enclose also two recent invitations to trip the light fantastic, as you might put it, Dad. The second one is from L. V., a buddy of Hug's (my escort at the Navy command performance dinner) and they get pretty creative in tracking us down.

Still well, busy, and happy.

Love,
Roses

Enclosures

**American Red Cross
IN GREAT BRITAIN**

12, GROSVENOR SQUARE
London W.1.
September ___ 1944

Miss Rosemary Langheldt
American Red Cross
_____ Hotel

Dear Miss Langheldt,

I am still remembering the visit which I made to your Clubmobile with Mrs. Sloan Colt last week, and how terribly impressed I was with the work you girls are doing.

Strenuous as it is, I know you must get tremendous satisfaction from it. It must be quite an achievement just to know your way around those docks so thoroughly well. Thank you very much for the time you gave us which I know you could so ill afford.

With best wishes to all,

Sincerely,

Miss V. F. Hichcox
Supervisor of Staff Health

Wednesday, August 30, 1944

Dear Rosie:

It seems the only way I can get in touch with you is for you to phone me. Will you call me at the Star this evening after 7:30?

The Court Royale Hotel, where I've been living, is having a dinner dance next Saturday, Sept. 9. The hotel is opening to the public the 11th and this is the initial dance. I believe it will be quite an affair. L. V. and two other officers and I have reservations, making a party of eight. Can you make it?

Here's hoping I hear from you this evening. L. V. called me Saturday eve and I tried for 45 minutes to get a call through to you with no success.

Hug

U.S. Naval Advanced Amphibious Base
Soton

Hants

Outgoing Despatch   Date: 18 September 44

FROM: Ensign L. V. (initials only) Assiter Star Hotel
ACTION: Miss Rosemary Langheldt
CLASSIFICATION: Plain (Rit by hand)
PRECEDENCE: Operational
ORIGINATED: L. V. A.
RELEASED: L. V. A.
INFO: Anyone concerned
DTG 181123 A

I have reservations at the Court Royal Sat. evening 23 Sept. for a Buffet & Dance. Can you make it?

Please call me some time Tuesday 19 Sept. I will be in from 0800 until 2400.

<hr>

Journal   *September 27, 1944*

It's been a yo-yo day all around, starting at the coffee kitchen. When the Army sent all field kitchens to the continent they left behind a colored unit for Red Cross coffee duty. It's hot, sweaty work as water to brew the coffee has to be boiled in huge galvanized cans on temperamental field stoves—a field kitchen setup in an old dock shed. But the men turn out great coffee and are efficient and cheerful to work with.

Several times we've spotted some of the guys with English dates up on High Street—there's a pretty blond we see with one of our detail one night and with a white officer or GI the next. How she manages her social life without provoking a riot intrigues us, as we know how vocal and nasty many GIs and officers are where race is concerned. But what choice do colored men have? The nearest colored Red Cross Club is in Winchester, too far away for men stationed here. Plus, the British seem to judge troops by manners rather than color. We've yet to see gross behavior by any colored man in town and we sure can't say that for some of the whites.

This morning when we pulled in to the kitchen for our first load, Ski hopped out to count urns and talk with the guys as I backed the Clubmobile around. Normal procedure. Only after we drove away did she blurt out, "Rosie, Jake asked me for a date. I was so surprised I didn't know what to say. I stammered around and finally told him I was going steady." She was very upset. "Why would he ask me?"

"He probably thinks you're British, Ski. You have a New England accent and our battle dress is the blue wool used for RAF uniforms. Don't worry about it." But we both do. I've been so sure I'm more open than most Americans or British but my first reaction when Ski told me was complete surprise. Why? I'm thinking that over now.

<hr>

September 30, 1944

Dearest Family,

Our APO situation is so mixed up I haven't heard from you, or anyone, for what seems weeks. Know you're writing, only hope my letters are coming through better than yours are.

Last week had to drive to London on business with our ex-captain Polly, who was going up to prepare to leave for the continent, and her Army friend, Lt. Watson. Lots of fun. We lunched at a little wayside inn with the usual thatched-roof charm and the usual unseasoned boiled potatoes and savoy cabbage. It was a thrill to get back to London, a wonderful city despite the new V-2s, which are Hitler's update on the buzz bombs. They're rockets and arrive so fast you can't hear them coming. There's no time for bells or warnings to take cover. This does simplify the matter. If you hear the explosion and feel the concussion it means you've lucked it out again. The damage they cause is appalling, whole city blocks leveled in some cases, and the explosions, noise, and shock waves are terrifying. Thank goodness they're not too frequent.

I reported into Headquarters to have a session with Mr. de Ganahl, a South African millionaire (gossip says) in charge of all Clubmobile activities. I requested lots of things for our work and, surprisingly, he okayed them all—including another Clubmobile, which I was to drive back from London. He promised to get more girls down to help as soon as possible.

It was early evening when I finished business at Headquarters and started back in *The City of New York* (another Bedford Clubmobile) with Lt. Watson joking about riding sidesaddle and lookout. It's somehow a fine sensation to drive along and look down on all you survey. After dark in the blackout was really an adventure as road signs have never been put back in place since the days the English feared a German invasion of England any day. The few signs remaining are deliberately turned to point in the wrong direction. Every time we'd come to a fork in the road I tended to go down the wrong fork. Watson enjoyed the whole experience enormously, but then he had relaxed completely with an ale or two at dinner we'd stopped for earlier.

He convulsed at me chewing gum and bouncing up and down as I peered through the blackness and prayed we were still headed in the right direction. Then we came to a place where the main highway was blocked off and a long detour followed. Watson said it's due to a British fighter airfield which operates only at night and closes the highway during flight times. The detour consisted of many miles on curving sheep-trail roads, rutty and really narrow. We must have covered most of southern England before we got back. What a drive!

Sorry I haven't sent a Christmas list, will soon, but offhand the Tabu creme cologne I was given before leaving home is such a success the crew comes by to use it before going out—outranks my Blue Grass in the theft department, probably because it conquers even the smell of coffee and doughnuts. I'd love a pink cashmere sweater, perfectly plain. And I could use some 3-thread hosiery before too long—not too sheer—and any good shampoo you can find. PX supplies are pretty basic and there's not much selection. Lifebuoy soap somehow doesn't fill the bill with us. And I'd very much like a pale blue or bright red soft flannel shirt to wear with battle dress in the winter. Or film for the still or movie camera. Now that should give you some ideas. A jar of peanut butter would induce profound gratitude in any of us. As you may have gathered, the food here is blah and tasteless. Any little treat like cheese or crackers.

Still loving every minute—and missing you very much. Kiss the boys for me please (tell them the dogs here don't compare) and write often.

All my love,
Roses

Journal *September 30, 1944*

It's way past midnight and Ski's still not back from her rendezvous with an old friend. With this unexpected quiet time (and any time without my roommate qualifies as quiet) I've managed to answer a few letters and write the family. Sure would have loved telling them about Ski's encounter with an armored division (a famous one I'd better not name) but the letter'd never pass the censors. So will preserve the details, the better to harass Ski with at some future date. At the moment she's trying to forget it ever happened. I'll never forget the scene.

The day after I brought The City of New York *down from London, Ski and I were using it on a very busy loading day when we ran out of supplies and had to head back to the coffee kitchen for more. Ski was at the wheel, driving with her usual verve along the Roman wall fronting the waterfront Hards where landing ships waited, bows agape, as the armored division loaded. Equipment jammed both sides of the road—*

little tanks, medium-sized tanks, huge tanks, bulldozers, earthmovers, traveling cranes, jeeps, all spilling over with tank men. It was a lovely sunny day and a typical Army "hurry up and wait" operation. Bored tank men, shirts open, helmets askew, lounged in the sun on all parts of their equipment, so greeted the sight of the Clubmobile with cheers and whistles that drowned out the sounds of Tommy Dorsey's "Marie" blaring out of our loudspeakers. They were in fine form. So was Ski.

"HI! Where you from?" she called out the window, waving with one hand, steering with the other, and chewing her gum madly. "We'll be right back with fresh coffee and hot doughnuts, don't go away!"

Ski drives through anything with enthusiasm, half leaning out the cab as she waves and talks, so as I waved from the left side I tried to keep an eye on the road yet still hear what she was saying to me. She's always carrying on an entirely different conversation with me—between greetings to the troops. It takes a bit of getting used to, but no matter how much noise and confusion surround us, her throaty voice carries clearly.

"Hi there! We'll be right back. Rosie, if you've ever flown a small plane . . . Hi there, guys! Back in ten minutes—don't worry, we'll catch you. They won't finish loading for hours." We were talking about her flying lessons and the thrill of the first solo and how she hated giving up the lessons when the Red Cross accepted her.

"Rosie, you've got to understand" (Ski always speaks with emphasis) "that flying is a matter of depth perception. Hi there, soldier! Anyone from Connecticut? Right back, guys. Rosie, to be a good pilot you've got to have perfect depth perception or you're . . . "

Ahead, a big crane was extending an arm over the road. "Slow down, Ski!" I said. "Stop!" I yelled. "That crane's low . . . "

She glanced ahead, not slowing. "Oh, there's plenty of room, it's a simple matter of . . . Hi, fellows! We'll be ri . . . "

There was a loud ripping sound as the crane arm caught the top of our cab. Ski jammed on the brakes and we jolted to a stop. Wild cheers erupted from the tank men as I heard the smash of cups and records crashing down in the back of the Clubmobile—undoubtedly the fresh supply of hits I'd just brought down from London Headquarters. I looked up and sunlight was pouring in through a gash in the top of our cab—a huge, ugly tear, maybe four feet long.

I couldn't help saying it. "Well, it was nice being a captain for almost a month anyway . . . " Ski didn't respond to my sarcasm. Stricken and shaking, she was huddled down behind the steering wheel.

"Are you all right, Ski?" Tank men were converging on us from all directions, whooping with delight at this break in their monotony.

She groaned. "Oh my gawd, what have I done?" She frantically started to push me out my side of the cab as she slid over from the driver's seat. "Rosie, please handle this. I can't face them. I want to die of humiliation. You know what a good driver I am. . . . " She was already fumbling around for her cigarettes as I climbed down from the cab to assess the damage and face the gleeful "woman driver" comments from what seemed like half the armored division.

The tank men were wonderfully helpful in spite of their gratuitous remarks, which I especially enjoyed as obviously I hadn't created the mess. I told them the pilot was inside and pointed to the cab. Within 15 minutes they not only had our Clubmobile free of the crane, they had lured Ski out of hiding to face their teasing. They were most attractive guys. To my credit, not once during our dash to the coffee kitchen for fresh supplies to go back and pay off the tank men did I bring up the subject of my roommate's perfect depth perception.

We headed for the Port Ordnance Shop the minute we finished serving the loading troops. It was Ski's bright idea, so I wouldn't have to go through the embarrassment and delay of a trip to London to get the gash repaired. As I drove into the cluttered mess of galvanized iron that's the Port Ordnance Shop, Ski scanned the faces of the guys running towards the Clubmobile.

"His name's Korowski, no Rogowski, and I slipped him extra doughnuts at Pier 43 while you were on the hospital ship that day, and he wondered why we never took care of permanent personnel, and he has a beer belly, and, . . ." her face broke into a radiant smile, her voice low and warm, "Well, Sarge! Here we are at last, just as I promised! Any of your men need a coffee break?"

The sergeant was so pleased his face turned quite red. GIs rushed to help us open up the back of the truck and lift the side serving panel. In moments "One o'Clock Jump" was blaring from the loudspeaker and what looked like the entire personnel of the shop was wolfing down hot doughnuts and fresh coffee. Before we had to switch to the second urn of coffee I sensed our problem was solved as Ski had Sergeant Rogowski entranced.

"Yes, every afternoon, Sarge," I heard her promise. "We'd love to come by. You just tell us when and we'll work it into our schedule somehow." And when they discovered they both are nicknamed Ski, it was only moments before we were in the middle of a discussion on the best way to repair the gash the lousy tank corps had made in our truck and which day the Ordnance Shop could do the work.

Suddenly a cross between a bellow and a roar interrupted our negotiations. "Rogowski!! What the hell is going on? Get that goddamn Clubmobile out of here!" It sounded like "ow da here." It sounded real tough.

Everyone froze as a tall lanky lieutenant stalked towards us, shaking his fist, his overseas cap cocked on the left side of his head, his face red with anger. His eyes seemed to bulge as he yelled at his men. "Don't you lousy jokers know we're supposed to be fighting a war!" It was not a question. He screwed up his face in an exaggerated grin and minced the last few steps towards the Clubmobile, his voice suddenly falsetto. "I'm so sorry, colonel, we're having a little tea party here," and lifted his hand and extended his pinkie finger to drink tea. "Do you mind telling the general we'll be a few days late getting his equipment repaired? We were invited to a tea party."

"Oh, no!" muttered Ski, as we frantically put away cups and trays and switched off the record player while he ranted on. "Now we have a clown to deal with."

"Get back to the shop!" the lieutenant bellowed, in what we presumed was his normal voice. The men got, and he turned to glare at us, his hands on his hips.

Ski smiled, held out a doughnut towards him and said, softly, "Care for a doughnut, lieutenant?" As he started swearing, she yanked back the doughnut and pulled on the support that held up the side serving panel so it flew down in his face. Her timing was perfect. We could hear his muffled roar as we slipped out the rear door to start around the other side of the Clubmobile. He followed us.

His voice was no longer a roar but still plenty loud. "Didn't you hear me? Get that lousy truck out of here!" Ski turned to face the mad bull and I jumped into the cab to start the motor. Her eyes were shooting out hotter sparks than the lieutenant's as they breathed fire and insults at each other from about a foot apart.

"Come on, Ski, let's go," I said firmly. "No use wasting our time on this joker. We usually don't serve officers anyway, if we can help it."

As Ski went to climb into her side of the truck he turned on me and snarled, "You wouldn't catch me dead eating any of your lousy doughnuts!"

I made an extra effort to smile pleasantly. "I'm delighted to hear it, Lieutenant. I'll spread the good news at Headquarters."

I slowly maneuvered the Clubmobile to snake our way out of the cluttered ordnance yard. Ski leaned out the cab and said, in her most well-bred New England way, as the lieutenant stood glaring up at her, "Tell me, Mr. Scrooge, how did you ever get to be a first lieutenant?" Then she quickly rolled up her window.

I couldn't tell in the rearview mirror whether he was shaking his fist at us or just laughing. Ski was livid. "Oh, horse!" she kept repeating. She claims this is not an expletive, but the way she says it has the effect of something far worse. "Of all the repulsive men I've ever met! Wasn't he awful, Rosie?" She had worked up a full head of steam. "Did you see his eyes, those beady green eyes?"

I had to admit I hadn't noticed the color of his eyes, I was too busy wondering how we could go around him to get our truck repaired, or if I'd have to take it back to London and explain the accident and, worse, go through the British Ministry of Works, which might put the Clubmobile out of action for weeks. She didn't hear me mutter, she was too busy describing the lieutenant—his long tall figure, skinny hips, broad shoulders, the way he walked. "Swaggered" is the way she put it. "He doesn't have any rear end at all!" She hadn't missed a detail. "And Rosie, why didn't you notice his eyes? He's got bedroom eyes if I ever saw them. Boy, I'd like to fix his wagon. . . ."

I tried to get a word in. "Ski, the problem is to get our wagon fixed in case you've forgotten, and now we've really got problems."

My roommate still wasn't listening. She was too happy enjoying her hatred of the lieutenant. She raved on until I agreed to go to dinner at the Officers Mess. The Port Army officers all eat there, but as it's only open two hours, three times a day, it's hard for us to get away from the docks during mess hours. The mess is a little restaurant close by the town Bargate (the ancient town wall gate halfway up High Street) and one of the few buildings to survive the Blitz. Service is cafeteria style. We switched ship loadings with Caroline and Ann so we could make dinner hours. Ski had a long list of remarks she was planning to fling at the lieutenant if she should see him. I was planning to run into the Army Port Commander or one of his colonels to find out if they would *help us get the Clubmobile repaired quickly—and dreaming of waving a repair order signed by the Port Commander in the lieutenant's face.*

But we were both amazed when guess who walked over to our table all polished up for dinner in his greenish Eisenhower jacket (which did, I noticed, set off his mean green eyes pretty well). We were still in the battle dress we'd been in for about fourteen hours as we were due back on the docks to work after dinner. Ski started in on him, as he calmly put his tray down on our table, before he'd even opened his mouth or asked to join us. This so shocked Ski she suddenly stopped talking in mid insult to catch her breath. Which gave him a chance to get a word in. "I'm Tom Carver," he said pleasantly, sat down and explained why he'd been rude.

Very colorfully. "Those goddamned Port colonels all want their sedans fixed yesterday 'cause they've got a date, and we have tank division emergencies coming out our ears. They've got to get their equipment repaired before they load." In two minutes we'd heard all the frustrations of his day and quite a bit about the importance to the Port colonels of their social life.

Ski listened, fascinated. I admit I listened avidly too. Then he told us his sarge had explained he'd invited us to come by and serve his guys. I'm not sure how, but within minutes we were all conversing instead of arguing. Within five minutes I was no longer looking around for the Port Commander, as Tom Carver (oh yes! he has the same first name as Ski's father and brother—her favorite name) had agreed to repair our Clubmobile.

Tom has a kind of Broadway or racetrack accent, and he's direct (blunt is really the word), honest to the point of insulting, cynical as to the realities of surviving Army life, funny to the point of crudeness. Ski asked him what his lapel insignia stood for, as we weren't familiar with it. It looks like a bowl with a flame coming out of the top. Tom beamed proudly and said, "It's the symbol of the mighty Ordnance Corps, a flaming piss pot." Ski looked shocked but couldn't help laughing.

Which may be why I wasn't surprised today when Ski told me she has a date with him tomorrow night, if I'll just adjust her schedule. Why am I thinking of Rhett and Scarlett? It's gotta be the attraction of opposites, as they couldn't be more different. But the Ordnance Shop did a great job on the Clubmobile. In just twenty-four hours, it looks better than it did when I drove it down from London.

Chapter Eight

Saturday, October 14, 1944

Dearest Family,

Have just deposited sixpence in our room heater so the gas fire will hiss and throw out a little heat and will finally start a letter before going to dinner. For some unknown (but wonderful to me) reason we have a big break tonight in the loading schedule. I'm sorry there's so little time to write but I've been busy yelling at Headquarters and all I get is promises to send down more crew as soon as they possibly can. My crew is wonderful (there are eight of us) but, as the English say, it takes a bit of doing to accomplish our ever busier schedule.

Keep wondering if I've told you about the strange woman who runs an ancient green electric lorry (flatbed behind a cab) around the docks, delivering supplies and equipment for the British. The lorry is a silly old-fashioned looking contraption but she fits it perfectly. Her name's Mrs. Lytton. She stands (Mrs. Lytton, not the truck) about 6 feet tall, has gray hair pulled back which she parts in the middle, is quite grizzled-looking. No makeup and always wearing an odd assortment of woolens—trousers and sweaters or jackets topped by a misshapen cloche type felt hat, her large feet encased in heavy wool socks and work shoes. Her voice is very deep. When she strides towards us, she reminds me of an old eagle or vulture.

Ski and I loved her instantly as she's always hovering around our dock coffee kitchen and we share coffee and doughnuts, and Ski her cigarettes, while we're waiting to have the trucks loaded. She speaks beautiful top-drawer English and her French is flawless (I heard her conversing with the Free French troops as they loaded). We invited her back to our hotel for tea one day when we finished early. Found out she lives in the New Forest with another old English woman, who turned out to be a caricature of what you always imagine English women look like. Right out of *Punch*—pencil slim, gray, carefully coifed hair, tweed skirt, sweater, a string of pearls, and an elegantly held cigarette—in a holder, of course.

Last week we finally had a free late afternoon and accepted their invitation to visit them. They share a lovely house, which they call a cottage, surrounded by a large and beautifully kept garden. The house has a thatched roof and is wonderfully furnished with antiques collected from all over Europe. The living room has a real fireplace, complete with cheerily blazing fire. You can't imagine the pang of homesickness Ski and I felt on being in a real home, even for a little while. They completely outdid themselves in serving us high tea. We had pastries, cupcakes, bread with vegetable marrow jam (sounds horrible and is delicious), chocolate cake, and fresh raspberries and cream! Of course we made pigs of ourselves and they loved it. We took them out enough sugar, cornstarch, chocolate, and cigarettes from the PX to more than make up for the rations we consumed. So we stuffed ourselves without a guilty conscience.

Mrs. Lytton, we discovered, had never worked before the war. She was born in India, as her father was a plantation owner and all of her family is English nobility. Her cousin is Sir Robert Vansittart. He's rabidly anti-German and generally conceded to be the most anti-German member of the House of Lords. He wrote the book *The Roots of Evil*. She showed us a huge photo album filled with pictures of her life since she was two years old. As she's seventy-four now (and looks about 174), you can imagine what a fine camera someone had. Her nursery was so huge and extensively equipped, it would worry the Emporium toy department manager today. And the pictures of her grandfather at eighty-five riding to the hounds from his castle in England are superb.

Her friend is just as interesting. She told us she'd never cooked in her life before the war as her husband was in the British diplomatic service. Her son is a commander in the Royal Navy.

The two of them were delightful together. We sat around the fire and they got to telling us ghost stories. Mrs. Lytton's friend (and we never did catch her name) told the most hair-raising stories with such complete British reserve and assuredness that we believed them completely. I was goosebumps all over as she described her stay in Hampton Court when Cardinal Wolsey, in his red robe, came to her bedroom—once his room—through an old secret passageway and talked to her one night. Then Mrs. Lytton made us believe her tale of the sound of coach and horses riding into the castle courtyard at exactly midnight at certain times of the year. Really, my deahs, it seems that all old English houses are haunted in some way or other and if "one lives in them it's only a matter of time until one meets a ghost." Of course.

By the time Ski and I headed back to work, the lovely St. Luke's summer afternoon (Indian summer to you) had given way to fog and darkness and it was an eerie, I should say spooky, drive back through the woods of the New Forest, which (have I mentioned it?) has been called that ever since the days of William the Conqueror. We couldn't get the ghost stories out of our minds and the fog swirling in among the trees and on to our windshield (oops! they're called windscreens here, my deahs!) only deepened the impression the stories had made on us.

Our work here is enlarging. I got a promise from London that Caroline and Ann and Ski and I can go to France together, but they want us here awhile longer. As eager as I am to get to the continent, I have to admit it's probably more important to stay put, as the Army considers our work essential.

I have a great crew—we seem to make up for our small numbers in effort and so far have managed somehow to meet every scheduled troop movement. They all have a sense of humor and work around the clock. I've told you about Caroline and Ann and Ski and Eloise. Slender, blond Kari from Maine is typically American but spent vacations in Norway with her beloved grandparents before Hitler took over the country so is bilingual and couldn't be more dedicated. I've paired her with Eloise, our delight from Connecticut.

Barbara, another New Englander, is fair and tall and willowy. She's an artist who paints and draws beautifully and was a model. She's been working in England several months and is dating a handsome British Navy lieutenant. I've paired her with Bettie, a Californian from Burlingame, who has naturally curly hair like Eloise and graduated from Cal a year before I did. Headquarters detached her from cross-channel hospital ship work to help us out. She was delighted when ordered to join us.

Room 15 is our gathering place for meetings and for the girls to pick up next-day assignments, borrow perfume, or just talk over the stresses or joys of the day. It might as well have a swinging door. Part of the attraction is that Ski and I have discovered our room's little gas fireplace is defective—we pop a six-pence in the slot and *wow!* the heat goes on but the sixpence slides out the return slot and we use it again when the time is up.

Might feel guilty about doing the hotel out of their due, but we have been residents here now almost three months. We turned in our ration cards so we'd be allotted two eggs apiece a month—but have only been served eggs *once* since arriving. By now we're noticing that when someone (British, and top drawer of course) is breakfasting at the hotel (on those days we're lucky enough to get back from night dock work to enjoy breakfast and mail at the hotel), they are served poached eggs on toast. I've complained to the manager, who wrings his hands like Uriah Heep, then tells me there are no eggs available.

I'm still scrounging around to get us more vehicles. Tom, Ski's new friend, an Ordnance officer who runs the shop where all Port vehicles are repaired, as well as vehicles attached to divisions going cross-channel, has just loaned us a Canadian truck left behind by an outfit shipping out. It's invaluable as it's small with a deep open bed which holds a lot of coffee urns and doughnut crates, a great backup for our regular equipment. We call it the *Joker*. We've become part of the Port family in a sense and completely involved in the way operations are run. Or are supposed to run.

The other afternoon, for example, I was driving in the dock area when I spotted about 800 or 1,000 men marching towards me. As I knew where all the ships were loading, I pulled up near the head of the column and a colonel came over. "Aren't you lost?" I asked him. "Hell, yes! I have no idea where we're going. No transportation officer met us at the station." He looked completely frustrated as he took off his helmet to scratch his head.

I asked him what kind of ship he thought he was loading on. "LSIs, I think," he said. "You mean LCIs, don't you?" I asked and he positively beamed, "*Dammit*, that's right!" He was headed in exactly the wrong direction, so I told him if he'd about-face his troops and march them to the Royal Pier, the LCIs and our girls were waiting there.

The other night I kept a date with Hug to hear the London Philharmonic. Basil Cameron conducting, it was a wonderful break in routine. He's invited me to go to London to hear Sir Thomas Beecham conduct but I probably won't be able to spare the time. I had to go to London on Monday again on business, and Sis, I got Marliss a birthday present which, with luck, may arrive before she's nine. She *is* celebrating her sixth, isn't she? Just wanted her to know I'm thinking of her.

Among unusual happenings to Rosie in the ETO, please file a cruise on a sunny afternoon to the Isle of Wight aboard a neat motor launch, with the Port Commander and some of his staff. It was a command performance as the colonel told me he needed to discuss future plans of the Port and how he intended to use our Red Cross unit when the Port is transferred elsewhere. Said I should bring along Ski and any other assistants if they were free as they'd enjoy the cruise. It took a lot of schedule juggling but Caroline and Ann and Ski came along for moral support as well as a well-deserved break. We "took tea" with the colonel and his staff on a terrace of the famous yacht club on the island and, being on best behavior, Mom, I managed to choke down the cucumber and watercress sandwiches that were served. They didn't change my opinion of cucumbers, but I managed not to burp on the way back!

The Port Commander went over the plans while we were cruising along. Seems the Army really likes the work of our Red Cross group and he's planning to try to get us permanently attached to his Port. If he can arrange it, we'd then go on with the Port to France or Germany or China or wherever the Port is sent. He was most complimentary about our work and went into the "ways and means" he'll use to bring about his plans. It does sound exciting as the colonel is already thinking about the Pacific part of the war, now that the Allies have crossed the German border. Career officers are always planning ahead. Have no idea if anything will come of his plans, but it's nice to feel he's satisfied with our work.

Say, Mom, if you can ever manage to send me a box with a jar of peanut butter and some tuna fish or sweet pickles or Royal Anne cherries or Philadelphia cream cheese or ladyfingers and such in it, I'll be grateful. Don't worry about weight, we're all losing it rapidly because of the work, or our mostly English diet. We hoard K rations and C rations in our room so when we come in late from work we can sit in front of the gas fire and eat. It's then we realize how good some peanut butter or Royal Anne cherries would taste. No rush—just anytime.

As I promised to write all I can, I'll mention that I was in a slight automobile accident a week or so ago and am only a little black and blue now. Barbara and I were in our little Hillman. I was driving back with Barbara from the muddy camp of a mobile hospital unit (miserably awaiting loading orders in one of the staging areas through three days of constant rain). She was at the wheel and it was long after blackout on a horribly rainy night. We ran right smack into an RAF lorry and trailer which had stalled in the middle of the road. There was no way possible to see vehicles ahead in the darkness as even the tail-hooded blackout lights, which do provide a tiny pinpoint of light shining down on the road, were not working. Barbara had five stitches taken in her head. I was hit in the forehead and bruised along the left side of my face. Wasn't knocked out but had a lump like an orange for a week. Gradually it turned black and blue and now I've a beautiful black eye. The GIs are having a field day asking who hit me.

My pen's running dry and we're out of ink, so had better close and stop by the PX on the way to mess to buy a bottle. Mom, I'd *love* to hear you play your "almost new" grand piano. I'm so thrilled you have it, and so proud of your work at Cutter Labs to make your dream come true.

I do love you all, I do miss you all, but I'm well and happy. Write often and please don't forget the peanut butter!

Your daughter and sister,
Black-Eye Rosie

P.S. Isn't it great that we are now allowed to tell you our location, so I can mention some of the historic places near the Port?

ᴗᴗ☺☺ᴗᴗ

Journal   *October 14, 1944*

Lucked out at the PX as they had good old Script blue ink which makes writing letters a joy. That watery stuff I've had to use takes half the pleasure out of saying hello to friends and family. It's bothering me that I didn't tell the family the whole story about our cruise with the colonel.

But, as Mom would say, and she's a world expert on euphemisms, I left a lot out about the cruise. No doubt because I didn't want the folks dwelling on the thought of me in the bow of the boat with the Port Commander holding my hand and giving me little pats and a serious pitch that didn't sound like Red Cross business at all. He did explain his plans and the complexity of his work, but then told me how he'd love to have me help him with his official entertaining of the many important visitors who come through the Port. He thought I'd be wonderful at it. Boy, did I scramble to get out of that one! I started babbling about the long hours we work and how little sleep we manage to get and how demanding my Red Cross duties are—all the time looking around for the girls to interrupt and change the subject. Finally glimpsed them, far aft, having a great time with some of the attractive younger officers on the colonel's staff, who help keep the Port running so efficiently.

Somehow I got the inspiration to tell him all about my handsome fiancé in the South Pacific (may both Bobs and all my other friends there I'm not engaged to forgive me). Described my fiancé in detail (a composite of every good date I've ever had) and had the colonel's eyes misting when I wound up explaining that even when I do accept an occasional date, my heart is elsewhere, and will always be. He easily, and very quickly, reverted to a father figure and said I—and I presume he meant the Red Cross—can count on him for any help we need in our work at all times. Sure was exhausted when we finally docked. Ski and Caroline and Ann had a marvelous time.

But I have to admit that ever since the cruise the colonel has been like a second father to us. Sometimes calls us his "daughters" when we see him in mess, and he often checks with me to be sure we're getting the cooperation we need to keep up "our splendid work." He couldn't be more helpful.

Saturday, October 20, 1944

Dearest ones,

Ski and I have just returned from three days in London. We were called up to go to driving school, the first step in getting ready to go to France. As we've been driving 2-ton and 2½-ton trucks ever since we've been here we weren't worried, but decided not to mention our experience, in case the course proved more difficult than anticipated. We were driven out to Wimbledon Dog Track, where the school is held, and the two of us were assigned to Mr. Cook, a Britisher, who was to teach us. He put us in a half-ton Dodge truck (we had been expecting 2½-half ton GMCs) and carefully explained about the ignition key, showed us where such important gadgets as the steering wheel, brakes, and accelerator were, then drove us down the road a ways to demonstrate double-clutching. While shifting gears, he stripped them more than Ski and I have ever done. Ski, sitting beside me in the front seat, punched me in the ribs gleefully as he did so.

Then he pulled up to the roadside and told me to take over, and to take it slowly. So I did and away we rolled; he was amazed as it was the easiest truck I've driven since we arrived. When he realized that both of us could drive he was overjoyed, and away we went on a sightseeing tour. We drove to Epsom Downs, where the English Derby is held, and watched the beautiful horses training. Then he suggested we could drive over to Brighton, so we did. En route, he fell asleep in the corner of the truck and we whipped along through simply lovely parts of Surrey and over Sussex Downs. It's just about the best time of October here and the tree leaves are in gorgeous shades of red, yellow, green, and brown. Ski says it's like a New England autumn.

Mr. Cook told us Brighton is England's most popular resort with the working people and it's quite a place, with wall-to-wall hotels facing the sea along a wide promenade. Despite the barbed wire, tethered barrage balloons, and evidence of bombing, it still has a fusty Regency air about it. Not sure which pub Mr. Cook waited in, but Ski and I did the antique and secondhand shops—looking for bargains in seal rings and tea cups—and enjoyed every minute.

The next morning back at Wimbledon Mr. Cook had us start off practicing parallel parking. It was Ski's turn. He instructed her to back into a space far larger than any space we normally use. When she casually reversed in on the first attempt he said abruptly, "That's enough! You'd better go home or you'll be teaching me to drive!" He said we were better drivers than he was and were no longer required at the school, so we got to come back a day earlier than the rest of the class. And now we have the necessary driving class certificate if we go on to Zone 5.

We stayed two nights in London at one of the staff clubs and it was lovely—even had breakfast in bed one day! These staff places are converted town houses in famous locations (like the Square, where a nightingale sings), run by the Red Cross and for Red Cross personnel only. One evening we had dinner with Emily—everyone calls her "Neme"—one of Ski's friends from home, the niece of a well-known general. She is a Red Cross worker at Rainbow Corner, which is the largest ARC Club, located right next to Piccadilly Circus. She took us through the Club after dinner.

Neme introduced us to Lady Cavendish (Adele Astaire), who also works at the Club. Everyone calls her "Delly." She is charming and, Neme says, very well liked. Makes no bones about being 44, and as she doesn't look anywhere near that age, I can see why she's proud of it. Apparently Lady C. told her that Lord C. was several years younger and died after being a drunk the last four years of his life.

Neme took us up to see the ballroom, which occupies the entire top floor of Rainbow Corner. The dance floor was packed with GIs from all branches of the service and their dates and a great GI band was playing so enthusiastically the floor shook to the beat of the music. We'd intended to just walk through as it was getting late, but a guy from Detroit grabbed me, a Southerner got Ski, and gosh knows what happened to Emily. About an hour later we managed to regroup and break away when the band finally declared an intermission.

Could go on for hours, but we're back at the Port and on the job. It's midnight now and the first ship to be loaded comes in at 6 AM.

Please keep writing and be patient—the letters will come eventually. At least that's what I keep telling myself.

All my love to all of you,
Rosemary

Journal   *October 20, 1944*

Maybe someday I'll tell Mom and Dad about the problem Ski and I had in getting back to our billets from Rainbow Corner the night we went to see Emily, but now doesn't seem the right time. Glad we carried our torches or I don't know where we would have ended up in the blackout. After trying in vain to grab a cab, impossible in the jam of servicemen and women milling around in front of Rainbow Corner, we decided to walk on over to Piccadilly Circus and try the Tube.

That was a mistake. Guess because we've only seen Piccadilly Circus in daylight we didn't realize what a flesh market it is in the middle of the night and how dumb we were to tackle it unescorted. The blackout was so complete it was hard to distinguish anything, and the Circus was absolutely jammed with raucously noisy troops and females pushing and elbowing through the mob.

Dumb us—we'd gone over to Piccadilly without a thought, assuming our uniforms would protect us, as usual. Almost without exception we've found our Red Cross uniforms ensure we're treated with respect and courtesy. But in that pitch black madhouse of jostling people we were just two more figures to be bargained with. Each time we got up courage to shine the torch towards what we hoped would be a Tube entrance or cab stand, all we succeeded in doing was getting grabbed and invited—think pressed in all ways—to do all sorts of things.

For minutes that seemed endless we wedged a way through the crowd. I shone my torch down an entranceway I was sure would be a Tube entrance but it was only a recessed doorway in which stood two couples (how would Mother say it politely?) coupling.

Ski gasped loudly. "Can you do it standing up, Rosie?"

How would I know, I thought. "Shut up, Ski!," I said, "and keep walking!"

At long last we managed to literally stumble on an entrance to the Tube, the wonderful Underground, and hopped on the first train. Actually it was going in the wrong direction, but we got off at the first stop and took a cab back to our lodgings.

After seeing Piccadilly Circus in full midnight bloom, I think I understand better the Brits' favorite lament these days, "The Yanks are overpaid, oversexed, and over here."

But even in that total blackout madness, the torch picked out more than American uniforms.

⚜

Monday, November 6, 1944

Dearest Family,

Did I ever get a wonderful surprise last week! Within two days I received thirty letters, so someone must have straightened out our APO situation. What a morale booster they were! Some of the other girls weren't as lucky, so I happily shared the best parts of the news from family and friends over a late breakfast at the hotel. We had been on the docks since the middle of the night so coming back to tea and toast *plus* a big mail sack from London was thrilling.

Mom, am glad you're keeping a scrapbook of my letters and the things I send home as I sure wouldn't have thought of it. Am keeping some other official papers and souvenirs in my footlocker—things that wouldn't pass the censors. Do leave some room for later additions please.

Yes, I'm hearing lots from Bob B. and he'd love to know about what I'm doing as I'm not managing any long letters, except to you. Sis has offered to mail copies of the interesting (?) parts of my letters so am sending one of Bob's recent letters with his address. And a big hug, Marty, for doing it. I feel guilty half the time because there are not enough hours in the day to keep in touch with so many friends who manage to keep in touch with me.

We had a big celebration here at the Port the other day—complete with news photographers. I was invited to a luncheon given by the colonel commanding the Port, as a representative of the Red Cross. A big event here, I discovered, is different from one at home. It just means everyone takes an extra half hour and eats upstairs in a private dining room at the Officers Mess with the colonels and generals, American and British, and with the mayor of the city (his gleaming chain of office outshining the brass of the senior officers present). The senior brass wore Class A uniforms, Rosie was clean and neat in fresh Clubmobile battle dress and boots as I was due back on the docks.

We ate the same food as downstairs (shucks!) but were served with a dessert spoon and didn't have to eat dessert with the same spoon we stirred our coffee with. This is quite a luxury, believe me. Then I was invited to ride to the dockside ceremony in a colonel's car (complete with green leather seats and uniformed driver!) behind a police escort and stand on a platform while speeches were made by everyone from the mayor (looking somewhat like a matador in his ceremonial regalia) to a British general (who resembled the bull), watched by hundreds of embarking GIs. Look for me in your local newsreels although I'd be surprised if they're ever shown. I was given a couple of official photos of the event and they'll go into the footlocker until it's okay to mail them home.

Oodles more to tell you but I'm terribly tired—will write again in a few days. I do love you all very much, so please keep your wonderful letters coming.

XXX OOO
Rosemary

✦

Journal　　　　　　　　　　　　　　　　　　　*November 6, 1944*

Before I collapse for the night should note that the ceremony I was hinting about to the family was a celebration of the loading of the Millionth Yank to go through this Port. A nice-looking private from Pennsylvania, the poor guy was overwhelmed with all the brass making a fuss over him and hanging a big sign around his neck. He's one of the many infantry replacements going over these days. Sure hope he makes it through, as we're hearing how much tougher the fighting is getting these past few weeks. Our work schedule is often around the clock as thousands of replacement troops are loading through here.

Happy thought: maybe London ARC Headquarters will now understand better why this small crew is using up so many supplies. They can't believe the amount of

Rosie watching the Millionth
Yank ceremony, Southamp-
ton docks, October 1944.

*flour and coffee that's flowing this way. Headquarters keeps checking me to be sure I
haven't made a mistake in ordering supplies.*

*Almost mentioned in my letter, but thought better of it, that the Port Commander
put his fatherly arm around me during the pre-lunch social chitchat and steered me over
to a sideboard in his private upstairs dining room. He told me he wanted to give me a
little present for having taken the time out from work to come—a compact. I was trying to demur politely, as I think Jane Austen might put it, when he pulled out a drawer
of the sideboard. It was loaded with compacts of all sizes, shapes, and styles. So I took
the easy way out and chose the least gaudy of the choices offered—a big round tortoise-
shell number. Boy, war is hell sometimes!*

⁂

Saturday night, November 11, 1944

Dearest Family,

Oh happy day! Joy, as they say in storybooks, reigned unconfined! That's right—
a package from home arrived. Ski was as excited as me. It didn't say Do Not

Open Until Christmas and Dad wrote he was sending film when he could find it, so we had an excuse to peek. Ski ripped it all the way open before I had time to let my conscience bother me. It was the package with Jordan almonds (they lasted almost a day as we both love them), a white blouse, gloves, stationery, and the darling travel chess- and checkerboard. Thanks! I'm desperate for white blouses as we wear them all the time. The tiny combination chess/checkerboard stole the show as Ski loves chess and has been wanting to teach me for ages, so the night it arrived we started playing and eating Jordan almonds. But I promise from now on I won't open any packages until Christmas!

Did I tell you that a cousin of Ski's, a Canadian flyer, was killed here in August? She felt terrible about it as her family is as close to their Canadian relatives as we are to our Pennsylvania ones. We finally had a break in schedule the other day and a chance to take a train to the cemetery where he's just been buried. We boarded the train dressed in Class A winter uniforms, wearing our red long john tops under our white blouses and our heavy lined topcoats over our uniforms, plus our lined boots and wool scarves and heavy gloves. And still we were shivering, Ski blowing her nose both from her cold and her sadness, although she blamed it on her cold. I brought along the chess set so we wouldn't just sit and stare out at the wintry gray landscape.

Four British men were seated (in their most reserved British manner) in the train compartment with us. After only a few miles of Ski explaining to me, again, the elements of chess the Britishers broke down and got into the act, kibitzing us hilariously until we came to our stop. We were enjoying it so much we darn near missed our station and literally had to jump out!

It was bitterly cold on the station platform and in the time it took to buy an armload of lovely baby white chrysanthemums we both were chilled to the bone. A cabbie took us out through bleak and flat countryside to the cemetery. The leaves, which had been so gorgeous the week before, were all the same dreary yellowish shade, and the winter sun only broke through the storm clouds occasionally. The cab turned into the grounds and drove past what seemed like thousands of rows of neat white crosses divided into plots; one for Poland, one for Norway, Czechoslovakia, the United States—a plot for each of the Allies.

When we came to Canada the driver stopped and we walked along a row of crosses towards a group of men placing sod around the graves. Ski asked a worker where we should look for the grave of a Canadian officer killed in August.

The man leaned on his shovel and removed his cap to scratch his head as he looked around at that sea of white crosses. "August?" he repeated, then turned and called to a worker a few graves away. "Where's the August ones? Them's July ain't they?" The other worker pointed across the field and we started searching.

I finally spotted the cross beside a small tree at the end of a row. It said simply, FLYING OFFICER W. T. SHANNON 8-8-44. Sod hadn't yet been placed on the brown ground. Ski was standing with her flowers, just staring at the rows when I called to her. She came over and knelt quickly and arranged the flowers on the grave. We stood for several minutes. I didn't look at Ski and was glad she didn't look at me. All I could think of was how many, many boys there were and how far away from home they were. As we walked back to the car Ski said, "It just makes you want to go out and buy all the flowers you can and put them on all those graves."

We didn't play chess on the train ride back. Instead, we stared out the windows at the depressingly gray and wintry landscape which so accurately reflected our feelings.

It's quite late and we start at six in the morning, so goodnight now.

All my love,
Rosemary

Chapter Nine

Journal   November 13, 1944

The frigid trip to the cemetery sure didn't help Ski's chest cold or my runny nose so early this morning after our first loading we stopped by the dock medical dispensary to pick up some cough medicine. A long line of enlisted men were standing around outside and Ski said, hoarsely, "See, Rosie, it's not me—everybody's catching cold in this climate!" She started over to greet the men when I noticed a sign and grabbed her arm.

"Ski, look." Black letters on a white arrow board pointed the way to the Pro Station. "It's not colds they're here for—that line's for prophylaxis after sex." Ski was aghast. "Oh, no, nooo!" she croaked. The length of the line shocked me too, so we hurried on into the building, trying to hide our red faces as Ski coughed convincingly enough to suggest she was harboring at least an advanced case of pneumonia.

Luckily, Colonel M., the Port's fatherly chief medical officer, spotted us as we walked in and steered us into a side office "I'm afraid you didn't pick the best day, girls," he said. "We're always very busy after the guys return from weekend leave." We'd already heard that the colonel is much respected in the Port and has an international reputation as a doctor. On this foggy morning he told us half the Port already has colds or walking pneumonia. He wrote our prescriptions and groused good-naturedly about his luck at ending up in this land of respiratory winters when his medical specialty is tropical diseases. Said he had expected the Army to send him to the South Pacific to treat malaria, elephantiasis, and other tropical plagues he's spent a lifetime studying. He chuckled. "But that's the Army. I'll bet the world's leading respiratory disease specialist is running around South Pacific islands with the Marines wondering why they sent him there."

* * *

Wednesday, November 22, 1944

Dearest Family,

I've been off to London on urgent business plus the Port is jumping. I feel terrible when I can't manage to write at least once a week, but do remember if there's a lapse in my letters it only means we're busy working. Sometimes we feel so physically drained when we return to the hotel it's impossible to get thoughts together to write. And our beds are wonderfully comfortable, which makes the urge to flop irresistible.

One of Marty's Christmas packages arrived the same day Ski received a package and we've been policing each other ever since. We removed, under surveillance, the outside wrappings and put the pretty packages on the mantel. Not once, but three times, I've caught Ski feeling her package, and *mine*. She reminds me of my sister in a great many ways. So stop worrying about Christmas parcels arriving. We each have a gift to open.

Ski and I planned to celebrate Thanksgiving by telling each other what our families would be doing—to put a sixpence in our gas fireplace, sit in front of our "fire," and talk about Thanksgiving at home, after eating our turkey dinner at the Officers Mess. We rushed to mess at noontime, our mouths watering at the thought of celery, olives, nuts, and cranberry sauce—only to be greeted by spaghetti. Turkey was to be served at night. So we rushed back at suppertime and did get turkey and dressing, but none of the trimmings we'd so looked forward to. It was probably the first Thanksgiving I've not eaten myself sick as the chow line was so long we didn't line up for seconds.

We were immediately recalled to work and spent the next few hours giving out doughnuts instead of turkey to the wounded. They were still very grateful. It was dreadfully cold and as they were carried off the hospital ship they *all* managed to express their thanks. I heard one say to his litter bearer, "I *knew* the Red Cross would be here." When we finally returned to Room 15 it was such a relief to have seen the day through unscathed by homesickness we decided not to tell each other about home at Thanksgiving. Instead we promised to visit each other if this war is ever over.

Caroline and Ann are leaving this week for another base in England—very near here—as a first step towards France. Ski and I are slated to be next, Headquarters keeps promising me. In some ways we all hate leaving as I feel we've built up a smoothly functioning organization, and it's hard to leave something you've helped start. The Army has been wonderfully cooperative, but I was floored the other day when informed by one of the senior officers that we are being sent an Army Letter of Commendation for our outstanding work. He said they'd tried to get us the Army Certificate of Merit, but it wasn't available to us because of the peculiarly unofficial status of the American Red Cross. Copies of the letters are being sent to ARC Headquarters and we're pleased that the Army is making the gesture.

Goodnight now—write often. At the rate mail is arriving this should reach you around Christmas. Hang the tinsel straight, Dad. Don't just throw it on and upset Mom!

My love to you all, and love and hugs to Marliss, Steve, and Bob. There's not a child in England who compares with *my* niece and nephews—tell them for me. And Marty, it's not true I send the boys more love than your kids. The boys are just dawgs, for Pete's sake (but don't tell them I said that, Mom and Dad).

XXX OOO
Roses

The huge amount of supplies we're using up finally has gotten the message through to Headquarters, as at last we're getting more girls. We've had some British Red Cross Club workers come to help out and last week a number of new girls arrived. For how long I don't know. The hotel manager temporarily bedded them down in the faded elegance of the high-ceilinged third-floor ballroom until he can work them into regular rooms. The incongruous sight of Red Cross girls in battle dress camped out with duffle bags and footlockers amid temporary beds and wardrobe closets resting on highly polished hardwood floors throws me every time I enter the ornately chandeliered room. Since Elizabethan days royalty have graced this ballroom with their presence and in the nineteenth century Jane Austen, Queen Victoria, and Thackeray attended the famous assemblies held here.

One night when I was completing our work schedules for the next day, Ski came roaring down from the ballroom and burst into our room. She sounded frantic. "Rosie, you've got to come up right away. There's a girl just arrived who's bad news. She's going to cause trouble, mark my words! She hated her last assignment and she's criticizing the Red Cross, and she's ugly and . . ."

"Wait a minute, Ski," I said (I say this a lot to her). "Hold your horses, it can't be that bad. I was just about to hand out the schedules, so calm down, will you?"

"You've got to come now," Ski insisted, not calming down. "I've never met anyone like her and she'll ruin the attitude of the new girls in another ten minutes. Wait 'til you see her!" So of course I went, as Ski with her impetuosity is a great help in keeping me abreast of what's happening, almost before it happens. Muttering and plunging up the steps ahead of me, she shoved open the double ballroom doors and burst in to announce, in her loud voice, "Here's our captain, Rosie."

I could have shot her. Kari and Bettie were chatting with three new girls they'd been crewing with all day and at Ski's announcement all conversation stopped and everyone turned to stare. Except for one girl bent over her duffle bag pulling out gear. All I could see was her rear end. She slowly straightened up and turned around to face me, hands on her hips. Ski was right, I thought, she's certainly not good-looking. Short and stocky with an uneven complexion, a noticeably large nose, and black hair streaked with gray strands. Probably ten years older than most of us. Her dark eyes bored into me from under thick dark eyebrows. She took a step towards me, then stopped. She wasn't smiling.

"I'm Lil," she said slowly and clearly. "I'm a Jew and I'm from Brooklyn and I don't like to take orders." It was a challenge, not a greeting.

I took a deep breath in the silence, then stuck out my hand and smiled, I hoped cordially. "Welcome, Lil. I'm a gentile, I'm from San Francisco, and," I groped for the right words, "I don't like to give orders, so we ought to get along fine." Turning as quickly as I could I walked out the door. Then stewed for the rest of the night trying to figure out how to work someone with that big a chip on her shoulder into our crew.

I needn't have worried. In a few short weeks Lil has become one of our most popular crew members, both with the crew and with the GIs coming through the Port. Her Brooklyn accent pleases all the guys as she pronounces bottle and shuttle as only a true Brooklyn native can. She's told us she took a leave from her job as an English teacher in one of the toughest high schools in New York to join the Red Cross. She's blunt about the rough time she had in her last Red Cross assignment, stationed with two girls who thought only of dating and how their hair looked, and not of what they're supposed to be doing for the troops (and we've all met a few, if only a few, of those in this organization). When it was time to make doughnuts or scrub out the dirty Clubmobile they passed the buck to Lil. She most resented, I gathered, their prejudice and plain meanness. Once she discovered we're all working almost around the clock here and pitching in, she's a different person.

Her talents are enormous as her maturity is seasoned with intelligence and experience and a great sense of humor, although she certainly doesn't present the typical image most men have of Red Cross girls. For she's not only the pal or sister figure the GIs expect us to be, she's old enough to be a mother figure to some of the guys from the cities. She can give a former zoot-suiter, big-city GI unvarnished hell in a few explicit words if he's out of line, as easily as she lends a shoulder to a scared young GI never before off the farm. She also jitterbugs better than any of us, which delights the guys, and when ships are late loading she shoots a great game of craps. She always has a pair of lucky dice handy in her pocket.

I found this out three days after she joined us when I pushed through a big circle of GIs behind the Clubmobile and caught her on hands and knees, a pile of dollar bills, English pounds, shillings, and pence in front of her, cleaning out a group of crapshooters. She admits she almost always wins but gives the money back to the men as they board ship—often with a lecture on the dangers of gambling if they're no good at it. She can handle anything and I wish I had three more just like her.

If ugly can be beautiful, you only have to know Lil. She's wonderful.

⚜

Journal   *November 28, 1944*

Guess I'll have to keep this new secret code in my journal for safety. It just arrived from London and at this late hour I feel like grousing as it's hard enough to figure out how many supplies to order without trying to guess how many supplies we'll need two weeks from last night (or the day after tomorrow) and then have to encode it. Maybe I should call General Eisenhower to ask why the advance has slowed down and so many replacements are pouring through the Port? With no other responsibilities I'd love playing this code game, but after too many hours on the docks my feeble mind rebels at *translating troops into Spam and jam. Now it's back to the Port loading office for information before I try to encode it.*

SECRET

24th November 1944

SECRET   CODE TO BE PUT INTO USE IMMEDIATELY

To Indicate:

1. Troops arriving from the States, start messages with the word SEND.
2. Troops arriving from France, start messages with the word REQUIRE.
3. Troops leaving for the States, start messages with the word PLEASE SEND.
4. Troops leaving for France, start messages with the word URGENTLY REQUIRE.

Numbers of Troops	500	CAKES
	2,000	HONEY
	3,000	JAM
	5,000	SPAM

To indicate multiples of 5,000 men, use the words CASES OF SPAM, i.e., 2 cases of Spam means 10,000 men, 5 cases of Spam means 25,000 men.

Day of Operation	Monday	NEEDED BADLY
	Tuesday	SUPPLIES LOW
	Wednesday	ARRIVING TODAY
	Thursday	PAY CASH
	Friday	BILL ME
	Saturday	CHARGE ACCOUNT
	Sunday	QUICKLY PLEASE

**BURN ALL PREVIOUS CODES IMMEDIATELY
ON RECEIPT OF A NEW ONE.**

**SAFEGUARD THIS CODE IN ACCORDANCE
WITH SECURITY MEASURES.**

Example of a Message:

Plain language: 6,000 troops leaving for France on Saturday
Coded message: URGENTLY REQUIRE SPAM AND BISCUITS. CHARGE ACCOUNT.

Journal   *December 5, 1944*

Finally official notification of a job I was given by Headquarters in September!

AMERICAN RED CROSS
IN GREAT BRITAIN

Telephone Number Mayfair 7234   12 Grosvenor Square, London W.1.

4th December, 1944

Miss Rosemary Langheldt
Captain, A.R.C. Clubmobile

Dear Miss Langheldt,

It is a pleasure to notify you that you have been promoted to "Captain 1st class," and that as of December 16th you will receive an increase in salary. May I congratulate you on this well-deserved promotion, and thank you for the loyal and unselfish service which you have given, not only to the American Red Cross, but to the thousands of troops whom you serve. I have no doubt that you will continue the fine work you are doing.

I also take pleasure in enclosing a Captain's flash for your uniform.

Very sincerely,

S. Keene Mitchell, Jr.
Director, Clubmobile Dept.

December 12, 1944

Dearest ones,

This little Christmas card with choirboys singing is a typical English greeting. I could find none that said I love you and miss you and wish I could spend Christmas Eve with you. I'm not sending gifts home for Christmas as I haven't been able to find anything nice enough for you, as the few things I thought you might like take "points" to buy (and we're not issued any English points), or are not shippable during wartime.

So I'm sending you only my love—but an awful lot of that. At this point Ski and I each have two packages ready to be opened. I have one from Marty and one from Eleanore, my store secretary, remember?

Between ship loadings the other day Ski and I drove out through gray fog to stop at a little white church in the New Forest we'd spotted before. It has beautiful holly trees on three sides, so guess what's sharing space on our mantel with the gift packages? It's a joy to walk into our room and see that touch of Christmas.

All my love,
Rosie

Dearest Family,

I can just imagine you all at Thanksgiving, and I'll bet the old songs sounded wonderful on your new piano, Mother. I can picture it in the living room, adding even more atmosphere to a room you've filled with so many warm and inviting touches.

I am propped up in bed writing this and planning to retire early, as we have been working a terrific schedule. I feel a little lost in the room as Ski is not with me. We took her to the hospital yesterday with pneumonia and she'll be in until Christmas anyway, I'm afraid. She had a temperature of 104 last night and is a pretty sick girl. At least she'll get wonderful care and a much-needed rest. Ski is one of those who can't relax—she never spares herself anything, throws all her energy into her work (in fact throws her energy into everything), and our hard work and this damp, cold climate finally caught up with her. I'll have to make her take it easier from now on.

Things have sure been happening here the past two weeks. All the big Red Cross heads have been visiting us to watch our operations. I couldn't quite understand why at first, as they never before have sent down the London bigwigs. The statisticians were amazed in checking our doughnut consumption figures—it seems we averaged 60,000 doughnuts per girl per month the past two months, and they couldn't believe the figures. Do you suppose the statisticians thought we were operating a black market in doughnuts?

The first visitors to "drop in" on us stayed two days and never had a chance to gather everyone together for a meeting (as they had planned) because we were working around the clock. Thank goodness I had talked to Buddy, our London Clubmobile boss, who warned me some officials might be dropping by, and checked back at the hotel every so often to take them in tow or parcel them out among the crews. They got an eyeful of our loading operations as well as hospital ships, hospitals, and marshaling area work. *And* were frankly amazed. It pleases me to report we ran them ragged and they were worn out after two days and nights of running around cold docks at all hours. But I think they enjoyed wolfing hot doughnuts and coffee with the GIs—if only as a change from the hot meals in lovely settings that I've enjoyed with them when I'm in London on business.

Then the head of the Clubmobile department, a Mr. Keene Mitchell, arrived in town, because it seems he couldn't believe the amount of work he was told we were doing. After seeing our operations he informed me he'd like to talk with some Army officers, if I could possibly arrange it, regarding future plans in order for him to know whether to enlarge our doughnut kitchen and equipment. I walked him right into the Port Commander's office without a minute's delay and the colonel spent a half hour telling Mr. Mitchell what a superb job we were doing. He said he had tried to have us decorated for our outstanding work, but the Red Cross is not eligible for military awards so he is sending us (the crew members here during the boom) letters of commendation. Everywhere we went the brass received us royally and bragged about our work. I was embarrassed, as it looked like a snow job.

Mr. Mitchell told me he had never witnessed such wonderful feeling between the ARC and the Army before—often there is antipathy and lack of cooperation. The upshot of the visits is we're getting more help, more equipment—including another Clubmobile—and lots of praise. Evidently we are the most important group in England. He has requested us not to ask to go to France right now as he thinks we're needed more here. At this point, it looks as though we will remain here for a while yet. I guess I don't care—except selfishly—where we are as long as I can feel we're doing necessary work. The comments the Port brass made to Mr. Mitchell about our work really were a morale booster for all the crew and put our long hours in a different perspective.

An amusing part of all this praise is that we seem to be the "happiest" crew in England. One of our new members told me she'd been told by three people how lucky she was to be coming here as "even the air is different—everyone's happy there." Mr. Mitchell kept complimenting me on the way the crew ran, so I mentioned the importance of sorting the girls into congenial combinations. Then, with such a busy schedule, no one has time to be unhappy.

To know our efforts are appreciated is a real tonic.

And, oh yes! I have been made a captain, first class (whatever that means), as of the middle of the month. It does mean a raise—I think $25 a month, but Mother, I was too surprised to inquire. The real surprise for me has been that money doesn't seem to matter much in wartime. As Red Cross workers our meals, cleaning, travel expenses, medical expenses, and lodging are all taken care of by the voucher system. Plus we're so busy there's little time to shop or sightsee. Think most of us feel richer than we ever felt working for decent salaries at home.

It's strange, Dad, that you should ask me if I've ever read Thomas Hardy or been to Stonehenge. I've always loved Hardy, especially *Tess of the d'Urbervilles*, and have always wanted to see Stonehenge. One clear but frightfully cold day, shortly before I got your letter, Ski and Bettie and I took a few hours off and drove to Salisbury. We had lunch at the Red Lion Inn, a medieval hostelry still going strong, and spent an hour in the beautiful cathedral. We poked and rummaged around in antique shops, then we drove on, over tiny, twisty roads lined with hedgerows and thatched cottages. Suddenly, it got colder and bleaker as clouds swept in and the scenery more plain-like (the Romans camped on Salisbury Plain). Just after it started to rain we came in sight of Stonehenge.

As Ski exclaimed, it looked exactly as she remembered from a woodcut on the first page of her English history book in grammar school—right opposite the paragraph on the oldest signs of civilization in England. We pulled up and started to get out when an Army jeep, containing GIs who'd been following us for some time, stopped and asked if we were lost. We told them we had come to see Stonehenge, so the GIs decided to go look at it too—said they'd never heard of it. We all walked across the plains into the wind towards the queer gray stones and were chilled through just in the time it took us to reach the circle. The scene was as coldly forbidding as the night Tess of the d'Urbervilles stumbled upon it. We all braced against the wind to stand in the midst of the circle of tilted stone monoliths. Ski shouted to the guys trying to explain what Stonehenge *meant* but she was drowned out by the engines of a flight of planes towing gliders passing overhead. The fragility of the gliders loaded with troops, buffeting in that high wind a few hundred feet above us, was even more chilling than the wind. For we knew they were preparing for a real drop soon. We were literally frozen when we got back to the Clubmobile but still glad we saw it as we did. Stonehenge goes best with a bleak landscape and a gray sky.

Enough for now. I'm tired and you're probably tired of reading. Goodnight—I love you all dearly and am so grateful for your wonderful letters.

All my love,
Roses

P.S. Here's a quote from Mr. Mitchell's letter to me after his visit:

"To say that I had a fruitful and most enjoyable experience during my recent visit with you and your fine crew would be to understate the case. The competent manner in which you conducted your operations certainly aroused my admiration. You and your girls are doing one of the finest jobs being done by the American Red Cross anywhere and you are to be congratulated on your unselfish and untiring efforts. I was also very pleased with the fine spirit of your whole crew, and the comradeship which exists among them."

Chapter Ten

Journal

December 15, 1944

Just returned from a drive over to Netley Hospital to see how Ski's getting along. The old hospital sits on a hill filled with ancient evergreens and looks out across the water towards the Isle of Wight one way and back towards the Port the other. All Port water traffic is clearly visible from its distinctive high windows. The huge building also features very high ceilings and wide corridors painted a sickly pale green. Doubt if it's changed much since Florence Nightingale was a nurse there. When I finally found Ski's room I almost walked past as she was obscured by three guys in bathrobes standing beside her bed. Then I heard her unmistakable throaty hoarse chuckle.

Propped up on two pillows she looked pale and fragile, her eyes especially sparkly, probably from the remnants of fever. In fact she looked like Camille receiving callers, and introduced me all around. Between hacking coughs, she told me about each man, including division, branch of service, and what caused him to end up in the hospital. As one man wandered out, another wandered in, so it was a while before I had a chance to mention that I thought this a weird way to recover from pneumonia and had she considered shutting her door occasionally?

When we finally got a few minutes alone together she insisted she was feeling much better and resting lots. She promised to save her voice and it's obvious how much she hates not being in on all the action at the Port. She grilled me on every last detail of the past days. Said she was going to get to sleep early and get rid of her cough. Relieved, I stood to leave just as Tom walked into the room wearing a fresh uniform and a great smile. He wore his overseas cap rakishly cocked over his left eye and carried an armload of lovely spring flowers. Gad knows where he found them in the middle of this winter freeze.

"Tom," sighed Ski, lingering on the word and gazing on him with obvious pleasure, "how sweet of you." The last words I heard as I walked out the door were Ski's, hoarse but only too clear. "Tom, maybe you can stay and walk me down to the recreation room. They're going to show that new movie Saratoga Trunk tonight and Rosie has to get back to the docks." And there went my more-rest-and-sleep theory.

All the way back to the Port I worried about their relationship. I had been so encouraged the day Ski and Bettie and I took off to explore Salisbury and Stonehenge.

For both Bettie and Ski have fallen in love and, it seems to me, spent most of that beautiful day facing up to the pros and cons of their romances. They finally made up their minds, I thought, to put romances on the back burner until they're transferred to the continent or the war's over. And then decide. They'd cool things, Bettie said firmly, and just be friends. No major decisions now. They both seemed relieved after they finally arrived at this conclusion.

"Invite them home after the war," I suggested, trying to be helpful, "and see them in a civilian setting. If it's really love, it will last—at least that's what Mother always told me."

"Easy enough for you to say, Rosie," Ski snapped. "You're not in love."

"And I have no intention of falling in love overseas," I said firmly, and concentrated on driving as they rehashed their situations yet again.

Bettie's going with a GI she met while working on a hospital ship and thinks he's wonderful. We've met him and like him and he obviously adores her. Jerry's a sergeant, twenty-nine, and a baker on the hospital ship with ambitious career plans for after the war. But Bettie's beginning to realize what completely different backgrounds they come from and is already worrying about how their feelings will hold up in a civilian world. Actually, she's agonizing over what they really have in common, except for a great emotional attraction. He's gentle, considerate, caring—and bakes her wonderful cakes and treats. She has a big sweet tooth, which, she admits, doesn't lead to clear thinking either.

The fact that he's an enlisted man has nothing to do with her problem. One of the things we like most about working in this Port is that the usual division between officers and enlisted men isn't strictly enforced. At least not nearly as much as in some of the line outfits filled with trade school (West Point) men. Ski's Tom calls them "chicken outfits," where a bird colonel or above (a bird colonel is a full colonel with the insignia of an eagle on his uniform) devotes his days to enforcing every last rule in the book. Even though the Port Commander is a West Point graduate, everyone here in the Port seems to work together without undue ceremony about rank, probably because most are not career Army men but here only because of the war. We Red Cross girls discovered right away that the insignia on the uniform hasn't much to do with the intelligence inside the suit. As Tom puts it, there are jackasses in both categories. And also wonderful minds. So despite our instructions during Washington training that we date only officers, it's a rule often ignored.

Ski and Tom's emotional attraction is so obvious it sends off sparks. And seems more intense every day. She finds him "kind of dashing," she tells us, and admires his sense of humor and his intelligence. His crude honesty (he calls it "cutting through the bullshit") delights her while often shocking others. She finds his background, which includes struggling through a broken family life to pull himself up by the bootstraps, absolutely appealing. His bawdy stories of worlds light-years away from her quiet New England town—tales of racetrack life, New Orleans, gambling joints, prostitutes, and the seamy side of life—have opened up a whole new world to her. His accent (what is it? Pal Joey?) bothers her, but not very much. Maybe it's his confidence. Whatever, she's still enchanted. What bothers me is she hasn't gotten around to mentioning one word about him in her letters home to her parents. Once she does that, I can let them *worry about it and won't feel somehow responsible. Bettie, on the other hand, says she's written reams home about Jerry, and of course her parents are worried she'll go off the deep end.*

After seeing Ski with Tom in the hospital tonight I realize I jumped too quickly to a conclusion that hasn't been reached yet. Gad, why did I ever agree to be captain and responsible for this crew?

✍✍✍

Journal   *December 19, 1944*

Just when I think I have the code mastered and can send orders quickly they send a new one—especially frustrating with all our sudden changes of schedules these days. It takes so long to figure the dumb things out—this time it's blotting paper and carbons, for Pete's sake! Looks like I'll have to drive to London to pick up a gross of envelopes if I follow instruction four. Damn!

SECRET

SECRET   NEW CODE TO BE PUT INTO IMMEDIATE USE

11th December 1944

To Indicate the Arrival of Troops at Your Port:

1. Start all messages with the word REQUIRE.
2. Follow this with the code word indicating the number of troops:

500	BLOTTING PAPER
1,000	LABELS
2,000	POSTCARDS
3,000	NOTEPAPER
4,000	CARBONS
5,000	ENVELOPES

To indicate multiples of 5,000 men, use the words BOXES OF ENVELOPES, i.e., 3 boxes of envelopes means 15,000 men, 5 boxes of envelopes means 25,000 men.

3. Then indicate the day of the operation:

Monday	URGENTLY
Tuesday	AT ONCE
Wednesday	IMMEDIATELY
Thursday	SHORTLY
Friday	SEND TODAY
Saturday	PLEASE SUPPLY
Sunday	WITHOUT DELAY

Example:

Plain language: 7,500 troops arriving on Saturday
Coded message: REQUIRE NOTEPAPER, CARBONS, AND BLOTTING PAPER. PLEASE SUPPLY.

**BURN ALL PREVIOUS CODES UPON RECEIPT OF
THIS NEW ONE.**

4. Acknowledge receipt of this code at once, marking your letter SECRET
   and placing it in an envelope marked SECRET inside another ordinary
   envelope. This should be mailed through the APO.
5. SAFEGUARD THIS CODE IN ACCORDANCE WITH SECURITY
   MEASURES, about which you have received instructions.

❧

December 20, 1944

Dearest ones,

No time to write but wanted to send this commendation on and see if it gets
through. Well and busy,

Love,
Roses

HEADQUARTERS 14TH PORT
UNITED KINGDOM BASE
COMMUNICATIONS ZONE
EUROPEAN THEATER OF OPERATIONS

APO 229, U.S. Army
19 December 1944
SLK/mjt

201.2
Subject: Commendation
To: Miss Rosemary Langheldt

I am sincerely grateful for the work you have done as Captain of
the Clubmobiles and trucks servicing the Hards since your arrival here
on July 31, 1944, and feel that you are deserving of the highest commendation.

The keen understanding you have displayed in the innumerable
problems which have confronted you has assured the success that the
Clubmobile Units attached to this Port have achieved. I am proud of
your superior supervision and untiring efforts which have been so outstanding in providing our American men passing through this area
with hot food and drinks.

You have, indeed, made a great contribution to the health and
happiness of the troop personnel and therefore to the success of our
men overseas. I am forwarding a copy of this commendation to Red

Cross Headquarters with a personal letter to further amplify your splendid work.

Sincerely yours,

(Signed) Sherman L. Kiser
Colonel, T. C.
Commanding

Saturday, December 30, 1944

Dearest Family,

Christmas is over and it's been a little hectic. We've been stationed here so long we had a cheery one in many ways as we know lots of people to wish a Merry Christmas. We're working day and night—our Christmas celebration was sandwiched in between loadings and hospital ships and emergencies.

Ski was released from the hospital on Christmas Eve Day and that evening, we had our Christmas "openings." Tom, the Army lieutenant Ski's been going with the past few months, came to our room about ten minutes after I got Ski back from the hospital bringing his pals, Tiny and Saari, two Port lieutenants. Tiny stands a mere 6 feet, 7 inches tall, Saari about 5 feet, 8 inches—but they whoosh around on a huge motorcycle doing I'm not sure what for the Port. I accepted a ride with Tiny once (I was dumb enough to say I'd never been on a motorcycle) and he whooshed me down the Hards and along the Roman wall so fast I was petrified. The three of them were lugging a darling tree about 4½ feet tall (planted too!) that Ski had made decorations for while in the hospital, so we quickly decorated it. Then had our "openings" while a stream of friends and crew popped in to welcome Ski home and say Merry Christmas. The traffic was pretty thick in and out of Room 15 in the short time we had to celebrate.

Ski and I each had four packages to open. I had Marty's package containing the wonderful film (I'm almost out!) and the chicken noodle soup, Willis's parents' lovely box of stationery, the scrumptious package from Mr. Robert at the store, and Ellie's huge box of fine airmail stationery, which I'm using now. It was such fun. Mr. Robert's package from the store, Mom, didn't hurt my morale a bit, especially the perfume. Tom gave Ski and me each a wonderful bottle of Cuir de Russie from France. That ought to take care of any lingering odor of coffee and doughnuts, right?

We managed to get to mess for a turkey dinner on Christmas Day, but our celebrating consisted mainly of amusing the GIs going through the Port all day and most of the night. I made Ski skip part of the night shift as she is still weak from her hospital stay, but our Clubmobile was bright with holly and greens and mistletoe and the GIs seemed so to appreciate our being on hand. Think the job Eloise and Kari did on their Clubmobile was the biggest hit with the guys. They decorated their truck with a little evergreen tree, then punched holes in the tops of C ration cans and threaded string through to hang them on the tree as ornaments. They wore adhesive tape on several fingers each when they finally got the holes punched and, as Eloise remarked, if anyone reached into the tree they might bleed to death. The final touch was tying mistletoe above the serving window so it hung over the GIs as they were served. The guys kept complaining it was hung in the wrong place as it was over them instead of over the girls.

It was, and still is, bitterly cold—hoarfrost weather, the English call it. Christmas Day was beautiful and freezing, all the rooftops and streets white with frost, but the GIs didn't notice the fine holiday weather. They were too busy feeling sorry for themselves being so far from home. When they talk to us and realize we're just as far from home it seems to cheer them up a little. One huge bunch of troops had the docks rocking with their "Jingle Bells" rendition before we finished serving them.

The European situation is certainly grim and we're seeing some of the most heartbreaking sights. The results of the German drive have affected us so directly, the stark horror of war impresses itself upon our minds more strongly each day. I wish I could say more as there's so much I'd like to write but it will have to wait until a later date.

Tomorrow's New Year's Eve and if we don't have to work late we may go to services at Winchester Cathedral. Ski and Tom—and I have a tentative date with Joe, if his LST is in. Joe's a tall, very handsome, and nice Navy lieutenant. He's twenty-seven, up for lieutenant commander, and fun.

I met him one night when I dragged into the hotel from work—dirty, tired, and completely a horror. Pam, our English friend who works in the Red Cross Club and has invited Ski and me to her country home so often, was in the lobby and insisted on introducing me to Joe. He couldn't understand why I wouldn't go out with him. I just kept telling him I was tired and was going to bed, which I proceeded to do, thinking as I made my exit what a dim view (as the English say) he must be taking of me. He couldn't understand a Red Cross girl turning down a date. I couldn't understand why he kept asking me out. Anyway, I finally dated him on a later night. The reason I'm mentioning this to my family (*only*) is because all the crew (and we have twelve girls now) think he's the most attractive Navy guy in town and I know my sister Martha, the family expert at snagging handsome men, will be glad that Rosie made good. Seriously, he's a nice fellow and exceedingly clean-cut in the Bob B. and Bob L. tradition. Has a wonderful sense of humor, too. The first time he called to pick me up for a date, he lifted Bob B.'s picture off the mantel, stared at it for a long minute (and you know how good-looking Bob is), then said, "Rosie, you didn't tell me your father was in the service too!" Ski almost died laughing. All of which is enough about Joe. Too much, in fact, as I'm not interested in him seriously—just wanted the family, and especially my sister, to know that war is not all grim. It has its fun times too. Sometimes I have to remind myself of that.

Goodnight now. I do love you and miss you, but somehow I always feel we are very near. Time flies over here we are so busy—and the work seems more challenging each day.

All my love,
Roses

P.S. Please send me *Forever Amber* if you have a chance. Kathleen Winsor was in Cal same time as me and married Bob Herwig, our all-American football player. I remember her beauty and would like to see how she writes.

Journal   *December 30, 1944*

Just sealed my letter home and am feeling frustrated because I can tell the family only light and trivial details of a Christmas week so shadowed it broke our hearts. Hope they read between the lines and know there are more important things going on than those I am permitted to write about.

The day before Christmas Eve we started work at 0400 to feed several shiploads of troops. Just as we finally finished, the boys were suddenly offloaded, and I was informed the ships were to reload that night with infantry replacements. A high-security operation and real rush job because of the German drive in the Bulge. I already had made crew assignments for Christmas week and knew several of us hoped to grab a few free hours to be with friends after finishing work. But when I asked for volunteers (sure to be six extra hours—at least—in the middle of the night on bone-chilling cold, damp, and foggy docks), all I got was the usual "Okay, coach, which piers and how many?" It's no wonder I love my crew.

The division being rushed over was the 66th. On December 23rd, they were yanked out of camp so fast—without any notice—they still wore 66th snarling Black Panther division patches on their uniforms. Usually all division insignia is removed if it's a high-security operation. The cooks had to leave stuffed turkeys and Christmas dinner preparations behind. They'd all had Christmas parties planned and suddenly they were eating K rations and headed for a channel crossing. Always especially tough in winter.

They dragged into the dock area exhausted and it was easy to see they were not in a happy frame of mind. They began arriving early evening and our crews were there to serve units before the Port started loading the two troopships waiting at Pier 38: the British-controlled ship Leopoldville, a huge Belgian passenger liner, and the SS Cheshire. It was so cold in the dock sheds some of the guys lit little bonfires to try and keep warm during the long wait. There seemed to be more than normal confusion in the loadings and we'd see an occasional "lost" platoon wandering through the piers trying to locate their company. The men seemed so young. Many carried Christmas-wrapped boxes or goodies that wouldn't fit into their packs and told us they were determined to celebrate Christmas wherever they happened to be.

I used the Joker, the wonderful Canadian truck Tom gave us, to check supplies and shuttle more coffee and doughnuts where needed. By the time I drove into Pier 38 the troops crowded into that huge cavernous shell were in full-voiced rendition of "White Christmas," the reverberating sound of thousands of voices seeming to swell the shed in a mighty plea. I broke out all over in goosebumps. Eloise and Kari were in charge of our main Clubmobile and I noticed their eyes misted over too.

For hours we served the men, and sang and talked and laughed with them. We did, as usual, a lot of listening and admiring pictures in wallets. We lingered past midnight to stand by the gangplank and wish the last units well and cheer them off as they finally boarded. It was so dark you couldn't see much, but every now and then a GI leaned over to kiss one of us on the cheek or give an awkward one-handed pat on the shoulder.

Most of us sleepwalked our ways through the loading schedule for Christmas Eve as it was just as busy—and just as long. The docks and Hards were full of embarking troops being poured cross-channel. Late on Christmas Eve, Eloise and Kari reported, they rushed over to serve a hospital ship that arrived unexpectedly. They spotted it coming in to dock ablaze with lights, white sides gleaming, a huge Red Cross symbol clearly visible on each side because hospital ships speed straight across channel brightly signaling their presence to friend and foe alike. Eloise kept thinking how familiar some of the walking wounded looked as they came down the gangplank and, being Eloise, bubbled out to one hollow-eyed boy in a disheveled uniform, "Gosh, you look familiar, friend!" and the boy said, "You're right. You just served us last night—on the Leopoldville." And that's how they heard that the Leopoldville had been sunk just before entering Cherbourg Harbor. Eloise was so shocked that the GI was gone before she could ask him anything else.

When Kari and Eloise finished work it was pretty close to midnight and they decided to go to church. They'd never discussed religious preferences but just felt the urge to go, so they attended midnight mass at a nearby Catholic church. It was lit mostly by candles and packed with GIs, British and American sailors, Royal Marines, and Royal Engineers in all sorts of garb. Kari and Eloise stood against the back wall and could see the only attempt at dressing up was that all the men had their hats off, the candlelight flickering on their freshly combed hair.

Eloise admits she had trouble sleeping when they got back from church as she suddenly remembered it was a year to the day since her older brother's squadron returned from Atlantic patrol duty and he showed up on leave in Connecticut. On Christmas Day. Then was lost at sea four months later. And a beau of hers (Eloise is very New England in terminology) had been lost in the Pacific during the year. She cried herself to sleep as quietly as she could when she heard Kari doing the same across the room in her bed. Kari's already told us that her fiancé, in the free Norwegian Air Force, was killed on D day.

Christmas Day was beautiful but freezing cold hoarfrost weather—and devastating as rumors flew around the Port about the Leopoldville. While I was checking our work schedules early Christmas morning at the Maritime Chambers, the Port loading headquarters, Colonel Jim told me the details. The ship was in sight of the harbor when *it was torpedoed and they feared at least 800 lives or more had been lost. Since I've been stationed here other ships have hit mines crossing the channel and been lost, but the* Leopoldville *was a large transport with over 2,200 troops aboard. The thought of it going down was horrible.*

When Barbara drove into the dock area for her very early Christmas morning assignment she spotted a British "dockie" holding a soggy life jacket from the Leopoldville. He told her it had just been brought in by one of the channel patrol boats. She sat down on the dock and began sobbing. Told me she couldn't help it as she remembered all the guys she had talked with and all those pictures of wives and girlfriends she'd admired and all the singing during that long night.

So Christmas Day was especially difficult. We served thousands of troops being rushed over to try and stop the German drive. It was obvious they all knew where they were headed. On the Hards, looking up into the clear sky, we could see literally hundreds of contrails from a flight of bombers rendezvousing overhead. The bomber flights had been grounded by fog for days, unable to help out with the German breakthrough. But since Christmas morning dawned clear and bright, they could again fly. When the big flight started to head off toward the channel, first a few GIs, then instantly everyone on the Hards, looked up, waved their arms, and shook their fists skyward as they joined in a shouting mass chant, "Go, Go, Goooo!"

That's why it was so hard to write home. The first chance we had, our crew finally got together to celebrate a late Christmas and share our feelings of the past days. Drew numbers so we each gave one gift. Barbara, our artistic one, decorated the tree in the room she shares with Bettie with gift wrap ribbon tied in bows and sparkling balls of crinkled wrapping paper, retrieved from Christmas packages sent from home. It was wonderful to share true feelings with our family—for that's what our crew has become.

Part Three

Falling in Love

Despite bitterly cold weather in England and on the continent, the Allied offense was again on track by early 1945. Good news greeted us daily—our 69th division had linked up with the Russians, Generals Patton and Bradley were pressing Germany from one side, General Montgomery and his forces from another, the Russians from the east. Both Patton and Montgomery claimed credit for crossing the Rhine first. But Hitler was cornered in Berlin, and for the first time certainty of victory seemed real. The war news was wonderful.

And awful, for as the Allies got deeper into Germany they ran into concentration camps and uncovered the worst horror of the Third Reich.

News from the Pacific was riveting. The Japanese were losing ground, slowly and bloodily, and flying suicidal kamikaze attacks on shipping lanes, but the Marines were about to take Iwo Jima. We worried over the experts' estimates of what it would take to conquer Japan—2 million lives and two years—and knew that even after Hitler surrendered, the other half of the war was far from over.

And then morale was buoyed with the advent of one of England's most beautiful springs.

Chapter Eleven

Dearest ones,

Enclosing a couple of things for your amusement so you'll know I think of you every day. The first is a "poem" (and I use quotes advisedly) circulating around the Port, a popular GI doggerel which describes general GI attitude in the middle of this very harsh winter:

Life in England

Where the heavy dew slips through the breeze,
And you wade in mud up to your knees,
Where the sun don't shine and the rain blows free,
And the fog is so thick you can hardly see,
England.

Where we live on brussels sprouts and Spam,
And those powdered eggs aren't worth a damn.
In town you eat their fish and spuds,
And wash them down with a mug of suds,
England.

You hold your nose when you gulp it down,
It bites your stomach and then you frown.
It burns your tongue, your throat feels queer,
It's rightly called "Bitters"—it sure isn't beer,
England.

Where prices are high and the queues are long,
And those GI Yanks are always wrong.
Where scotch is watered four bits a snort,
And limey cabbies ne'er stand short,
England.

Where most of the girls are blond and cold,
And think Yank pockets are filled with gold.
"Piccadilly Commandos" with painted allure,
Steer clear of 'em boys, or you're ruined for sure,
England.

And those pitch black nights when you stay out late,
It's so damn dark you can't navigate,
No transportation, so you have to hike,
And get knocked on your can by a damn bike,
England.

This Isle is not worth saving—I don't think,
Cut loose those balloons—let the damn thing sink.
I don't complain, but I'll let you know,
Life's rougher than "Hell," ask GI Joe,
Believe me, bud, that is England.

Also sending on this note to show you how wolves operate in the ETO. Toss it after you read it, as I'm ignoring the invitation. It's from one of the Port Commander's fair-haired boys. From what I hear the major's happily married but likes Red Cross girls. His invitation for me to come to the subport where he's operating for a long weekend and bring Eloise and Kari and Ski "if I like" to ride in his heated sedan and stay in the best hotel, get "slightly irrigated on some Haig and Haig, and eat the best steak I've ever eaten" is ridiculous. And this, after always telling me when he's here at the Port that we're working too hard.

As you, my parents, must know, I haven't had a steak in ages or Haig and Haig for as long as I can remember. I hope you realize I'm not in the habit of getting irrigated on anything, given the chance. Honest, Mom and Dad. Some people win the war the easy way, don't they? Oh yes, he has a boat—the goat! As you can see from the note he is friendly and charming (and I hear a very efficient officer) but I wonder how he's going to explain all these extracurricular activities when he returns home to his family and real life, as Ski's friend Tom puts it.

※◎※

Journal   *January 12, 1945*

They say this is the coldest winter in England in a century and I believe it. Three of us, including me, got over our "walking pneumonia," as the Port doctor called it, without missing work. But Ski's back in the hospital, this time with acute sinus problems. Tom offered to go see her with me if I could get away for a couple hours, as she's in an American Field Hospital and he knows the way. He suggested we take the Joker, the Canadian lorry he gave us, to surprise her with the improvements his shop made on it. After Ski went into the hospital again Tom told me he needed to service the Joker and

Rosie with troops on the Hards after snowball fight, winter 1944.

would loan me a jeep for the day. When I went back to pick up the truck, Tom was standing beside it, a silly grin on his face. He'd had his men stencil a smiling Donald Duck and the words "City of Moosup" on the sides of the hood. Moosup is Ski's tiny hometown and Tom was delighted with himself, sure Ski would love this accolade to her New England village.

She certainly did—she laughed herself into a coughing fit when she saw it. The great news is she's much better and hopes to be discharged in a day or two. Caroline and Ann are back and a wonderful addition, but we're still swamped.

⚓

Journal   *January 15, 1945*

Maybe the cold winter makes me view things too harshly. I find myself regarding the word "quaint" with different eyes than when we first stepped into this historic hostelry and were charmed to our eyeballs by the look and feel of old England. For one thing, the smell of cabbage or brussels sprouts permeates our rooms at night. We realize the English have little choice in selection of foods, but why are only the smelliest ones served?

Our room, on the floor right above the mews, is most noteworthy for the sound of rats scrambling under the floorboards every night as we huddle under comforters trying to warm up enough to fall asleep. Even clad in red long johns, flannel pajamas, with our wool overcoat liners over them and heavy GI wool socks on our feet, we often still can't shake the chills for a while. Voices of drunken servicemen, drifting up from High Street rendering, and I do mean rendering, enthusiastic choruses of "Lily Marlene" or "Roll Me Over" also changeth our perspectives, especially at 2 AM.

Last night about 3, I woke up to realize I should have trekked down the hall to the row of water closets before going to bed. But we look so ridiculous in our nightwear, I had decided to wait until morning to visit the loo. Ski was sound asleep and, angry with my own vanity in not wanting to parade the hall to the john in nightclothes, I threw on my overcoat liner and dashed off alone without my flashlight. The two lightbulbs dangling from the high ceiling outside the row of toilet cubicles are 20 watts at most. I hastily pushed opened a door and turned to latch it, just as I realized I was backed up to the back of someone else. Know I set a record in getting out of the cubicle and rushing away as a gruff voice bellowed expletives after me. And I do mean bellow, the swear words so colorful I knew it must be a resident sea captain as I couldn't understand half of them. Had to wake up Ski to accompany me the next time—after a suitable wait. She wasn't much happier than the sea captain, but at least her language was lady-like.

Then, not long ago, Ski and I trudged down to the hotel mews about 4 in the morning to take out the Clubmobile for an emergency loading. It was so cold our hands were numb, even with lined mittens, and our breath hung in clouds when we walked out into the frigid air. The Bedford refused to start. This happens often, so while Ski checked under the hood, I took one of our serving pitchers and pushed open the nearest mews door hoping to find hot water to unfreeze the necessary parts. We've used hot water before and it works. Have no idea why, but it does.

I stumbled into the working kitchen of the hotel. This is where foods are prepared before being sent up to the serving kitchen adjacent to the elegant second-floor dining room. I groped for a light switch then instantly regretted it. Even in the yellowed light of naked bulbs dangling down from the high ceiling, it was clear this kitchen hasn't been renovated since its origin in the reign of whom? Henry VIII? It looked as though it hadn't been touched since Jane Austen attended assemblies in the grand ballroom. And the odor was appalling.

The pale light failed to hide the spiderwebs festooning the ceiling and the spiders working the webs. Roaches or some kind of bugs ran on the walls and along deep cracks in the broad wooden counters, cracks full of decaying remnants of potato peels, brussels sprouts, and cabbage. The reek permeated the huge room. Rows of rusty utensils stacked way up on high shelves were also festooned with cobwebs.

I managed to find a hot water spigot, fill the pitcher with water, and leave, sick to my stomach. At least the water was warm enough to start the truck and we made the loading, but the memory stalled in my head.

Other memories linger. Some fester. They have nothing to do with the British, they're about our guys. I've noticed Ski and I keep dredging them up at odd moments when we are alone, as they're hard to file away and forget. One day during the rush to pour troops cross-channel to stop the German breakthrough, I got word of yet another group embarking from the Royal Pier. It was a loading unlisted on our schedule. I had the Clubmobile restocked and grabbed Ski as she drove into the coffee kitchen from another job, and we raced over. Instead of the whoops that usually greet our arrival, armed guards met us with rifles pointed towards us, bayonets affixed. Only then did we notice lines of men standing in stiff rows, completely encircled by other armed guards. An officer started to walk over, rifle at the ready.

"Turn off the record player, Ski," I said as he approached. "Looks like a problem."

"You'd better get out of here, girls," the officer ordered, just as I started to alight from the cab. I stepped down anyway to face him.

"We're American Red Cross," I said, trying not to sound self-righteous. "We serve all the men going through the Port." He stared at me stone-faced, so I tried another tack. "Look, you don't want to get us fired, do you?" I smiled, what I hoped was a conciliatory one. "This is our job, sir. Wouldn't you like a cup of coffee and a warm doughnut with your men? It's darn cold on this pier."

The officer's grim expression didn't change, but he hesitated a moment as Ski, standing right behind me, glared at him. Then he decided to level with us, measuring his words. "Look, girls. These men are not just soldiers. They're from Leavenworth. That's the federal penitentiary. They're military prisoners who are doing big time—for major crimes. Some are up for life, some have a death sentence hanging over their heads. They've been given a last chance, to volunteer for frontline duty or face execution or life in prison." The officer looked tired and his eyes were gaunt. "I've got to deliver these men without incident. For your safety I suggest you leave now."

"With your men standing guard, sir, can't we at least give everybody some hot coffee?" Ski broke in.

"We'll make it quick," I added.

He thought that over. "Okay, but make it fast."

Ski and I never worked faster, nor with less pleasure, as the guards with rifles at the ready filed the men past the Clubmobile. Some didn't look at us as they reached the serving window. Others stared right at us or through us with eyes we can't forget, mostly hard, cynical, bitter eyes. Yet every so often a man looked at us directly, smiled, and said, "Thank you."

We finished quickly and left. We discussed it later. Did those just-released men, still virtual prisoners in transit, make the most of this last chance and soldier? Or did an officer get shot in the back, given an opportunity? What happened to the few who looked as though they were in this group by some cosmic mistake? Have they turned their lives around? Have they survived?

Eloise says she won't ever forget the day her Clubmobile stopped at the dock gates to let a freight train go through. Flatcars lumbered by, heaped high with crushed piles of smashed and burned-out tanks, crumpled like toys. Idly at first, she noticed names painted on their sides. "Some stood out clearly," she said, "Victory, Intrepid, Trafalgar. I thought they must be British, probably disabled in the relief of Calais. Then I spotted other names—Sword, Juneau, Abilene—and I remembered the faces of all those great tank guys we fed when they were loading to go win this damn war."

Another memory Ski and I can't erase is a day we were working the Hards as MPs herded German prisoners off an LST in droves, like cattle. The PWs, crammed together, had stood for the entire channel crossing and came straggling out of the ship's maw looking as gray and bedraggled as their uniforms. One of the MPs guarding them ran over to the Clubmobile and put down his rifle to reach for coffee and doughnuts. Each finger on both of his hands was loaded with rings.

I couldn't help asking, "Does your CO know you have those?"

The guy laughed and put down his coffee, waving his hands in front of us. "No problem. It's called war loot. Need a ring, girls? I'll give you a good buy, nice war souvenir. Or do you need a watch?"

Quickly unbuttoning his sleeves, he held up his arms to reveal rows of watches, strapped high up both arms. "In fact I'll give you one. Go ahead. Choose!"

Ski thought quickest. "We have watches, thanks, but we won't forget your offer." And we haven't, but we sure wish we could.

⚜

8:30 PM, January 24, 1945

Dearest ones,

First of all, your wonderful Christmas package arrived about a week ago. The unexpected thrill of an arriving Christmas package in mid-January makes it even more fun to receive.

"Susie," the darling paper doll little Marcy asked you to put in with your letter, Sis, has already become famous. I took your letter when I went to visit Ski in the hospital, and Susie fell out. A Navy officer from the ward across the hall begged to borrow her for a few days to be his pinup girl. So for three days Susie was tacked on the wall above his bed, the most popular pinup in the whole ward, putting Hedy Lamarr and Rita Hayworth to shame.

After the strain of December's heavy and heartbreaking schedule, Buddy, our Clubmobile London superior and a great gal, ordered Ski and me to take a three-day leave in January, and our long-overdue week's leave as soon as our schedule will permit. Ski and I didn't argue. Ski had to go back in the hospital for a brief stay, and I've been tiring more easily than usual. We both were ready for a little time off and the thought of getting away from coffee and doughnuts for three days was lovely. I chose Bettie to take over while I was gone as she knows all the ropes.

We decided to go to Torquay, which is said to be one of the nicest resorts in England. It's in Devon and an easy trip from where we're stationed. So last week, at the last minute as usual, we *just* caught the train and left for our three doughnut-free days.

When the train pulled in we opened the first door marked First Class and sat down in a compartment with two British sailors (gunner's mates) and a French Naval officer. The train wasn't far past Salisbury before the two sailors had us convulsed. One had a wry and delightful sense of humor, and with his musician friend, they entertained us all the way to Exeter, only stopping their nonsense long enough to pop out at way stations to buy us cups of tea. Ski, in her usual offhand manner, had brought nothing practical along like comb and lipstick, but as usual had her purse full of sugar lumps. So that made our tea party perfect. The French Naval officer spoke excellent English but didn't say much. He spent the whole trip just sitting back and enjoying the sailors' remarks, his face wrinkled up with silent laughter.

Our reason for choosing Torquay was because we were told south Devon is always much warmer than the rest of England. We stepped off the train and disappointedly slushed through snow and ice to get to the taxi stand, thankful we had on our fleece-lined boots. It was a beautiful night, though. A brilliant moon shone on the snow and the sea and the lovely hotels along the promenade. We soon found out that this was unheard-of weather for Torquay. For the entire three days the natives talked of nothing else. To me it was exciting, as I've never had my fill of snow. Ski was not quite as enthusiastic.

We had reservations at the Palm Court Hotel and thank goodness our room had a sixpence heater (the Brits call it a "sixpenny fireplace"). Like ours at the Dolphin, we discovered we could just turn the knob and the flame renewed itself, without having to deposit a sixpence. So *no* pence kept us warm three days which is some kind of record.

Before we left we decided we wanted to really rest and we did just that; we slept the clock around, ate, and walked along the seafront. I took writing paper but relaxed so completely I didn't even get it out. It was marvelous. The meals were British, so file them under brussels sprouts, fish, hare, pork, boiled chicken wings, soup, cabbage, and pudding (usually semolina or rice). But they were served by courteous help, which was a real surprise, and to the hackneyed but valiant tunes of an ensemble. The leader played the violin and misdirected the piano and xylophone players. After so many months at the docks it was quite jolly—quite! We felt elegant. If we had been given napkins we would have felt ourselves lost in utter luxury.

Here are some snapshots we took. You can see from the lousy picture of Ski that she's been quite sick and still looks a little peaked. It was wonderful, frankly, not to see any GIs for a few days. We went to hear *Faust* our last night there. Although the manpower draft was obvious when you looked at the chorus (for that matter the principals too), it was an elegant evening. Mephistopheles had a lovely costume and looked like the devil, even if he did sing flat. I guess you can't expect Ezio Pinza to winter in Torquay.

As you probably notice from the ink changes, I've been interrupted many times in the days since and I'm afraid this is disjointed. I'll try to do better next time, which should be real soon now that I'm rested and back on the job.

I enjoy your letters more than I can tell you. So do the crew. Some of them haven't been lucky in the mail department. So please keep sending those wonderful words from home.

All my love,
Roses

Just sealed my letter and suddenly realized how long my lapses are becoming between letters home. At least two weeks or more. More guilt-inducing is the thought of the many subjects I'm skipping entirely.

I thought of telling them more about Ski and Tom's relationship and her letter to him while we were in Torquay (after much anguishing and many nail-biting rehashes of the whole matter with me in front of our fireplace). She finally wrote that they'd better not get too serious until after the war. At one point in our fevered discussions I even suggested she and Tom go off together for a weekend (as the British seem to be comfortable doing) if their passion was so great, shocking myself even as I said it. I kept trying to sell her on delaying any permanent decisions until she was back home and her family could get to know his sterling character. And now that I think of it, what do I know about grand passions? I'm the girl with lots of friends, great friends, but the one who hasn't yet seen a man she'd think of spending a whole life with.

Tonight Tom and Ski are out again and the docks are quiet for a rare change. The fact that Ski's letter to Tom only increased, if possible, his ardor makes me realize it didn't accomplish one damn thing. At least she's finally faced up to writing home about Tom and their falling in love. Now that she's written her family, the captain of this crew can eschew responsibility and forget it, I keep telling myself.

Except none of us can. Ski has us all involved at this point and Tom is becoming a fixture in Room 15. Lil, our marvel from Brooklyn who taught English in the New York public school system for years, has even volunteered to give Tom speech lessons. And he accepted! Now that's getting serious. My gawd, Lil's Brooklyn accent would choke a horse and I have no idea if Tom will sound any better with a Brooklyn accent than he does with his Pal Joey one. But his enunciation and grammar may improve. Guess I'm likely to find out as, of course, they're planning to hold these study sessions in Room 15. So glad I've discovered the music room at the end of the hall. I've had to take refuge there quite a bit lately to concentrate on schedules and coded reports, but Gad, the furniture is uncomfortable. And I hate missing all the action.

Another crisis electrifying the air lately I've not mentioned in letters home is front and center now that Ann and Caroline are back from their work at the subport. They've both dated a lot, since being friendly and congenial is expected of all of us, on or off duty. It's part of our jobs. After all, if we become unsociable and nasty to someone, the Red Cross is almost bound to lose another supporter. Caroline is always charming in a Southern way, even if at first she was only going through the motions as she adjusted to the realization that her husband's sub is lost forever somewhere in the Pacific. Now that she's had enough time to work through her grief and face her loss, she's finally beginning to enjoy life again and look to the future.

Ann, our sophisticated, slightly older, beautiful blond from southern California, has loved socializing from the beginning. That is, once she adjusted to her disappointment when the Red Cross sent her to the ETO instead of the Pacific where her Naval officer husband has been serving for three years. She accepted her bad luck gracefully and is witty, fun, and a great worker. "It sure beats sitting around two more years doing war work and waiting for letters," she told us. "And now I have lots to write him about."

Soon after Caroline and Ann arrived at the Port, Tom talked Ann into going out one night with his friend Jack, a motor pool lieutenant in the Port. Tom had tried to line me up with Jack right after he first began dating Ski, to make a convenient foursome no doubt. But when Jack grinned into my Clubmobile window (I thought he was leering) with those big brown cow eyes, his black hair sleeked with hair tonic, and asked me to join the group, my reaction was to cross him off as a typical redneck Southerner. Obviously a Texan, judging from that drawl, he was good-looking if florid-faced, but his invitation was effusive to the point of repulsion. Too eager, and it didn't sound like dancing was uppermost on his mind. I pleaded heavy duty on the docks.

When I confronted Tom afterward he laughed and told me it was a good thing I refused as Jack is married. Said he had only just found it out, even though he's been billeted with Jack for months. Jack finally told Tom he took off his wedding ring the day he left the Panhandle, or wherever he came from in Texas. He explained that he got married only a few weeks before he was sent overseas, but he sure planned to make it up to his bride when he returned. To Jack, that was a perfect Texas justification.

When he invited Ann out she called his bluff immediately. Told him she knew he was married and she was too. Ann said they got to sympathizing with each other, then laughing together about the problems of lonesome marrieds, mateless overseas. That's when she agreed to go out with him once in a while to share a little off-duty fun—if he stuck to her rules. "Always with a group and just for laughs," she told him, and she told us. It did sound logical. You can't help liking Jack, we all agree, and Ann's a party girl who loves a good time.

The two of them have added sparkle and fun any time we gather. At mess they brighten up any meal. Or at Ma Hubble's pub out in the New Forest, one of many where Tom's on familiar terms. He knows everyone by name and they think he's great as he comes in the door bearing extra cigarettes, sugar, or butter rations to pass around to his British buddies. Or at the Polygon, the hotel where Port officers are billeted and the one social event of the week is Saturday night dinner-dancing in the ballroom. Ann and Jack's friendship has seemed light and gay, nonthreatening.

When Caroline and Ann were sent off to the subport, Jack suddenly disappeared, and we heard he'd finagled detached duty at a subport. Didn't have to ask where. Now that they're back, Jack is back, magically reattached to the Port. It's a remarkable coincidence I attribute to knowing how to pull strings in the Army. Or to Jack's winning drawl and grin as he snaps to attention when the Port Commander requests something and Jack salutes extravagantly before he says, "Yes, suh, Colonel, suh, anything you say, suh!"

Equally remarkable is the change we all notice in Ann and Jack. The ground rules have been lost. So has the light attitude they exuded. We're at the quiet conversations off in a corner and hand-holding stage. It's obvious they've fallen in love.

I've had time to go dancing a couple of Saturday nights at the Polygon now that our crew is growing daily. Ann and Jack are much in evidence and you'd have to be blind to miss the attraction—face it, the magic—between them. Their lingering glances and complete absorption in each other as they dance when the orchestra plays Ann's favorite song, "I'll Be Seeing You," is poignant, sweetly painful to anyone with eyes and a heart. By the time the song ends, "I'll be looking at the moon, but I'll be seeing you," I find myself thinking of all the years ahead and blinking away tears. And I'm not the only one.

We all realize they're bound to be separated soon and there's no future for them together. This improbable love of theirs is sure to become a guilt carried home, a war memory. So why do I find myself feeling glad for them when I see them together, even as I feel guilty feeling glad?

❧

Journal   January 26, 1945

Sure had fun this morning. Ski, Bettie, and Caroline went with me when I checked Maritime Chambers to update today's loading schedules. In fact they insisted they go. We'd been working adjacent docks all morning, and Caroline and Ann, in a lull between troops, ran through their choices as to the most attractive men in the Port. They decided one young major won hands down. For some reason they thought it hilarious when I wasn't sure which one they were talking about. They accused me of being absolutely blind where looks are concerned. That got my goat, no doubt because it's true. All men look great in uniform, I said, too defensively. My pulse rose as high as anyone's our first few weeks on the docks. But after months of working daily with, and being surrounded by, thousands of men all dressed alike, the novelty tends to dim.

"I know and like them all, but I don't go to socialize," I protested. "I go to get ship information." It sounded dumb even as I said it.

That's when I got the volunteer escorts. The troop movement guys like it when I bring some of the crew along, but I attempt not to interrupt their work. Bettie, who loved taking over while Ski and I were off in Torquay, had other ideas today.

"Come on, Rosie," she said, as we walked up the stairs of the old Cunard building just inside the dock area, "let's pep things up a little. If we see the officer Caroline and Ann were talking about, I'll give you a nudge."

The men in the office greeted us immediately and enthusiastically. Two rushed over to say hello. Colonel Jim is a suave older bachelor with a moustache like Adolph Menjou's who dates classy, top-drawer British ladies. Port gossip has it that he made a fortune in southern California real estate, but would have made more if he had taken a few chances. We call him "Colonel Worry Wort" as he stews constantly over every last detail of every operation.

Then there's the major we sometimes call "Pop," a thirtyish officer from southern California who has become our Red Cross adviser on social matters. Not only because he's Christian Scientist–friendly, but because he's one of the few married officers here we've spotted who isn't out having a high old time away from home. He'll show pictures and talk to anyone about his gorgeous wife, Inez. He doesn't drink or smoke, yet he's gregarious and participates, alone, in any Port gathering. He's a good pal and listener and we've come to trust his advice.

I stopped a moment with the girls to greet our friends, then went on over to the planning desk. Bob, a captain I often get ship information from, sat there concentrating on something he was reading. I waited for him to finish. Usually he looks right up and our conversations start off with a laugh or joke before we get down to ship-loading schedules. It looks like a church bulletin, I thought idly. I glanced again as he turned a page, and it was a church bulletin. I was surprised, and impressed.

Often if I have to wait more than a moment in any office, the men aren't working on Army business and schedule changes. They're fielding telephone calls from British girls wanting a date. The direct pursuit of American servicemen by all too many English "birds," as our men call the girls, is hard not to notice. We know the cream of British manhood, since the war started, has been away serving in Burma, India, Africa, Australia, in all the far reaches of Empire. So it's little wonder the women left behind to defend home and family alone through Blitz and V bombs have welcomed the arrival of our troops. But so heartily? To us they seem overly aggressive in their search for a date.

Must admit an even bigger shock has been discovering how our guys love all the attention. Some take off wedding rings to pass themselves off as single; far too many, we think, jump at any chance to kick up their heels while safely distanced from home and family. It's been disillusioning.

Just then Caroline, Ski, and Bettie slipped up behind me. Bettie gave me a big poke and said, "Okay, girls, all together!" and started singing "You Are My Sunshine." I sang along, seething inside, as I talk to Bob almost every day. When we started singing, Bob looked up and took off his official Army glasses to stare at us, frowning slightly. His eyebrows wiggled a little, but the stern look remained.

That's when I noticed a gold major's leaf on his collar. He'd been promoted, which explained everything. No wonder I didn't know whom they were talking about. He was a captain when Ski and I went off to Torquay. I sang along with more enthusiasm.

Bob's eyebrows really were wiggling as he struggled to hold that quizzical stare. The rest of the staff was loving the performance and demanded an encore. Ample time to notice that he is good-looking, does have those blue eyes the girls were talking about, and is quite attractive. Nice wavy hair—is it light brown—and well cut. When we finished, his thick eyebrows arched once more before he smiled. His teeth were good too, I noted.

"What brought all this on?" he asked, obviously embarrassed. Then we laughed and joked a few minutes before getting down to schedule changes.

As we left the Maritime Chambers, Bettie was still gushing about the major. I said, "Face it, Bettie. I know him and like him. We laugh all the time about meeting at 9 for a date. But it's a joke. He's got to be spoken for or married. He must be twenty-nine or thirty and definitely too attractive not to be married with a wife and three children at home. Use your head. Forget it." And so we went back to work.

It's been wonderful these past two weeks to have time for some laughs. During the breakthrough it was often impossible to retain a sense of humor, and we all had to work at it. Now, new crew members are arriving every week so I should be able to plan a more normal schedule for everyone. Our responsibilities are increasing but I'm promised enough crew to get the work done without everybody working around the clock. The Army's starting a leave-train program and wants the Red Cross to meet every train that departs from or arrives here. Some of our crew will ride the leave trains back and forth to London.

Replacement troops pour across the channel in vast numbers now that the Allied offense is on track again and chasing the Germans back towards Germany. The guys who've been in the thick of the fighting are beginning to return for brief leaves. Wounded have not ceased arriving since the invasion started. So I continue to pester Headquarters for more crew, more equipment, more supplies, and a larger doughnut and coffee kitchen to handle it all.

Journal   January 27, 1945

Realized I forgot to note that the 2,000,000th Yank embarked from this Port on the sixteenth, with appropriate ceremonies. Similar to those held for the 1,000,000th Yank whose departure we celebrated last October, that shy young private from Pennsylvania. I still see him standing halfway up the gangway, very embarrassed as the British and American brass singled him out and presented him with a new mess kit, hanging that 1,000,000th Yank cardboard sign around his neck. We just heard that he was killed six weeks after he landed in France. I sure hope this guy has better luck.

Journal   January 29, 1945

What a fun way to end a long cold month! Went to the dance at the Polygon Saturday night. I almost blew the invitation. Saturday morning Ski and I were finishing breakfast at mess when Pop S. and Bob brought over their coffee to join us. Then Caroline and Ann stopped by the table to find out if we were all going to the dance. Ski said she and Tom were, I said I wasn't. That's when Bob asked if I was free to go with him.

Ever the Miss Priss, I started to blurt out my standard speech, "Sorry, Bob, but I don't go out with married men," when Pop interrupted me in midsentence.

"Oh, I think you should, Rosie, by all means. You all should go and have a good time." He grinned and added, "Just be sure you all come right home after the dance, kids."

"We will, Pop," Ski chortled, gleeful at my embarrassment, knowing I'd caught Pop's signal.

So I told Bob I'd enjoy going with him and he left, saying he'd get together with Tom about picking us up. I looked at Pop. "You don't have to worry, Rosie," he said. "Bob was separated from his wife long before our unit left New Orleans."

All day Ski kept insisting we ought to get out of uniform for the dance. It took some persuasion as I'd sent home almost all my civilian clothes when we got overseas orders. But she was right, it was nice being a civilian again for a change, once I retrieved my black date dress, dressy shoes, and a last pair of nylons from the bottom of my footlocker. Dressed in "civvies," we proceeded to get hysterics elaborately com-

plimenting each other on our loveliness. By the time Tom and Bob came to pick us up, both particularly dashing in Class A uniforms, billed caps, and dress overcoats, our good moods only improved. Think we all felt like a new cast of characters.

The Polygon ballroom is large, with tables encircling hardwood floors, and the most popular action in town on Saturday nights, war permitting. The British band dresses in tuxes and plays well, both American and British hits and all the old chestnuts. Usually Port Army officers predominate as they're billeted at the hotel, but there's always some Navy and their dates, and WRAFs or WRENs in uniform. Many local British couples attend in evening dress, and once the music starts, the dance floor is instantly alive. The British, it's evident, take dancing seriously. Standing very erect, yet almost welded together at the hips, hands extended precisely in the correct position, their feet fly over the floor with grace and precision. In the process, the evening wear they've carefully preserved in closet bags through this long war and only take out for an occasion, sends out a faint odor of mothballs.

When we arrived the band was on a break. I'd warned Ski I planned to ask Bob a few leading questions (at which she agrees I'm an expert) to ease my mind about his marital state. But just as we reached our table the band burst into a fast and furious version of that real oldie, "Tico, Tico." Bob grabbed my arm and I discovered he's a marvelous dancer. That ended my research. Don't think we sat down more than twice all evening and we didn't have time to talk much, we were having such fun.

"Where did you learn to dance?" I asked him, after we'd flown all over the floor together.

"With a pillow," he laughed. And he wasn't joking. Said his beautiful big sister Ruth made him practice dancing around the living room with a pillow before he caught the bus to high school in Indiana.

So all I know now, as it slipped out between dances, is that he's from Indiana, has wonderful blue eyes and a real sense of humor, and comes from a family of four brothers and one sister. But I'm sure glad I went, as I can't remember when I've had a better time.

Chapter Twelve

Sunday, February 16, 1945

Dearest Family,

Eureka and hallelujah! What a ten days this has been. All told at this moment twenty-three Christmas packages have arrived, just when I had given up hope. Not only yours came but lots from friends, which I didn't expect. It's been wonderful and aside from my slightly dim view (to be British about it) of making time to write all those wonderful people, it's been even more fun than having gifts at Christmas.

First, my shaky handwriting is because I'm on the London Express, and you know how I write on trains. Read on at your own peril. But I love to take the train up to Headquarters as it's two hours to catch you up on all the news I haven't time to tell you about when I'm working.

Three more packages came from you, Mom and Dad, and they were marvelous. Have to mention the movie film you sent, Dad, and Mom, the packages for Ski and Caroline thrilled them.

As for the nightie and jacket, Mom, wow! So silky and lovely, I feel like searching for some Clark Gable to run off to the south of France with. When the weather warms up and we stop sleeping in red long johns (under our regular pj's) they'll certainly be an improvement on my blue knit pajamas. I'm considering renting out this enchanting ensemble by the week as several of my crew are on the verge of marriage. You should have seen their eyes pop when I opened the package. You may be the incentive for several weddings, Mother, as the main reason three of the crew haven't married before is they don't want to do without the frills they could have at home.

Gifts have been pouring in—truly! Now have a cache of lovely items like Monteil soap, books, perfume, hosiery, and lipstick. Even the mail has been arriving in torrents, thirty-eight letters in a three-day period and I loved every one of them. Marty, yours are so amusing Ski asked if she could send one home so one of her sisters might get the idea of how to write a letter.

Time flies. I'm now on the way "home" again, having made a two-hour stop in London for business, caught a bite to eat at the Grosvenor House Officers Mess, and bought "a hyacinth to feed my soul" (remember your favorite Japanese proverb, Mom?) in the form of three bunches of narcissus at 5 shillings a bunch. What extravagance!

Yesterday Caroline, Ann, Bettie, and Eloise were called in to go to France. Ski and I weren't. I immediately phoned Mitchell (he's head of all Clubmobile operations), and he said I was completely indispensable, in charge of the largest operation in the UK (United Kingdom). He needed me more than ever with the leave trains and all, and as I've been in charge of the civilian hiring at the base, and blah, blah, blah, I had done too fine a job to go to the continent now.

So today I went up to London and raised hell. I told him and Buddy, my immediate boss, it was nonsense that I was indispensable. Now that the system is running well it should be simple to get someone else to keep it running smoothly, and if they do think I've done a good job they should let me go on to the continent. The more I argued with Mitchell the more he complimented me on the work we've done at the Port and talked me into being a good Red Cross soldier. I really gave it the old school try, but the answer was negative. We're not going with this group, but Headquarters promised to send someone down for me to train, before they send Ski and me on. I have their word but Mitchell didn't say when. Buddy told me after my conference with Mitchell that Polly, the captain I replaced, is now assistant to the head in the combat areas on the continent, and she'll contact her about working on getting us over.

I'm sitting in this train wondering if it's vanity on my part, this wanting to get to the combat areas, to see it all. Am I being selfish? Mitchell made me feel guilty for asking to go. Said I'm doing much more for the war here. Ski and I really do love the work and so, in a way, don't mind waiting, but we'd love a crack at the other.

You know, I can't get over how long I've been in England. I still feel a little thrill of pleasure when I settle back into a red leather-lined cab on the way to Headquarters from Waterloo Station and look at the fog hovering above the Thames, or notice the bomb patches in the Houses of Parliament and Westminster Abbey. I'm actually used to thinking in pounds and shillings and pence, to hearing V-2s explode in the distance, to seeing horse-drawn carts rattling over crooked, cobbled streets, and to passing bomb-blasted areas everywhere and scarcely noticing them.

When I go into a centrally heated U.S. hospital I feel stuffy and cooped up, and wonder if the British are right when they say central heating is unhealthy. If I saw a napkin now I'd have to remember to use it. When using an English phone, I even press button A and B and stand without impatience for the eight to ten minutes required before an operator answers. One adjustment I can't make is to British newspapers. I'll never get used to having everything from Bile Beans to Liver Pills advertised on the front page, right next to the German breakthrough.

I'm enclosing the theater program from *Hamlet*. Kari, one of my crew, took me to see it the other night for my birthday. We came up in the late afternoon and caught a late train back. It certainly was worth the rush and effort. John Gielgud is rated the greatest living Shakespearean actor and boy, he is! I saw Maurice Evans's *Hamlet* in San Francisco a few years ago and thought he was great, but Gielgud is magnificent. He's handsome and wears black but divinely! Polonius was wonderful too and you should have seen Ophelia go mad. Exquisite. I loved it so I'm going to try to get up to see it again, but what with giving out 260,000 doughnuts a week (no joke) I may not find time.

The narcissus beside me smell lovely and it's so mild out I can't believe that a couple of weeks ago we had nothing but snow and I was colder than I've ever been in my life. We did have lots of fun though. One day Ski and I were serving a bunch of GIs along the Hards and we started making snowballs. A convoy of vehicles went by, driven by a bunch of GIs who are stationed here and drive vehicles to loading ships. We hit about every one of them in the face. About an hour later when we drove into a pier to serve another group of men, we ourselves suddenly were deluged with snowballs. Our driver friends had gone to our next destination ahead of time and just waited patiently for us.

They are really our pals now. That day one of them let me drive a Bren carrier (looks like a small tank) down the road and into the net to be hoved (heaved?) aboard ship. About seventy-five GIs watched and made bets as to whether I'd drive it into the net or into the water. I don't know what odds they were giving. But they were quite impressed, may I add with all the modesty of a truck driver. Most fun, of course, is driving big vehicles into the mouths of LSTs. The drivers say Ski and I belong to their union and I'm always pleased when they yell, "Hey, Rosie!!" as I drive around the docks. My pride rises because they just don't take anyone into their group. So there!

Oh yes! In line with the Red Cross Drive in March, you may see pictures of our girls on leave trains and hospital trains. Ann and Caroline are in lots of them, so let me know if you happen to spot any.

The train's slow tonight (hence time for this long ramble) but now the fog's thickening and I must be almost "home" so it's back to work for me.

Goodbye now, wonderful family. I'm convinced I have the best one in the world, as despite your busy lives you always manage to write. I love you all and Sis, tell little Stevie *yes*, I'm keeping my face clean.

All my love,
Rosemary

Journal   *Late! February 16, 1945*

Why on earth Mother sent me that sexy, sheer, black peignoir outfit has puzzled me ever since I opened the package. The crew thought it wonderful. But my conservative, ladylike mother?? It's very unlike her. Thought keeps occurring that she always must have known I've never been really in love, despite infatuations, friends, and devoted dates parading in and out of my life. Is she sending some kind of a signal?

Don't really believe that, yet keep thinking about it, maybe because my birthday's next week and I'll be twenty-six. Yikes! What is there about twenty-six? Twenty-five seemed such an on-top-of-the-world, now-I'm-a-sophisticated-adult occasion. The thought of turning twenty-six doesn't make me glow at all. Is it because I'm discovering how many answers I still don't have?

That's ridiculous. Guess I'm affected by all the love affairs going on around me. Bettie's still half in love with Jerry, but she's just been given time to think it through by being sent on to the continent. Ski and Tom are head over heels in love, their sparks affecting everyone around them. Barbara's seriously involved with Derek, her handsome British Navy officer, and has been for months, so they're bound to marry soon. Maybe the atmosphere's contagious around here. As Mother Hen of this crew—that is, captain—I find myself these days spending as much time clucking over my chicks as I do over our work. At least the war is going well at the moment. Bradley and Patton really on the move again, Monty's pressing ahead, the Nazis backtracking, the Russians advancing from the east. Perhaps at last we're getting somewhere.

≈⊕≈

Journal   February 20, 1945

Today was a hard one. Caroline, Ann, Bettie, and Eloise left to report in to London and go on to the continent. I rushed up from the docks to wave them off at Southampton Central just a few minutes before the train was due. Ski arrived from another dock. Jack and Ann were standing together off to one side, under a sign on the station platform that features a large glass of foamy brew, a smiling face atop the foam. Big white letters above say KEEP SMILING. *Below the glass it reads,* GUINNESS IS GOOD FOR YOU. *All I saw was the Keep Smiling right over their heads. But they weren't.*

Jerry was there to see Bettie off, and several Port men to bid Godspeed to Eloise and Caroline. The girls looked great in Class A uniforms, trench coats draped over their shoulders, and smiled bravely when we heard the train coming down the tracks. Bettie reminded Ski and me of our vow, that day we went to Stonehenge, to meet after the war in New York City. At the Waldorf. To reserve the best suite, to spend everything we've saved on the most elegant outfits in the city. To go everywhere and see everything. And have breakfast each morning in bed, before even thinking of getting up. We quickly renewed our pledge as the train eased in, we all hugged, I snapped a couple of pictures as we promised to write, and they promised to pull strings to get Ski and me over. We promised eternal friendship and they hopped aboard the train. I rushed away so no one would see me cry.

Ski was right behind me but we couldn't bear to look at each other as we hurried back to our trucks. She headed to the new docks, and I to the old docks. On the way I pulled up beside the old Roman town wall to fix my face, then sat a few minutes. I thought of Caroline, my first friend in the Red Cross since that first day of training in Washington, D.C., and of Eloise, who came over with us on the Liz adding pep and sparkle from the day she joined our crew, and of Bettie, who left the hospital ship to join us and keep us laughing, and of Ann, who's been in the middle of everything since

Eloise Reilly, Bettie Gearhart, Ann Logan, and Caroline Drane leave for duty on the continent, February 1945.

the day she arrived. As the memories flooded back of all the terrible and wonderful experiences we've shared, I gave myself a few more minutes to brood over the slim chances of our ever being reassigned together again.

That's the hardest part of this Red Cross duty. The friends you come to treasure are suddenly snatched away and all you can do is carry on, as the Brits say—and keep smiling.

February 23, 1945

Dearest Family,

It happened! Yesterday I was twenty-six. Funny thing, I never felt better in my life. I had a lovely birthday, very cheerful in fact. It started off well as I received Marty's birthday letter! That floored me. I felt like writing the APO and thanking the postmaster personally. Ski gave me a silver British lion for my charm bracelet. Bettie gave me a lovely leather compact before she left. Keene Mitchell, our Clubmobile head, sent a telegram.

Last night the 14th Port held its second anniversary dance. Marty expressed interest *again* in our social activities in her last letter, so maybe this is a good place for a play-by-play report, especially as it happened on my birthday. About two weeks ago the director of Port operations, a young lieutenant colonel, invited me to the anniversary dance. Scott's single, a Louisianian, extremely blond, about 6 feet tall, was a Phi Bete and football player at Loyola (all this information is the result of last night's research, Sis) and was twenty-eight years old on the twenty-first. I've never paid much attention to him as I thought he'd undoubtedly be conceited and a wolf, being a colonel at his age. He asked me so far ahead I didn't realize the Port was planning to celebrate an anniversary. Then two others invited me. One was the Port surgeon, a fatherly man about fifty-six, and the other a young major in the planning office. Bob's a darling fellow of twenty-eight I've enjoyed going dancing with a couple of times recently.

Yesterday afternoon as I was whipping along the dock road, a colonel's sedan started chasing me and out jumped the colonel. It seems he had been calling me hourly and was driving all over the docks looking for me. There was a slightly irked note in his voice as he told me I was the only girl he'd ever chased. Anyway, he wanted me to go to cocktails and dinner with him as Colonel K., the Port Commander, was giving a small party before the dance.

For the occasion I wore my good black dress and my coat with the nutria collar, really the only outfit I brought overseas, and my Delman shoes. My hair was just clean and did what I wanted it to, all of which is quite remarkable. Scott and his driver called for me at our humble abode in his shiny sedan and away we went. It was a small party in the Port Commander's dining room above the mess. About nine couples. One brigadier general, two full colonels, and the rest lieutenant colonels. One look at all the brass and I wished I were back with the GIs.

It was fun, once I realized again that high-ranking officers are usually just gray-haired men with lots of ego, energy, delusions, and pet theories, and not necessarily brilliant. If you're a good listener, they think you're charming, especially if you don't interrupt or try to get a word in edgewise. Scott and I were obviously the babies of the affair. We enjoyed a *swell* steak dinner too. Just as I was munching a french fry, the general and colonels (is this beginning to sound like the Hatfields and the McCoys?) burst into song and sang "Happy Birthday" to me. I blushed as capably as possible and finished the steak, my appetite getting the better of my emotion.

The dance was such fun! Ski and I know most of the men in the Port, having been here so long. Not long after we went to the ballroom of the hotel where the Army is billeted, Ski and Tom joined us. I think I got to dance with Scott twice, as many others cut in. Of course, that made me feel terrible. It's very bad for a girl's morale! Most of the Port officers always see us in uniform— usually in boots and battle dress—and they certainly were receptive to the change to civvies and Delmans, gotta admit.

It's funny what gossips a bunch of men are. The few I've dated spread the word that I'm the best dancer in England, and you can't imagine how many people have asked me out on the strength of that idle rumor. As I've told you before, we go out very little because of our working hours, so I've refused most invitations. At the party they all wanted to dance with me and judge for themselves—or at least that's the line they gave me. I danced with the adjutant general, then he went from table to table, I was informed later, and told everyone to be sure and dance with me, they wouldn't regret it. It was heady stuff. My shoes are being resoled this week, *no fooling*. Even Colonel K., the Port Commander, cut in.

In the midst of the fun, the band played a Happy Birthday to me. Everyone sang it and the Deputy Port Commander called on me for a speech. I was horror-stricken but managed to take the mike and say, "Thank you very much, Colonel (he had just made a flattering speech about me and the work we've done), but I'm getting too old now to start making speeches." Everyone, no doubt because of what they'd been drinking, thought that was funny. It was just one of those wonderful nights when you can do no wrong. Oh yes! Scott was a swell date. He was a perfect gentleman in every way too. He's invited me to go for a boat ride in his launch as soon as I return from my leave.

And that's the next thing. I'm finishing this letter in London. Ski and I are actually having our week's leave. We're going to Cornwall tomorrow.

Goodnight to you all. I love you so. I hope this letter doesn't sound too smug, but you asked me to report, Sis. Don't worry. I'm still the same girl. I looked into the mirror after the dance and I still look more like the pumpkin than Cinderella.

All my love,
Roses

Tregenna Castle, Cornwall
February 28, 1945

Dearest ones,

My head is so full of things to tell you I can't decide which should come first. Yes, Ski and I actually are having a week's leave (now that our second week off is way past due). We weren't sure we could get away until the very last minute. Ski and Tom made it to London Friday but I couldn't leave with them as planned, so came up late Saturday.

I had a fun ride to London I won't soon forget. All the first-class train compartments were full when I boarded, but four British majors jumped up to make room for me when I opened one compartment door and started a conversation. Or rather one of them had a dog who started the ball rolling, a darling brown miniature long-haired dachshund. The minute I sat down, "Jill," who was sitting on her handsome master's lap, just walked over to mine and lay down. Her master looked surprised and said that Jill didn't usually take to strangers.

They were the best-looking and most sociable Britishers I've met. They wore superbly cut, obviously hand-tailored uniforms, each man perfectly dressed, down to an equally superb handkerchief stuffed up under the left sleeve between uses. I couldn't help wondering if they were returning from Lord Louis Mountbatten's estate near Romsey, but of course I didn't inquire. Two of them were lords, I know for sure, the others rich if not noble. They might have been noble too, I just didn't see any coats of arms dangling! One of them carried a book, *Thoughts on Hunting.*

We chatted gaily, that is, I mostly smiled, exclaimed, and listened through such diverse topics as the campaign in Africa, the campaign in Burma, "my friend the Viceroy of India," and "remember the time I sold old Pasha so-and-so my matched set of clubs for £50" (that is 50 pounds, I've been here too long myself!). Also we touched on skiing in Austria, dear old Paris, and "Isn't it a shame that I shall have to sell my tenth-century house because that fellow next door (mind you) has sold his 1,800 acres to be subdivided among the *nouveaux riches*, so the only thing to do is to buy a small house, with stables, of course, and retire to it after the war."

Ho hum. One of his lordships, the nice owner of Jill, desperately needs golf balls. He gave me his card and invited Ski and me—because he asked me where I was headed—to run up to Surrey some weekend to visit his estate. (I wouldn't think of hunting without my red coat—the Brits call it pink. Please send it air express, also my hounds, Fathah.) Seriously, Dad, if you ever run across two brand new golf balls, I'd give them to the poor old lord. I know he'd love them as they are a war casualty here—nonexistent. It's not that they couldn't afford them.

Jill monopolized my lap and her master my attention all the way to Waterloo. Never enjoyed a British train ride more. Grabbed a cab to meet Ski and Tom. Hotel reservations are practically impossible to get, especially at Claridges, the Savoy, or the Dorchester. After trying for hours, Ski and Tom got rooms at the Hotel Russell in Russell Square.

You should have seen it! It's a huge hotel which must have been *some* stuff in Lillian Russell's time. I kept wondering when Diamond Jim would appear. It's furnished in such completely horrible taste it's magnificent. Nine shades of marble, bronze, and alabaster statues strewn among stained glass windows, pillars and potted palms on red velvet carpets, converted gas lamps, and, naturally, the original plumbing fixtures. The rooms are just as Victorian (or is it Edwardian?) but extremely clean, and the beds comfortable.

Ski, Tom, and I had dinner Saturday night at our hotel. He's with us so much he's known as the dean of the Red Cross girls at our base. Whenever an officer comes to town and wants to meet any of us, or extend us an official invitation, they always see Tom first. Ski and Tom insist I do things with them even if it isn't a double date. They are seriously considering marriage at this point and I've already told them I refuse to go on their honeymoon with them!

Sunday morning Tom went back to the Port and Ski and I had lunch at Claridges Causerie. It's such fun to use napkins. They're a casualty of war here in England that we especially miss. After lunch we took a cab over to Knightsbridge to hear the London Philharmonic. Royal Albert Hall was all I expected, in fact more. It's like being on the inside of a Christmas silver ball. The symphony was wonderful, more wonderful than the conductor. After the concert and after we refused the dinner invitation from the 8th Air Force officers seated next to us, we went back to the hotel for dinner.

Monday I went shopping in the morning and pretty well covered Regent Street. Spent lots of time in Libertys, Mom and Sis. It's an exquisite store, with acres of beautiful wood paneling—San Francisco's Gumps on a grand scale. I had a couple of points, as we do get British ration cards, so bought you each a pure silk Liberty scarf. Their stock isn't large, no British hunting scenes left, but think you'll like these. Will send them home soon.

After tea at Claridges and another night's sleep, Ski and I were feeling wonderful the next morning. We had made appointments at Elizabeth Ardens and we two little country mice came out of the salon three hours, two manicures, two permanents, and £14 later looking like city mice. That's about $25 apiece.

Later, we ate fish and chips at a Lyons Corner House and then took in a movie. It was Irene Dunne and Charles Boyer in *Together Again*. Our morale definitely higher, we managed to get stall seats for Noel Coward's *Private Lives* at the Apollo. The cast was marvelous. We missed dinner to see it as London plays start at 6:30 PM, but we survived on the coffee served in one's seat between acts. Then we ran for a cab as soon as the curtain fell. Finally caught one in the Piccadilly blackout, no mean accomplishment, and got to Paddington Station in time for the night train to Cornwall. We'd hoped for a sleeper but the ministry released none that night. At least we had a first-class compartment to ourselves.

Cornwall is gorgeous, by far the loveliest part of England we've seen. Luck was with us and we arrived at St. Ives on a beautiful spring morning. Even the air is different. It's soft and light and smells of the sea. The sky is blue and the fields are green, full of yellow daffodils and tiny white lambs gamboling after their mothers. Lovely rock walls divide the fields and all the houses are of stone.

St. Ives is a fishing village nestled on hills overlooking the sea, about the most picturesque place imaginable. Narrow houses, squeezed together, with cobbled streets that wind up and down the hills. The lanes, too narrow to be called streets, teem with life and color. Indelible impressions—a housewife, scarf wrapped around her head, sweeping her doorstep and tending to her flowerpots; a fisherman returning from the sea, yellow slicker slung over his shoulder. And cats, we saw at least forty of them, basking in the sun in every doorway or sitting, tails curled, on walls.

Remember "As I was going to St. Ives, I met a man with seven wives"? No wonder it's a famous artists' colony. I'm sending some color cards which don't exaggerate its charm one bit, but can't convey the wonderful salty sea smells.

You can imagine the effect the sunshine, the dazzling brightness of it all had on us after so many months of cold, damp weather. We had no reservations so started with the best and were lucky enough to be taken in. Tregenna Castle is one of the finest local hotels, sitting high on a hill looking down on the town, the harbor, and the sea. We're told it was originally the castle of the squire of St. Ives, but it has been a hotel now for many years. The service was excellent, and the food, if still the inevitable pigeon, porridge, sausage, and brussels sprouts, very well served. We were given a beautiful front room overlooking the harbor.

We spent the whole sunny afternoon walking. Down through a forest full of singing birds to the town, along the tiny, twisting streets to the harbor, into bookshops and art shops, past fish shops and through the Sloop Inn, the old inn where pirates used to take their loot to divide it. As we strolled, we took movies and inhaled the wonderful air. Of course we ran into the inevitable, two sailors and two GIs also taking snapshots and exploring. They were very nice, quiet guys who walked with us up the hill called St. Ives Head. A friendly dog joined the six of us and got into the pictures we took of each other. Ski and I left the boys after a sufficient length of time and wandered back down to town to have tea in a tiny inn. It served wonderful fresh bread and honey, cakes and tea, on quaint Devon pottery. We practically inhaled it, everything was so fresh and good.

Tregenna Castle is such a British hotel that it suited our resting purposes handsomely. In the best British tradition, no one speaks to anyone else. Staid old men and women stomp stoically through the lobbies in knickers and tweed suits by day, and by night, in stiff collars and formless dresses sit and watch other people walk by. Only once was our peace broken. A youngish man, complete with tweed suit and pipe, rushed into the lounge where we were having our coffee in front of the fire.

"I say," he said breathlessly, "can you help me? What is the capital of New York?" "Albany," Ski and I answered in unison. He smiled. "Thanks awfully. I've won a wager you know. My friend thinks it's New York." And off he ran.

Having Gilbert and Sullivan in mind, the next day we dutifully trekked to Penzance on the way to Land's End. We took a bus that passed through the lovely Cornish countryside, all green and gray, then through part of a moor full of bracken and stones and gorse bushes. As we rode, the sky became overcast but the moors and countryside were as beautiful under a gray sky as under a blue. The remarkable thing about Cornwall is the light and color.

Penzance proved more charming in fiction than in fact—a dirty little town. Wonderful old Mount St. Michael, standing right off the coast, is the most exciting thing about it. We finally succeeded, with spare pounds, in hiring a limousine and driver to take us to Land's End. He drove us past Celtic crosses, past "The Last Inn in England" (which when we looked back reads "The First Inn in England"), and stopped at the end of the road, the beginning of the rugged cliffs. The driver said he'd wait while Ski and I got out to walk, into a brisk wind, to the very edge of the cliffs.

Ski said, "We're as near home as we can possibly get, Rosie, let's wave!"

And we did, wildly in your directions. Then blew our noses before we hiked on along the cliffs for a couple of miles. The country reminds me of Carmel near Cypress Point, wild and jagged and gorgeous. The sea smells added to our touch of homesickness.

I could go on for hours about Cornwall. In fact it seems I have. Started this letter in the spell of Tregenna Castle, but now we're back here at the base.

Goodnight. I love you all and wished so often you could have been with us. After the war we'll do it again, together.

All my love,
Roses

Journal   March 5, 1945

Surprise! This note from the handsome British major I met on the train to London was waiting when I returned from leave. It is kind of nice to know the major enjoyed the trip as much as I did.

Dear Rosemary,

You probably won't know who this is from but you will probably remember the chocolate and tan dachshund. I am really writing to apologize for not getting you a porter and a taxi the other afternoon. I was in the devil of a hurry to catch a train the other side of London. So please don't write me down as being very bad mannered.

I do hope you and your friend have a good holiday and enjoy Cornwall.

I would so like to meet you again. Perhaps you would let me know if you would like to dine in London one night. Perhaps your friend would like to come and bring someone to make a four. Anyway let me know how you feel about it. I won't be able to get to town for a few weeks, so let me know if you are coming up in about a month.

It is seldom I meet someone I really like and I don't like losing sight of them.

My best regards to you.

Yours most sincerely,
Jim

March 14, 1945
A few minutes snatched from the day

Dearest Family,

Harrison, the red-faced and jolly Britisher who drives for the Red Cross, came into the room Sunday night to find out which of the new girls he was to instruct in driving the next day. I told him, then asked how he had enjoyed his day off at home in London.

"Topping," he said, in his fascinating London accent, "up until last night when we almost 'ad it."

"What do you mean?" I asked.

"A bloody rocket bombed us out again," he said, puffing on his cigarette. "That makes the nineteenth time, and the fifth 'ouse we've lost."

Harrison stood there calmly smoking as though he was reporting on the new girl's driving progress. I was appalled. "Is your wife all right? Was your family hurt? How close was it?"

"My wife's a good sport, she is. She just laughs anymore. We've lost all our possessions. The only thing," he thought a moment as he warmed himself in front of our sixpenny fireplace, "the rest of our furniture and wedding presents went last night. It's lucky I was standing by the french doors instead of 'er. When they blew off they 'it me in the nape of the neck and knocked me silly for a minute. It might 'ave killed my wife." He suddenly laughed. "The ceiling came down on old Joe and when I looked about 'e was just sitting there. 'What are you thinking about, Joe?' I asked and old Joe rubbed 'is 'ead and said, 'I cawn't think, sir, to tell the truth.' "

"Who's old Joe, Mr. Harrison?"

" 'E's our old dog, been through the whole Blitz with us." Harrison finished his cigarette. "It don't seem quite fair, do it? Nineteen times? The dog 'as a fox-hole under the table 'e always goes to even before we can 'ear the rockets. If we're in bed 'e runs across the bed before 'e gets into 'is 'ole.

"The buzz bombs are fairer, you know. You can 'ear them comin' at least and take cover. The rockets—swish, boom—you've 'ad it! The first time we was Blitzed, the doodle blew all our clothes off. Even my wife's shoes."

He lit another cigarette. "Before my pub was Blitzed it was full of Americans one day. A bomb landed across the way on a store full of kiddies buying the first ice cream they could in five years. It was a direct hit. Your American chaps rushed out of the pub, left their coats and wallets and everything, and ran over to 'elp remove the children. It was no use. The roof 'ad fallen in and as they was removing the rubble the kiddies caught fire. You know how dirty you get working in that rubble and mess," he added, looking at me, his eyes misting over. "Well, your American chaps 'ad black all over their faces by the time they came to the kiddies. And not one of them, you know, but was crying and the tears made little white trails down their cheeks."

He put out his cigarette. "Well, cheerio. It's been a beautiful day, 'asn't it? Simply smashing. I'll see you in the morning."

Sometimes I get so provoked at the British I can see why some GIs joke about cutting the strings to the barrage balloons that fly overhead everywhere and sinking the island. And sometimes I think the English are magnificent.

Have to get back to work now. Keep writing, please.

All my love,
Roses

Chapter Thirteen

March 15, 1945

Spring is busting out everywhere and it's affecting us all in lovely ways. Think we'd almost forgotten the feel of warm sunshine. Just the other day Ski and I got back from the docks to find a present waiting at the hotel desk, with this note attached:

> USS LST 508
> c/o Fleet Post Office
> New York, N.Y.

Rosie & Ski—

Not exactly what Mother used to make—but o.k. At least—fresh apples! Hope you enjoy it.

Bill

Good old Navy, those LST guys are terrific, and what marvels come out of their kitchens. We carried the huge and still warm apple pie up to our room, inhaling its fragrance every careful step of the way. Tired and dirty though we were, we sat right down to devour the pie before any of the crew came by. Luckily, Lil and Kari walked in just as we were deciding whether to try for thirds, and probably saved us from gaining about ten pounds in ten minutes.

And then there's Joe. What shall I do about him? His notes are coming in again and will keep these until I figure out how to tactfully phase him out of the picture:

Dear Rosie,

Being of sound mind (?) and perfectly sober, how about seeing you tonight at 6:30—at least long enough to discuss the possibilities of your attending the brawl at the Polygon with me tomorrow night. I'll call at 6:30—sober. How about trying to be around?

Joe

Dear Rosie,

Sorry I didn't get to leave this yesterday, but be tolerant with me til I learn new habits. Dinner is from 1800 to 2000 at the Star tonight, and the dance at the Polygon is from 2000 to 2400. I'll pick you up at 1800—o.k.? Shamrocks are in order—also green stockings, etc. . . .

Joe

I didn't need green stockings as we were working. He's a nice guy but think he's long overdue for a leave. He's landed that ship so often on so many beaches it's high time he had a break. At first we were a convenience for each other for an occasional social occasion. Kind of "pals time" as I'm not in love with him, nor he with me. He's a decent dancer, interesting, and good company—but not when he drinks too much. Not long ago I went with him to a Navy party at the Court Royal (the only other modern hotel in town) and a favorite Navy hangout as a lot of the Navy is billeted there. Joe kept ordering drinks and I kept refusing. He ordered one for me anyway. Rather than argue I poured mine into his glass, when he wasn't looking. He was far enough into his cups to not even notice.

It can't have been two days later Ski rushed up to inform me (Ski manages to catch all the rumors) that she heard one of the Army officers (a very unpopular one) gossiping at mess about seeing a Red Cross girl deliberately load the drink of a Navy officer.

I said, "Ski, that was me!" and we laughed as I explained the situation. I had noticed the officer who spread the rumor, sitting alone at the Court Royal that night. Gad!

Perhaps because this world of the Port is such a closed society, it is a gossipy setting. We all eat in the same place, at the same times, work in the same area, see each other at all times of day and night. The men, especially, separated from lifelong surroundings, with too much time on their hands, seem to revel in passing around each detail of everything that happens in and around the Port. They watch the Red Cross girls with especially proprietary and supervisory eyes. If we turn down a date, no matter what the excuse, even more attention is paid to reporting our moves, what we wear, where we go. We've laughed about the gossip, but it becomes a concern as, always, every minute of the day, we bear the burden of remembering that we are representing the American Red Cross.

So remind yourself again, Rosie, to follow Mom's sage advice. Next time I'm caught in this situation I'll manage to leave an unwanted drink on a windowsill or a grand piano or in the base of a potted palm. Mom gave me this tip just before I entered college in\order, she said, for me not to be caught in an argument with a drunk who insisted I have another drink.

March 19, 1945

Dearest ones,

A note while sitting in London Headquarters waiting to see Mr. Mitchell as we're in the midst of an exciting game of cops and robbers regarding the disappearance of Red Cross supplies from our big warehouse on the docks. So in addition to regular stuff your daughter is learning to be a gumshoe. And that's all I'm allowed to say at this moment but think we're closing in on the culprit. More when permitted.

(Pause for slight three-hour interruption.) Now I'm back on the train going home. Been meaning, ever since our leave, to tell you about my patch jacket. The GIs insist on giving us presents, usually cheap lipsticks and *always* "patches"—division shoulder insignia—from their outfits. Have seventy or so now, including some the Free French gave me as they left to retake Paris. Even two of the German PWs, who manned our coffee kitchen for a brief time, handed me theirs. The patches have been piling up for months, so I started sewing them onto my GI jacket when off on leave. It was too cold to wear GI jackets over our Clubmobile battle dress during the winter. We wore Navy fleece-lined jackets instead as they are even warmer than Clubmobile car coats. Face it. No matter what we wore we were cold. Despite my lack of sewing skills, the jacket's already become a constant reminder of all the great outfits we've served as they pass through the Port.

Also been meaning to write you about Saturday, a week ago, when Ski and Tom and Bob (the handsome major from Indiana I know I've mentioned before) and I enjoyed a lovely day together. We went to London! I've been there about a hundred times but this was for pleasure—just a day off. We laughed from start to finish and had a marvelous time. No V-2s went off too near to ignore, so it was perfect.

We took the morning train up and went to Claridges for lunch. Because it was a holiday we even had drinks before lunch. Naturally, we ate in the main dining room! As Tom put it, we bought a new Persian rug for the place. We felt very elegant indeed as a top-hatted doorman in his livery hailed us a cab to catch the matinee performance of *Private Lives*. We followed that with tea dancing at the Grosvenor House. Bob is the best dancer I've met in years and we have wonderful fun dancing. After the Thé Dansant, we strolled along Park Lane, skirting Hyde Park as the sun set red and flaming behind the dark silhouettes of the trees and tethered barrage balloons. Then we walked along Piccadilly to the Berkeley (as in Barclay, my dears) for dinner. There was a great orchestra playing so we danced until time to catch the 10:30 train back. Talk about squeezing everything we could into one very full day!

Until today, when it is again rainy and foggy, it's been lovely and all of us have more than a touch of spring fever. The British say it's darned unusual weather—the best they can remember. Some think it's a portent of victory. I surely hope so.

Please keep writing and I will. Please keep loving me as much as I keep loving you. Please catch yourselves thinking of me as much as I catch myself thinking of you. No, Mom dear, I don't feel we're miles apart. We're closer than we ever were, because we are a *very* unusual family!

All my love to all of you,
Roses

P.S. Have you mailed my "hounds" yet, so I can go hunting? Dear dogs, tell them I miss them so.

Journal   *March 19, 1945 (still on the train)*

The letter home is sealed and the train's not nearly back to base and I sit here feeling guilty. Why didn't I tell the family more? Why didn't I mention in passing that their daughter may have fallen in love—despite all her vows, resolutions, and best intentions? And despite all the easy speeches and free advice I've dished out, ad nauseam, *to my crew these past months about not rushing into romance overseas?*

Now that I think of it, I didn't mention that my wallet was stolen from my Red Cross shoulder bag, sitting right on the seat beside me in the train compartment as the four of us returned from that wonderful day in London. My wallet that contains the basic essentials I need for life overseas—my AGO military identification card, Red Cross credentials, Social Security card, and British ration card.

Worse, I only discovered the loss when Ski and I were finally back in Room 15. And then we remembered the British sailor in the compartment seat beside me. Bob was sitting by the window, I was next to him, and then the sailor. Ski and Tom were across from us. The sailor smelled of beer and was slumped down in his seat drowsing, we thought, so Tom pulled up the blinds and turned off the dim lights of the compartment to watch the world go by. At least that's the excuse he gave at the time. What with the blackout outside and no lights inside, I didn't hear much conversation from their side of the aisle but I wasn't paying any attention. Bob and I were talking quietly and happily at first, then not talking, gently, at last. Clearly, we were completely oblivious to the sleeping British Navy at my side. I don't care about the pounds in my wallet, but my identification will take all kinds of effort and red tape to replace.

More guilt-producing is that I didn't level with the family and tell them about the walk Bob took me on, just before we went to London. After our first few dates—think it was shortly after Scott aced him out by inviting me to the Port anniversary celebration first—Bob said we needed to talk. We must have walked for two hours through a gorgeous, warm twilight (it doesn't get dark now until about ten or so) around and across and again around the commons before he got it all out. He told me about himself, his family, the mistake of his impulsive marriage on graduating from Officers Training School, the baby they had in an effort to rescue the marriage, and his wife's return to her home state from New Orleans, once they realized the marriage would never work out. This was long before he was sent overseas, but they agreed there'd be

no divorce until after the war. Pop, now Colonel S., who was stationed in New
Orleans with Bob at the time, is the only officer he's talked to about this.

He put the blame on himself. He was so obviously sincere I said there was no reason we couldn't date. I'm on leave from a career I love and plan to return to. I told
him about my college friends, who seem to anticipate my return too. Did we ever talk!
I assured him that later there'll be plenty of time to get serious, if his feelings last. But
I'll enjoy his company while we're both here. After the war here ends, there's still the
raging war in the Pacific and the Port's already mentioning having our Red Cross unit
transferred with them. Besides, he might just think he's in love with me. So we agreed
to date, and wait until the war is over and our lives get back to normal, to get serious.

It sounded fine at the time. With each passing day I'm discovering it's not that
simple. I find myself more involved and, yes, more in love. All of this emotion is really
not in my master plan for life. I came overseas so confident of returning to my career
and then, my plans ran, vaguely, sometime after the war, I would decide if any of my
other friends might be a man I'd want to spend a lifetime with. Now I'm realizing life
doesn't work out that way. So much for logic.

I should have told Mother and Dad at least some of this. I should have also mentioned that my patch sewing is rapidly slowing down. The problem is that although, late
at night, I still take out the jacket and start sewing, Bob is showing up as regularly as
Tom, with Tom. He says he's come to help me sew (while Tom and Ski are bundling).
That's not how it's working out.

I must write home soon. Or should I procrastinate until I'm positive this isn't
just an advanced case of spring fever? Thank goodness, the train's coming into the station. Only thing I do know is I've never felt like this before and it scares me.

⚓

April 14, 1945

Dearest ones,

Am stealing a few minutes to write as we've just heard of President Roosevelt's
death, and somehow I want to be in touch with you. We were all stunned here
yesterday when the word spread. Including the British. Everyone, almost without exception, felt terrible—somewhat as if all the windows and doors of your
house are knocked out. An intense insecurity was evident everywhere. Even
people I have heard bitterly condemn Roosevelt while he lived seem genuinely
sorry that he had to die now, at this crucial time. The really surprising thing is
how deeply the British have reacted. They are so damn self-assured and unemo-
tional about most things that their open display of feelings amazes me.

His death was announced over the midnight news on BBC, but we first
learned of it the next morning. The manageress came up to me to offer condo-
lences as though I were related to him. She was the first of many to offer sympathy—and questions. People talked of little else. I walked into the hotel serving
kitchen in the evening to get some boiling water for Ski to soak her hand in

(she had just put a rusty nail practically through her left hand) and the kitchen maid who boiled the water immediately spoke of Roosevelt's death.

"Isn't it terrible about your President?" she began. "I was serving in the saloon lounge today" (a men's bar attached to the Dolphin), "when one of your soldiers came in. There were about fifteen or twenty men in the saloon and he ordered drinks all around."

She stopped pouring water and came over to face me. "And what do you think he did when he had paid for all the drinks?" She shook her head in wonder. " 'Gentlemen,' he said as he raised his glass, 'may I ask you to drink to the late President of the United States.' And everyone in the room stood up and drank to President Roosevelt."

She returned to her water pouring. "It must have cost him eighteen bob," she added, very impressed. Then she stopped again to turn and look at me. "Have you anyone to take his place over there?"

It's a question on everyone's mind. How is it at home?

Back to work.
Love, Roses

April 17, 1945

Dearest Family,

Again I'm full of news but often find it impossible to grab time to write. I realize more every day that living in one room must be like being at boarding school. I swear there are sixteen to twenty people in and out of our room nightly, unless we're working. I never have a minute that's really my own. In one way it's lots of fun but often I wish I could dig a hole to write letters in. Half the time the girls drop in for schedules and stay to gossip, or Tom and Bob drop in, or I'm called to the hotel's one phone down in the lobby. Something's always happening. Or if we shoo everyone out of the room we get a rush call to work before I have the writing paper out.

Ski's Canadian cousin Dean, a captain in the Canadian army, has been here the past few days visiting Ski. He spent the last two years in Sicily and Italy with the British 8th Army and is in England awaiting orders home. Ski is the first close relative he's seen since leaving home in 1941, and he is so glad to see someone from home it's touching. He's been with us for hours at a time and loves to sit here, drink beer, and tell us all the things he's been storing up for so long. He's twenty-six, tall and thin, with a pencil mustache. Despite all his awful combat experience, he's managed to keep his sense of humor and love of life.

I've been wanting to tell you about Easter. Bob asked me to go to church a week or so ahead of time, which I thought a lovely idea. He also persuaded Tom into taking Ski—a feat as Tom's never been exactly what you'd call a churchgoer. So on the evening before Easter (we had promised to go dancing with them) we came home from work at eight. We were to be ready at 8:30! We found not one but two corsages for us. Yellow roses for the dance and three green and rust orchids apiece for Easter!! Corsages are unheard of over here, so we almost fainted. Naturally, we got the grease off our faces and really scrubbed up to wear the flowers.

Easter Sunday we put on our dresses and coats (the ones we brought overseas with us) and the orchids. Bob and Tom looked smashing in Class A uniform. We walked up the hill to St. Michael's, a tiny church built by Norman monks around 1100. If the first service I saw there was high, you should have seen this one! A darling little choirboy rang the bells from the center of the nave. The processional was preceded by *three* incense swingers, who swung the bright gold incense lanterns in circles by their long chains. Very dextrously too. Little choirboys followed, then very old choirmen. The pageantry was beautiful and the church robes very old, ornate, and colorful.

Despite the many, *many* gettings up, kneelings, sittings, standings, kneelings, and standings again, it was worth the effort to see the medievally intact service unfold. With all the ostentation, it was very moving.

It was the first time Bob has been to the Church of England. Being a good Presbyterian at heart, he was quite taken with the singsong chants of the rector, or is it priest? When we walked towards mess after the service, he suddenly intoned, in a high-pitched chant, "Play anybody here a game of dominoooooooeeessss. . . ." We almost died laughing because it was a perfect imitation of the chants. Bob is at present engaged in a little research to find a somewhat lower church to take me to, as he says he'd like to go again but keep the crease in his trousers.

Gotta get some sleep. Plan to write news, of which there is oodles, on Thursday. I have to drive a Clubmobile to London early tomorrow.

Goodnight, all of you.

I *love* you,
Roses

Journal   *April 17, 1945*

Sleep can wait awhile longer, as I can't get over my surprise at finally meeting Ski's cousin Dean. Ever since we've been overseas, whenever Ski and I got disgusted at the carryings-ons of some of the married officers in the Port, she'd fume about it and end her diatribe by holding up her cousin Dean as an example of a real man.

"Rosie, he's been overseas for almost three years in the midst of the action. He's married and wonderful, but he wouldn't carry on like this! Not my cousin Dean! He has principles!"

When I heard he was coming, I half expected him to arrive carrying a Bible. The surprise is his sophistication and urbane presence, and I don't think he looks tired only

Bob and Tom Carver off for
Paris leave, April 1945.

from combat. He mentioned a very nice lady he's seeing here in England, and he may mean that in the titled sense. Think she's putting him up at her country house. Ski has not used her famous quote once since Dean came to visit.

Unfortunately, both Tom and Bob had left for a week's leave in Paris when Dean surprised Ski, so they haven't met this paragon of virtue. I have a hunch Dean is a match for both of them and they'll like him instantly. He's a great guy, but I don't expect Ski to keep touting him as an example of pious rectitude. Can't wait for Tom to meet this future relative. The guys are due back tomorrow, now that Dean has returned to his lady friend.

Know he'll come again if Ski and Tom decide to marry in May. Ski received a loving letter from her dad after she finally wrote her family about Tom. Her dad told her if Tom is really a diamond in the rough, that's no problem. The polishing will come with a happy marriage. Or words to that effect, but I'll bet the next move her dad made was to write Dean asking him to check Tom out.

Some days the personal crises of my crew seem almost as complex as our work efforts. Guess that's the charm and challenge of this job.

Wouldn't you know! Tom and Bob arrived back from their leave in Paris soon after Dean left town, full of their adventures together. Just as they got to Paris, Bob ran into an officer he'd known in New Orleans who sent them to a marvelous hotel taken over by the Army. Because of his friend's influence they ended up in a luxurious room with two large beds and mirrors on the ceiling. Tom was the one who insisted they rent bicycles to sightsee. They bicycled all over Paris, with frequent stops at the sidewalk cafes, even cycling out to the elegant racetrack several times. That, of course, was Tom's idea. Bob couldn't get used to horses running the wrong way around the track. They hit the nightclubs, including two visits to the Folies Bergères. Then ended up having bacon and eggs at a nightspot, about four in the morning. And woke up each day, heads heavy, to stare up at the huge mirrors covering the ceiling.

Ski and Tom's wedding is definitely on again, for sure this time I think. Have never seen two people happier to see each other, and I have to admit it's wonderful to have Bob back. What really floored me were the gifts he brought. A darling bracelet with gold charms strung around it—individual hearts, each one inscribed with a part of a French phrase: "Je t'aime—Aujourd'hui—Plus qu'hier—Moins que demain." Even my limited French instantly translated that into "I love you—today—more than yesterday—less than tomorrow." Then he produced a bottle of perfume he'd chosen for me. It was huge, a round blue bottle (the largest I've ever seen) of my favorite one, Worth's "Je Reviens." Don't recall discussing perfumes. I've never before been given such thoughtful and touching gifts.

~≈⊙≈~

April 26, 1945

Dearest Family,

Since Lil's been here, our wonder from Brooklyn, she's specialized in taking candid shots of us (more candid than I like in most cases), and at the moment I have about fifty snapshots to send home.

San Francisco is on everyone's lips and minds these days with the convening there of the first United Nations meeting. Even the staid London papers headline it "Frisco," though, which galls me no end. Sis, you asked me about feature stories in English papers. Ha! I'll send you one just to show you that in newspapers as well as every other material thing I can think of, the British are years behind. I'd like to write an essay on England and the British Empire but am afraid it would be censored. Not that many aspects aren't charming. For instance, coming to a typical English town is like stepping back in time. However, middle and lower classes here don't know what modern comforts and conveniences are, and that's not because of the stringent controls of wartime.

The other day at a movie a "short" was shown on new gadgets for the home to be produced after the war. The Yanks in the audience guffawed, for they were all things long passé at home. A lot of their cars are dreadful, but of course we don't drive the Rolls or Bentleys. We have fixed our Hillman pickup with bobbie pins (no kidding). There are more horse-drawn wagons passing in one hour on High Street than I saw in three days when I was six and waited for the ice wagon to come along California Street. I must have told you about the WCs (as in water closets, loos, or johns). You can tell exactly how long you've been here by how many times you have to pull the toilet chain to flush it. Ski and I pride ourselves on our one-pull ability. Some rural areas don't have plumbing, and carts go through the streets emptying the pots (sometimes referred to as "honey pots") into the cart. You can imagine the odor, as the carts are open.

Remember, Marty, when we were children and they had all those inoculation campaigns? The English are just getting around to that. Signs like Diptheria Is Deadly are on billboards everywhere.

They are so tradition-ridden that sometimes their common sense seems paralyzed. For example, every morning about 6:30, if I happen to go down the stairs to the lobby, there is always a scrubwoman polishing the woodwork, cleaning the stair carpet, and shining the brass rods that hold the carpet in place. At first I thought how wonderful that with the tremendous labor scarcity in England and half of High Street still rubble, management manages to keep the bannisters shining in wartime. But what good is it to have clean stairs if cockroaches pour out with your tea?

That recently happened to me in the main dining room. Scud, one of our new crew members from Hyannis, has a somewhat sardonic sense of humor. She immediately started an analytical discussion on whether I had a locust or a cockroach swimming in my teacup. I asked one of the liveried waitresses (black uniforms, starched white aprons) to bring me another pot of tea, which she did, grudgingly. She's the one I had noticed polishing the silverware on the tables she was setting with the same dirty cloth she had just finished wiping off the legs and backs of the period dining room chairs with. Another reason we eat at the Army mess most of the time!

The English emphasis seems to be, always, on what has been done in the past, not what it is important to do now. To me, this is their main weakness, and the reason I can't help feeling the British Empire is fading and keeping its place in the sun only because of the bulldog tenacity and stubbornness of its leaders.

Don't misunderstand me as this sounds harsh and I'm sure no expert after my few months in this blessed and blasted country. I love tradition, and have loved, almost worshiped, every moment spent in the great monuments to the past I've been privileged to visit. But England seems deathly afraid and jealous of change. Contentment with our surroundings is commendable. Smugness that amounts to blindness is dangerous, and that's a malady affecting most of the British upper class. So Britain looks backward while the rest of the world looks forward. The only thing I'm sure of is that the English will continue to stop regularly twice a day for tea, even if they happen to be on the road to oblivion.

Let's be nice for a while now. The foregoing criticism was no doubt brought on by the brussels sprouts and toad-in-the-hole I ate in the dining room tonight. I was looking forward to a rare night alone to write without interruptions. But I think my stomach's upset as the toad (sausage) that comes out of the hole (mashed potatoes) was at least 95 percent pencil shavings and it didn't sit well. It seems to have settled down now.

According to an old trashman I was talking with today, this is the loveliest spring England's had in thirty years. It's been simply heavenly. Robert Browning was right when he said, "Oh to be in England now that April's here." England's blossoms and spring loveliness are enhanced by the beautiful surroundings. Apple blossoms and wisteria are twice as charming around a thatched cottage as they would be around a hot dog stand. I do love England so, dear ones, which is probably why I get so cross with the idiosyncracies and the class system.

Bob and Tom and Ski and I had a wonderful afternoon recently cycling in the country, and had tea in the New Forest. Scott, the one I spent my birthday dancing with, invited us all out aboard his boat last Sunday. It was perfect. I can't tell you where all we went, although think it's safe to say we were around an island famous for its yachting.

Ski's enclosed check is for £s (pounds) I loaned her. Please deposit it. She may likely be married on May 11th if they can arrange it, although I'm not recommending she marry on a Friday. You can see I'm trying to perpetuate our family superstitions about lucky and unlucky days of the week! She and Tom remind me lots of you, Mom and Dad, in their vastly different approaches to life. I wish you could see the two of them. They keep deciding for and against being married overseas in wartime, but I think they'll end up being married anyway. I'll let you know in my next letter. What would you do?

Goodnight now. I love you all so *very* much. I wish I could take you riding through the countryside and we could all stop for tea.

All my love,
Roses

P.S. Isn't that wonderful about the 69th's linkup with the Russians? They're one of our favorite divisions. They came from the United States and we fed them, they left with our coffee and doughnuts inside them, and we've had lots of their wounded. They're a swell bunch and a wonderful division.

P.P.S. On reading this over I want to be sure you know that I don't think the English are dumb! We pay for every 2 cents that we use over here through lend-lease, and prices, rentals, charges seem exhorbitant. The lend-lease amounts charged for everything used by us Yanks is above reason and is, of course, credited toward reducing their debt. So what? So the United States ends up billions in the hole and the Brits probably end up with us owing them money. Leave it to British shrewdness that they profit by it; they are the world's greatest traders. Seeing the tons of U.S. equipment, supplies, and weapons pouring through this Port reminds me that we will be "paying off" for years the billions of dollars of supplies we've provided to our Allies. On the other hand, what is the price of freedom? I find the English difficult—many of them absolutely wonderful, some of them singularly unlovable. But they've endured through years of impossible horrors with character and fortitude, and the whole free world will forever be in their debt for hanging on.

Journal   *April 26, 1945*

Pages written home, and I didn't tell them more about Bob. It seems to me the main reason I distanced myself tonight was to write home. Trying to not rush into anything, I again asked Mr. Mitchell last Friday about my chances for going on to the continent and, again, he turned me down. Am I afraid to commit myself? I think so. Then why am I so happy knowing I'll have to stay here awhile longer?

And I didn't really tell them about the fun we had when we bicycled to tea in a place in the New Forest Tom knew about called the Angry Cheese. I built up in my mind the romance of this old English name as the establishment looked like it had been there for ages. Then the proprietor told us he named it after an American mystery novel he'd read. So much for old English tradition. We really had a delightful day. For the first time we bicycled right along with all the Brits instead of cursing them out from our trucks as they hog the road, four and five abreast, never giving an inch. This time we joined along with them to hog the whole road. It was a refreshing change of viewpoint.

April 29, 1945

Dears,

Just a note with more enclosures. The war news is wonderful today. If it's really over here within the next few weeks, I may as well plan to remain in England for months as we'll certainly be busy. The senior officers here have brought pressure to bear on Headquarters again to have Ski and me attached to the Port. They don't want us to leave as they like the way we're doing the job.

Am also sending home the note that handsome British major wrote, after I shared my seat on the train with his dachshund, Jill, en route to London as I started on leave. Imagine a staid Britisher sending a note like this. I was amazed. Sonia, our Britisher from Kenya, who's married to a full colonel in Africa (with the title "Chief Military Advisor to the Emperor of Ethiopia") wrote her husband to ask if he knew this man, as she was terribly impressed that he would write me. Her husband wrote back that "Jim" was in his class at Eton, was a regular ball of fire (a very complimentary English phrase), unmarried, and rich. The 7th Hussars is the most aristocratic outfit in the British Army. Well! It did my morale worlds of good to have a man with a twelfth-century estate invite me to dine. He probably only did it because I was so nice to his dog on the train.

Gotta get back to work. All my love to you all.

XXXXXXXX
Roses

᠁

Well, I've done it, sent home the note from the British major for my souvenirs. Faced the fact I'll never get around to answering it. Think I've delayed, wanting to be sure of my feelings for Bob. With each passing day I'm more sure.

᠁

Everyone's on tenterhooks these days wanting it to be officially over, a roller-coaster of emotions as we scan headlines and listen for the latest reports on BBC and Armed Services radio. New rumors fly daily—Berlin's fallen, no, there's still fighting in the streets, Hitler has disappeared, Hitler is dead. No one seems to know anything for sure. At least now we're finding out the truth about concentration camps. Herald Tribune reporter Marguerite Higgins's chilling account of entering Dachau with the U.S. 42nd division is all over the newspapers, gruesome photos documenting absolutely incredible horror—so stunning in sheer evil and inhumanity it's almost impossible to absorb.

But in a peculiar way it reaffirms the importance of all these years of struggle and sacrifice to destroy Hitler and his Third Reich. So much for the apologists who said the rumored camps were just civil detention centers to humanely rehabilitate criminals! Refugees who fled Germany in time told far different stories, but no government spoke up. Including ours. Why? We all are wondering.

᠁

Chapter Fourteen

May 10, 1945

Dearest ones,

Things are happening so thick and fast lately I feel breathless half the time! We've had a very busy day but I keep wondering how the reaction to VE day was at home.

Here, it was a slow reaction. We've been terribly busy all week and particularly during the two-day VE day holiday. This telegram from London Headquarters (OWING TO THE NATURE OF YOUR OPERATION PLEASE CARRY ON YOUR WORK AS USUAL DURING VE DAY HOLIDAY) is a laugh. I returned to the hotel at 0900 (that's ay-em) to receive it, after we'd already been working four and a half hours on the docks. There were so many false VE day rumors that any great sudden or joyous surge of emotion was out of the question. It was almost too big a thing to take in all at once. A day everyone had so looked forward to, so anticipated, was almost an anticlimax. People kept talking about it in order to impress it upon themselves.

The day before VE day was officially proclaimed, Ski and Tom and Bob and I took a jeep ride out into the New Forest after supper. With double British summertime the sun stays up until past 10 PM, and we went for a walk down a country lane. It was a heavenly evening. Hedgerows of bridal wreath and blooming blackthorn and gorgeous wild purple rhododendrons lined the lane, and wild ponies wandered about the groves. When we finally returned to town the announcement had been made.

I must have driven a hundred miles the next day we were so busy. Slowly the realization sunk in. I noticed shopkeepers hanging out flags along High Street. Then the pubs began to fill with whole families—red, white, and blue bows in the women's hair or on their lapels and flags in the children's hands.

On my next trip up High Street from the docks, I stopped by the Dolphin in time to see two sailors clamber out on the balcony and rehang the American flag, as it had been hung backwards by mistake.

By 10 AM, the main street was full of families walking, cycling, and standing in the street around the pub entrances drinking bitters or ale.

Rosie, as troopship loads for the
States, Southampton docks,
VE day 1945.

By noon, excitement was really in the air. Flags hung all over the Dolphin lobby and a Japanese flag covered the floor at the entrance. Everyone entering duly wiped his feet on the rising sun. Saved-up liquor rations were unlocked in all hotels, inns, and pubs, and voices were gayer and louder. Ships which had been working up steam all morning began blowing their whistles—all kinds of whistles—even the *puuurp—puuurrrp—purrrrpp* of the destroyer (like in the old radio ad, "and on the sea").

By afternoon there was a steady exciting hum of voices, shouts, and chatter in the air. And by evening, ships added rockets and flares to their whistles. By the end of the second VE day holiday, there was an almost feverish excitement everywhere. But everyone, drunk or sober, was good-natured and orderly.

One of our jobs that day was loading boys to go home—Navy, Army, and Air Corps, and patients, both walking and litter. For the occasion I put on my patch jacket with its division and corps insignia. That day it was especially fun. Of course, most of the guys are quite numb; even the most boisterous sometimes turn meek and quiet when they actually see the ship that's going to take them home. For two or more years they've dreamed, thought, and talked of the day, but when the day finally arrives they just can't grasp it, and stand about quietly and look happy.

What really gave me the biggest thrill was the face of the first combat soldier I saw walking up High Street. He was one of the boys who came here for a 7-day leave. As a 29th division guy, they've had a tough deal ever since D day. His smile made me feel good all over.

VE day night, the Port had a reception for officers and guests at the Polygon. After we finished work at 8:30 PM, we cleaned up and Bob and Tom took us up. We stayed about an hour and a half and then came home, as we were dead tired and most of the officers had methodically set out to get dead drunk. For years they've been saying, "Boy, am I going to get drunk when VE day comes." It came and I think they all felt obligated to keep their boast. So we had a drink or two and chatted with everyone and when the lounge became raucously noisy, we left.

It was on the way home that I knew the war here was over. The street lamps were lighted on High Street! Great big, blessed, glaring lights—magnificently horrible old street lamps. It was marvelous. They thrilled me more than the flares, fireworks, blares, and whistles from the ships.

Each day now our work is like a picnic. I don't have to keep forgetting that many of the boys we see will be dead in a few days, because they won't be.

All my love,
Roses

Monday, May 14, 1945
Aboard the London Express

Dearest Family,

What a week! VE days, booming business for our expanding crew, liaison work for London, finding housing for new crew members—*and* helping put on a wedding, give a reception, and be sister, mother, and friend to Ski. Yes, Ski is married! She became Tom's wife at 4 PM Saturday, May 12th, in St. Andrews Presbyterian Church.

Bob and I gave them a small reception afterwards at the Polygon Hotel, for about fifty, before waving them off on the train for a long weekend. Headquarters managed a reservation for them at the Connaught, most posh and British of London's hotels.

The week went from busy to chaotic with the wedding preparations. What started out to be a small ceremony developed into a large affair as soon as Ski made up her mind. The word spread like wildfire and the whole Port got involved. Engraved invitations being out of the question, our GI friends in the Port offices fixed up a lively, if unorthodox, one. They mimeographed and folded one sheet of paper, illustrated with simple line drawings (and I do mean simple), to vaguely resemble the size of a wedding invitation.

Two days before the wedding, Ski and Tom realized a ring had to be bought. As Tom was saving his time off for the wedding trip, Ski needed help in selecting one. So, a day was spent in London exploring Bond and Regent Streets, from Cartiers to Jensen, until she finally found the diamond circlet she wanted in Aspreys.

The most comical of all the preparations, *just* among the family, was getting her ready hygienically—is that the right word? As you know, if there's anyone in the world a person shouldn't come to before marriage for advice, it's me because I'm ignorant. Well, Ski is ignoranter. Thank goodness, we have Lil, who was briefly if unhappily married in Brooklyn years ago. She's the one who brought up the subject or Ski probably wouldn't have thought of it until after the wedding. Away we raced to the chemists (as in drugstore), in panic now, with Lil in tow to ask for whatever was needed to prevent Ski from jumping into motherhood overseas as well as marriage.

We came away from the chemist's with a douche bag with attachments. Lil assured Ski that's the nearest the Brits have to what she needs. You should see the wartime model. The bag part is a glass and metal contraption that looks like a coach lamp. Talk about bulky—Ski had to wrap it in her jacket to carry out, as there's no packaging here. Safely back in Room 15, Ski decided she ought to practice and involved me in the procedure. This is called being a real war buddy. We spent thirty minutes getting all the various parts together. I handed it to Ski, finally, and she immediately broke the glass nozzle by tapping it gently against the washbasin. We were both so angry we just stood there, and then couldn't stop laughing. By the time we got another nozzle, Ski had misplaced a connecting link. After only three trips to the chemists she was all set to go—and I was all set to have her go.

One day before the wedding, the crew jumped in to do their part. We have every type of girl in the crew, from ex-artists to ex-wedding arrangers. Barbara, the artist, volunteered to do the flowers for the church, and Alice, a brand new member with a beautiful voice, agreed to sing "Ich Liebe Dich" and "If God Left Only You." Everyone was eager to help.

We planned to go foraging for church flowers in midafternoon, when our work allowed. Ski was in such a high tension state I took her off earlier for a quiet walk around Beaulieu Abbey, for one last soul-searching. Also took Brother along, Lil's newly acquired little cocker spaniel pup, to wander around the beautiful grounds with us before joining some of the crew to search for flowers.

Way out by Lymington we passed a gorgeous mansion, the front of which blazed with rhododendrons and azaleas in full bloom. We drove in the gates and found out it's about the nicest Red Cross GI rest home in the UK. What luck! The girl who greeted me as I entered the tremendous pickled-pine living room remembered me from a chance meeting in London last October and offered us all the flowers we wanted and practically gave us the place. From a distance it resembles Manderley, only lovelier. It belongs to a 12-year-old boy, left him by his family and lend-leased to the American Red Cross.

What luxury! Four floors of sheer comfort, elegant banquet halls, gaming rooms, everything. The GIs are furnished civilian clothes when they arrive and can do whatever they like. There are 500 acres to ride, swim, fish, or play golf or softball in. You can't help loving it. We stayed for tea, then roamed through the marvelous grounds and picked rhodys and azaleas to bank around the church altar. We left with the Hillman and jeeps filled with blooms.

Got back in town to find Cousin Dean had arrived and planned a small bachelor party for Tom, with Jack (Tom's former roommate, who came up from Weymouth for the occasion) and Bob. Dean and Tom get along famously since they've met, and the four of them went tooting off to Portsmouth for the evening, leaving Ski a new cause for concern—whether they'd return in time and in proper condition for the wedding.

The big day arrived, with most of us almost sleepless from the combination of our work with wedding preparations. It was sunny and warm. Colonel K., the Port Commander, was to give Ski away, Jack to be best man, and Cousin Dean and Bob to usher. I stood up with Ski and we wore our summer uniforms.

Colonel K. picked Ski and me up to drive to the ceremony in his sedan, giving Ski a fatherly pep talk on marriage all the way to the church. He had a very calming influence. I went down the aisle first, then the colonel escorted Ski to the altar.

The minister was fine—kindly, intelligent, and no pomp. He had prepared a beautiful talk, reading from *Sorrell and Sons* about people entering the gate of marriage expecting a garden and finding brambles and thickets instead, and of how people must work as hard at making their marriage a success, a "great concerned ship," as they work at their careers. He ended with that lovely quotation (1st Corinthians 13): "Love believeth all things, love endureth all things."

He couldn't have chosen more fitting words as Tom and Ski will either have the best or the worst marriage in the world. They are sincerely and deeply in love. Over here they are so completely removed from their environments I wonder if they can bridge the gap when they get home. There is no class society here, everyone is in uniform, and everything appears workable in this light. But it's going to take the deepest love in the world for Ski to struggle along with Tom, and for Tom to try, continually, to live up to Ski's background. They both realize the challenges and want to try, so more power to them.

Ski brought about as many nice things with her as I did, which means none. With the help of the crew we managed to have her start off with a trousseau. Mom, dear, naturally the black nightie you sent me was borrowed for the occasion and Ski looks darling in it. She tried it on, as she tried on everything else, several times while deciding what would fit into the suitcase. I also loaned her my black slip, my good coat with the nutria collar, my flowered blouse. We intended to put her on the train in my fluffy white blouse and her lovely beige-brown gabardine suit. At the last minute she decided she'd better be in uniform, as her wedding is unofficial, but left on the white blouse, which made her look completely like a bride. Other crew members donated a white nightie, a pink

Ski and Tom leaving for London honeymoon, May 1945.

one, a new bra and panties to fix her up for their weekend in London. She had enough choices to take a cruise around the world. Oh yes! She carried "something blue" at the ceremony, the hankie you sent her, Mom.

As silver is twice as expensive here as at home, and there is no selection, everyone contributed money toward a purse. It amounted to £50 or more, so they can buy something nice when they're ready.

Really, Ski never looked lovelier, nor Tom happier. They called me Sunday from the Connaught. Tom wanted me to bring up his Oxfords today when I came up on business and meet them for lunch. I did, and to say they looked radiant—both of them—is an understatement. Ski is one of the few brides I've seen who looks more beautiful after marriage than before. Which speaks well for Tom and augurs well for their marriage. By the looks of things they're off to a wonderful start.

Please send more film if you can find any, Dad, as I may have a leave in Scotland soon and I have no film of any kind at this point.

I love you all and have heaps more to write but I got up at 3 for a real early deal and I'm exhausted. Goodnight.

XXXXXXX
Roses

Journal
May 15, 1945

Train's still not arrived and I sit here almost drowsing, smiling at the remembrance of the sight our bachelor party boys presented at the wedding—well-groomed in Class A uniforms, freshly shaved and hair slicked into place, but so quiet the deep circles under their eyes confirmed that they'd really "done" Portsmouth with dear Cousin Dean. Bob told me, after we'd seen the bridal couple off, that Dean knew every spot in Portsmouth and was hailed as a buddy everywhere. He recalled with wonder that as the night wore on Dean rode astride the hood of the jeep like it was a horse and thinks Jack joined him on the hood, leading Bob and Tom on to yet another stop. Even Jack, the original party boy, looked worn out at the wedding. Bob thinks they got back to the Port about 5 in the morning, but he's not quite sure. He was very happy to return me to the rare and unaccustomed quiet of Room 15. Everyone's exhausted.

May 20, 1945

Dears,

We're certainly in a state of flux here. Within the next month I'll decide whether to go on to the continent or handle the expansion here first. Ski and I have screamed so often about it, Headquarters called me in Friday to tell me we've done such an outstanding job here, they felt bound by their promise to give us a chance. Mr. Mitchell said we can be transferred to Le Havre if we're still determined to go, but we're needed here now more than ever. Didn't it seem we could do much more staying here at least a month or so to organize the big work ahead? Buddy, our personnel head, who sat in on the meeting, said we'd have a chance that way to use our leave time too. So I agreed—for a month.

Obviously, Ski and Tom would like a month or so together before being separated. Another consideration is that Ski and I have an overdue week's leave, and if things go well we may go to Scotland before departing the UK. Bob has always wanted to visit there too, and now that Ski and Tom are married, all four of us could go to Scotland with perfect propriety.

We're so busy again we won't be sure we can get away until the last minute. I'm trying to arrange billets for new girls as the Dolphin can't handle any more and we may have to use civilians in our coffee kitchen—lots of things to line up.

Ski has always been a tremendous help in our work, so I've recommended her to be a captain as the operation expands. Also Scud, the Hyannis redhead who came down from an 8th Air Force base in the spring, as she is efficient and capable. They're both invaluable. It takes more than one pair of eyes to keep tabs on the girls and the work. We may have to get civilians or use PWs to make doughnuts in our coffee kitchen. We need a larger space, so organizing eats up a big part of each day.

Back to work. All my love to the best family in the world,

Roses

⁂

Journal   *May 20, 1945*

Why didn't I tell the family my decision to stay was made easier because I'm in love? Then I could have told them I think Buddy euchred me into this decision as she suspected this, so helped Mr. Mitchell ease his conscience by making an offer. When am I going to face up to the facts?

⁂

Thursday, May 24, 1945

Dearest Family,

Big news is we've moved to the country, to a huge Victorian wooden mansion sprawling over lovely grounds on the outskirts of town. Headquarters asked me to get more billets for the crew, and I found this. Quiet and peaceful and wonderful. At night cuckoos and nightingales sing into the window of my very small bedroom. The grounds are spacious and full of huge trees, azaleas, and rhododendrons. Tom and Ski loved it on first sight and joined me, and two more of the crew will move next week. I'm giving our "old" crew first dibs on coming here, then will have room for our new crew in the Dolphin.

It's called Lordswood House, is 12 minutes from the docks, and such a relief from the bustle of the Dolphin I can't believe it yet. The two little old ladies who rent the rooms out are dead ringers for the two ladies in *Arsenic and Old Lace*. Both about seventy or more, tiny Mrs. Airey manages the house and tall, thin Miss Needham runs a riding school from the stables behind the house. As I drove in the gates today I almost bumped into Miss Needham trotting out in her small pony cart pulled by a very large horse. She waved her buggy whip at me and said she was off to do errands. The two of them are so sweet and quaint, I'll not be surprised if they pull out their elderberry wine any day now.

Grounds, stables next door (we'll probably never have time to ride, but it's nice knowing we can), and pretty countryside surround Lordswood. The rambling house has several large reception rooms and many bedrooms, mostly small. My tiny room barely has space for a single bed, a wardrobe, a china water pitcher with blue edging, and flower-painted chamber pot sitting on a commode—and me. But the bathroom near my room has piping hot water and the johnny flushes. We may breakfast if we wish, and the ladies tell me we're welcome to tea in the afternoon whenever we're free. And all this is as cheap as the Dolphin!

Lordswood House, Mrs. Airey explains often and with great pride, belonged to Sir Neville Chamberlain for years and years. Old Sir Neville, a famous British general who distinguished himself in India and the Punjab and Afghanistan, was made a field marshall in 1900, my dears! He came back to Lordswood to die over forty years ago and after his death the property passed out of the family. We've somehow been given the feeling that perhaps even the chamber pots are distinguished around here.

Just the other evening Tom brought Bob out and the four of us had a rousing game of croquet on the beautiful croquet lawn. Mrs. Airey is very serious about the game and delighted that we knew how to play. But first she recited a whole bunch of technical rules before leading us to the mallets and retiring behind the french doors of the breakfast room to keep an eye on the game from afar. After our hilarious and contentious game, which saw one or another of us scrambling under huge rhododendron bushes for balls deliberately whacked out of bounds, she invited us to try her homemade gooseberry pie! It was absolutely delicious and still warm from the oven. Guess we weren't too noisy as she invited us to use the croquet court any time we wish.

I shall now take a hot bath, open my window to hear my nightingales and cuckoos in the garden (nightingales at night, yes, but cuckoos?), and get a good night's sleep. How about that—sounds good, doesn't it?

I love you all so *very* much.

Goodnight now,
Roses

Tuesday night
June 14, 1945

Dearest ones,

Today your daughter returned from her leave in Scotland and what a wonderful leave it was! As usual, up to the last minute I expected something to interfere, although Headquarters urged us to go before the *Queens* start docking here in their home port. The enclosed clipping about the *Queens* from the *Stars and Stripes* explains why it's been hectic reorganizing and enlarging our whole setup to handle so much business.

We had planned to catch the 4:20 PM train for London and then the night train to Scotland. As luck would have it, on Tuesday Tom had to go to Exeter for an ordnance conference. So Ski packed for both of them and we were to meet Bob at the Polygon at 3:15 to sweat out, as the GIs say, Tom's return.

Rosie and Bob, day off
in Bath, 1945.

Bob, Rosie, Ski, and Tom playing croquet at Lordswood House,
May 1945.

The sisters, Mrs. Airey and Miss
Needham, Lordswood House,
fall 1945.

Newlyweds Ski and Tom,
Lordswood House grounds,
summer 1945.

Kari Lund, Rosie, Ski, and Lil Keit playing croquet at
Lordswood, 1945.

He arrived at 3:30, just as Bob was telling us we had a chance to take a boat trip up. Good old Scotty, Colonel M., had arranged for us to go by sea if we wished, on an empty troopship! We jumped at the chance—the only catch was the ship was due to sail at 4:00. We tore down to the docks in the Austin and Tom followed in his jeep.

We got to the pier at 4:05 and drove up beside the ship. It was all ready to go, just one hawser and the gangplank between it and departure. Scott was standing by, calmly holding the ship until we arrived. So we whipped up the gangplank making quite a spectacle, looking like we were going round the world at least. Each of us carried a heavy suitcase or Val-pak, and odd bits of Tom's Class A uniform. Our original plans called for him to change just before we caught the train, but there was no time for that. Ski almost dropped his good shoes overboard in her rush up the gangway, but somehow we made it and the ship sailed.

Can you imagine four passengers on a troop ship capable of carrying 1,500? Talk about a private cruise! Ski and I had one stateroom complete with bathroom and Tom and Bob each had a cabin, on the other side of the ship. It was a historic ship. We know her well from our work here. She's lucky and called the *Bloody B.* Don't think I'd better tell you her name. She's been in every invasion since North Africa and never been hit, although ships all around her have been hit and blown up.

It was the chance of a lifetime as she was going up to Leith for repair, and when do most humans have a chance to sail up the channel through the North Sea and into the Firth of Forth? We knew there was an element of danger in the voyage but I was still shocked when we passed a mine floating only 100 yards to the starboard. Bob and I saw the lookouts spot it as we stood on deck after supper and joked about it being a black-orange crate—until the tracers and big guns on the ships escorting us opened up to blow it out of the water with a very satisfactory explosion.

The evenings are very long with double wartime and the farther north you get, it's as light as Alaska in summer. So when we passed the white cliffs of Dover we could see them well despite the deep twilight and, the only ones on deck, dared to sing a chorus of *the* song in their honor. Next morning, we picked up a convoy because of the dangerous waters at the mouth of the Thames and it stayed with us most of the way, slowing us down considerably. It was such fun having our own ship, we really didn't care how long it took.

The awesome thing about the voyage was the sad feeling that swept over us when we passed buoyed area after buoyed area, markers circling the sites of sunken ships, the masts forlornly sticking out of the water. After seeing mast after mast after mast, we began to truly comprehend the enormity of the toll that mines and torpedoes have taken. And the lives lost. They can never be replaced and it will take years to salvage the shipping and clear the loose mines.

But we had a wonderful time aboard. The meals were superb. We'd get to 7 AM breakfast, take a turn about the deck, then sleep until lunchtime, spend the afternoon on deck, eat dinner, go to the movie with the crew, or play bridge all evening.

One day, the only sunny day, sparkling and clear, the four of us were on the flying bridge with the ship's officers when three submarines came into sight. They signaled us then maneuvered all about us and cut all sorts of didoes—submerging, circling, turning, and putting on a wonderful show.

Thursday evening we sailed into the beautiful Firth of Forth. Now I have sailed into Scotland from both sides. It was rather hazy but we could see the Firth bridge plainly. After lunch Friday, the ship still out in the Forth off Leith, we clambered down a rope ladder (really a ship's net) into a small tug, to be taken ashore. That really doesn't tell the story.

This was no easy maneuver. The water was very choppy and the tug was bouncing up and down against the also-bouncing *Bloody B.* Worse, Ski and I, ladylike in Class A uniforms (complete with skirts and stockings and pumps as our mothers had taught us to travel), could see dignity as well as modesty had to be forgotten if we were to wiggle over the ship's rail, grab the coarse and heavy rope net to back down towards the tug, groping with a foot for each foothold while not losing our grasp on the thick rope of the cargo net. Two tugmen smiled up encouragingly, but their grins didn't encourage Ski.

"Look how they're leering *up* at us, Rosie, they're right *under* us," she wailed. So I went first, and shouted encouragement as Tom and Bob urged her on from the deck. Finally, Tom lost the "gentleman and officer" conduct he had managed to maintain during the trip and loosed a few choice swear words, and over the side she came.

From Leith, our trek really began. As Tom and Bob struggled with the heavy bags, they kept reminding us that it was all *our* fault. Tom told Ski she should have been able to put it all in *one* bag. Bob asked me why I decided we should all bring boots along. (Actually, it was his suggestion.) Eventually we got hysterical laughing at the caravan we presented—in one dinky cab with four of us and four huge bags.

We caught the train from Edinburrrr to Glasgow all right—a small miracle for which we were all grateful, for none of us knew our way around. In Glasgow I mentioned that I'd heard there were several bus stations and we should be sure to catch the right bus. Ski simultaneously was telling Tom to get a porter and Tom said he couldn't tell goddamn porters from trainmen as they don't wear red caps over here!

As usual, Tom and Bob listened to neither of us and, as expected, we wound up at the wrong bus station. We had fifteen minutes to reach the right station and catch the *last* bus to Inversnaid on Loch Lomond, our destination. We couldn't find a cab, there were none around, the minutes flew by and turned the drizzly atmosphere electric. A nice Scotsman at the bus station tried everywhere to get a cab for us, while Tom and Bob were circling the block searching for a cab, and the Scotsman finally hailed an empty, open-backed lorry. Ski and I had just piled on with the four bags when Tom and Bob came round the corner with a taxi in tow. So we piled off the lorry and into the taxi. By then it was 4:15 and we had missed the bus.

The cabman said he knew where we could hire a private car, so off we went for it. After twenty minutes dodging horses in big collars pulling wagons, we found the private car was not available. So the cabman, who looked like Mortimer Snerd but didn't have his brains, remembered that we might catch the bus at Dunbarton and off we sped. Halfway there he decided we couldn't make it and suggested stopping at the police station for a special permit for him to drive us to Inversnaid.

Bob went in with him but the police had no authority to issue permits. That's when our smart cabbie said he'd take a chance on driving us to Balloch, at the foot of Loch Lomond, and maybe we could get a connection there. Again, off we sped through the Scottish countryside in the funny old cab.

By this time, tempers were slightly on edge. Tom, optimist that he is, sat in his corner muttering that we hadn't a chance of making it that night. Ski mentioned that she and I had *never* had any trouble when the two of us traveled. I remarked caustically that I should have brought my father along to *organize* the trip, and Bob said, well, how did he know the cab driver would be stupid enough to take us to the wrong bus station? He'd said "Inversnaid" clearly enough, hadn't he! So we all had candy bars retrieved from Ski's purse and I bet Bob two shillings and sixpence we would get there.

At Balloch we hired a private car (I won't go into details) and a whiskey-soaked driver who was jolly as all Scotland. He knew exactly how to get where we were going. It took him two minutes to get us all laughing. His burr was so thick we couldn't understand half of what he said at first, but he talked all the way, cracking joke after joke and laughing so hard himself that tears rolled down his cheeks, and he'd gasp, "Oh, dear, oh dear, oh dear," and go into gales more laughter.

The jokes weren't very funny but he was priceless. Sample joke, after long, burry buildup: "Do ye know why Scotsmen hae the thistle as their flower?"—taking his eyes off a road that had the old tunnel road in the Berkeley Hills beat for turns but not for width. We hastily chorused no, so we wouldn't drive right into the loch.

"Because," and he started laughing again, "the Scotsmen hae so many fine points." More gales of laughter.

He'd speed down the narrow road tooting his horn on the straightaway but never touching it on the hidden hairpin curves. It had been raining on and off all day, but as we drove along the beautifully *green* shores of Loch Lomond, the loveliest rainbow I ever hope to see appeared suddenly—its right end in the middle of the lake—and, brilliant and breathtaking, followed us all the way to Ben Lomond.

Just past Tarbet our driver stopped in the middle of nowhere and pointed out the hotel directly across the loch—with its white, old-fashioned wooden exterior and a pretty waterfall cascading down into the loch beside it. There wasn't a person in sight but there was a public telephone booth in front of a small building on our left. The guys found out we had to call across to get someone to come for us. Eventually we saw an old rowboat heading across the loch towards us, rowed—with long oars—by a little man in a tweed jacket and cap.

He jumped out at water's edge and pulled up the wide old rowboat, grabbed our bags and loaded them, then helped us aboard and carefully balanced us against the bags, pushed off with his long oars, and worked for a while to fire up the old outboard motor for the short trip across to the landing. The motor fired on the fifth attempt and off we putted. Jumping out as he beached the boat below the hotel, he directed us towards the entrance and said he'd bring the bags.

We paused a moment to admire the view and share our amazement at having arrived at our destination. By the time we'd walked up and entered the hotel, he was waiting behind the desk to sign us in, in a white jacket now, before escorting us up to our rooms. As he opened each door to show us around and tell us dining room hours and hotel schedules, the correct bag was waiting beside the correct door.

Our rooms were quaint and very comfortable. Ski and Tom were given the bridal suite down the hall from the other rooms in the corner of the building, with wonderful views of Loch Lomond from all windows. My room was large, high-ceilinged, and charming, with a big double bed, large wardrobe, and nice view of Loch Lomond. Bob's was large and roomy too, very similar to mine. It was wonderful to have arrived and to be able to unpack the darn bags for a few days and hang up some fresh clothes.

When we came down to eat, the same little man, now the bartender, offered us cocktails, made suggestions as he presented the menu after we adjourned to the dining room, and served the dinner when we had ordered. As we entered the lounge after dinner, to review our day and what Tom was already calling "The Battle of the Bags," our little man was waiting to suggest a dart game, cards, and other ways to spend the evening. He always turned up at our elbows, even before we knew we needed him. We never did figure how he managed to be so many places at once.

After dinner we went for a walk. Loch Lomond and the country around it are the greenest places I've ever seen. Bracken, clover, and fern cover the ground and in every direction there are springs and rushing mountain streams and craggy little mountains (we'd call them hills at home) rearing up suddenly. Lovely bluebells mix with the bracken and small yellow flowers highlight everything else.

From Friday night until Wednesday we had a heavenly time. We climbed mountains and wandered all over, in battle dress now and those combat boots we had lugged along, perfect attire for exploring the countryside. We rowed up the loch to Rob Roy's cave and climbed all over it. Dad, you remember Sir Walter Scott's *Rob Roy*, don't you? Inversnaid is the real Rob Roy's property, and his cave is exciting, as are the few remains of Fort Inversnaid. After dinner, we'd take a walk, then play bridge during the long evenings, and have beer and sandwiches at ten or eleven.

Ski and Tom, Loch Lomond, June 1945.

Sunday was our one perfect day and it was superbly clear. We walked up to a priceless little church nestled among the hills and surrounded by trees. Those wonderful Scottish mountain sheep—white with black faces and legs, sometimes black tails, and curling mountain sheep horns—and their adorable lambs were everywhere on the hillsides.

The church bells began to ring as we drew near the church. Oh, how I wished you could have been there with us—seen the brisk, homespun-clad woman pound out the Presbyterian hymns on the squeaky little organ—seen the little man in the orange tweed suit take up the collection—heard the gray-haired minister fill the tiny church with his booming voice, even though there were only two others there!

It's now past midnight and I have to be up at 6 AM, so I'll start another letter tomorrow.

All my love to you all,
Roses

P.S. Mom, here is a Scottish bluebell I pressed for you.

Journal

June 15, 1945

Come on, Rosie, in my letter I skirted around so much. Why don't I just admit I'm head over heels in love? Why do I delay? Because it changes my often and loudly stated plans? I've got to write them about Bob soon. Then I could share all that made this trip so enchanting, exasperating, challenging, difficult, and absolutely wonderful.

Know they'd appreciate my surprise when we boarded that big empty troopship and Ski and I were shown to a cabin. I was dumbfounded. "Ski, you and Tom should be together, you're married, for Gawd's sake! There's no reason for you to bunk with me. Who arranged this?"

"I did," Ski said, primly. I hate it when she gets that Miss New England proper tone in her voice. "Rosie, I'm still officially single and we're traveling in uniform."

"So what!" I exploded. "This is ridiculous. Go talk to a ship's officer and tell him you're on your honeymoon. I'll go talk to him!" I was so envious of her marital status I couldn't control my voice. "You're married in the eyes of the church and in the eyes of the Red Cross, even if it's unofficial. You're wearing a wedding ring! Here we are on a ship with room for thousands. Why can't you and Tom, your husband, let me remind you, be together on a voyage few others could dream of? Just because your marriage is unofficial doesn't make it illegal." When I blow my top I do tend to be sarcastic.

But Ski, determined to preserve our Red Cross image, held her ground and said they'd manage time together. They sure did, I give her points for that. We often couldn't find them, not that Bob and I were looking. Even though we long since decided what our relationship must be until after the war when we're free, I stewed the entire week before we left, half hoping it would be impossible to get away. Then almost panicked when we had the last-minute chance to take a slow boat up.

I was right to worry for with each passing day we grew surer we were right for each other, in all the ways that count. We survived the Battle of the Bags with our humor intact, only to be confronted with what we now call the Problem of the Key. For just after I was shown to my hotel room and started to unpack, trying to fit my clothes into the old-fashioned armoire, I noticed another door and thought it a built-in closet. I opened the door and there stood Bob, unpacking his suitcase. He looked up and then we had to laugh. Our efficient little hotel man had indeed covered everything.

This slowed down our unpacking awhile. We lingered to inspect each other's rooms and compare views of Loch Lomond. Eventually I remembered we should finish hanging up our clothes and go meet Ski and Tom for dinner—and that the key must remain on my side of the door. It was a burden to carry all week.

⚜

June 15, 1945

Dearest Family,

It's now 5:45 Friday evening and I'm riding the rails again, this time on the return London Express. Had a rush call in middle of our busy day and hopped next train to London, boots and all, for a three-hour conference with Mitchell.

The gist of everything is that Southampton will be terribly busy and he wants to be sure I'll stay and see the operation through rather than opting to go on to the continent now. He obviously and sincerely wants me to remain in charge of the operation, so think I'll probably decide to do so. He brought up another point which I hadn't realized: on July 15th I will have completed one year's overseas duty, and after eighteen months overseas all ARC personnel are eligible for thirty days' leave in the States. So about next January I may be able to come home on leave. How would you like that? That is, of course, if transportation is available at the time. It gives us something lovely to look forward to, doesn't it?

I'm so tired sitting in this stuffy carriage I won't try and finish this. Will save details of the rest of our Scotland leave until I can mail a few pictures and small gifts home.

Goodnight and sweet dreams.

All my love,
Roses

Part Four

Victory at Hand

On May 6, 1945, the Germans had surrendered unconditionally and the occupied countries were liberated.

Russian forces, who were allowed to enter Berlin first, reported the death of Hitler and his staff in his bunker, but this report was unconfirmed for several months. We began to hear of other Nazi leaders being seized for war crimes.

After VE day, our Red Cross responsibilities increased to servicing battle-weary men on short furloughs and leaves, troops and divisions being redeployed, and young replacements being sent to Germany to take over for the combat veterans returning.

The joy of the troops boarding ship for home was tempered by the fear that they'd be sent on for an expected invasion of Japan. When atomic bombs were dropped on Hiroshima and Nagasaki and the Japanese finally surrendered in August 1945, the joy was not tempered.

The war was over at last.

Chapter Fifteen

June 21, 1945

Dearest Family,

Tonight I'm writing a letter just to the family. You've all asked about Bob and I've been wanting to tell you about him. He's been here longer than I have and works in the Maritime Chambers, where I go daily to get all the information for the following day. He's a person you can't help noticing—about 5 foot 10 plus, wavy hair, and lovely blue eyes. He's muscularly built and stands very straight; not handsome but attractive (although my crew think he's very handsome). He's all business when working and extremely well liked by the other officers as he's conscientious, intelligent, reliable, and has integrity. I know that sounds strange, but there are so few men with scruples over here they are always highly respected.

As he's a person you can't help noticing, I noticed him immediately! He was sitting at his desk reading a church bulletin from home and I filed him mentally under "Fine type—some woman is very lucky." Bob was always pleasant and used to jokingly ask me out; said I was working too hard and I'd agree to meet him at nine o'clock and we'd laugh.

One day, Bob and Colonel S. (we call him Pop as he's married and doesn't go out at all so we girls respect him) were sitting with us at mess when some others came over to discuss a dance that night. Out of the blue, Bob invited me (I thought still kidding). I glibly started to say for all to hear, "Oh, I don't go out with married men."

Pop S. hastily said I should make up a foursome with Ski and Tom and have fun. So I accepted and that night really dressed up in civvies, Delmans, and perfume, instead of in uniform, which always seems to retain that lingering odor of coffee and doughnuts.

We had a wonderful time. We danced every single dance as Bob is a marvelous dancer. (After all these years Rosie finds a wonderful dancer with brains too!) We often went to the Saturday night dances after that and had wonderful times. Then one gorgeous spring evening he asked me to go for a stroll. We walked for miles and I'd see him screwing up his courage to mention the purpose of this hike, then lose it again. Finally he suggested we stop in a pub for a beer. We were now 8 miles away from our starting point and I was amused, interested, and thirsty.

When at last he came to the point, every word seemed an effort. He told me Pop S. is the only other person he's talked with about his personal life, as he always thought he had pretty good judgment—but his marriage proved he didn't. Bob said he married the day he graduated from Officers Candidate School to a girl he'd known, gone with, and broken off with. He said, "I can't imagine why we married. Thinking back, I was away from home, she started writing me, and my newly married roommate kept telling me what a wonderful thing marriage is and I should try it. We started writing each other, I thought I was in love, and we got married."

Within a month they both felt they'd made a mistake. They had not much in common, there wasn't even enough feeling between them for them to be angry with each other. But Bob comes from a very happy background and wanted to make his marriage succeed. His wife did too, and they planned a baby. After Bobby came (now almost 2 and adorable, judging from the picture Bob carries in his wallet), it wasn't long before they agreed it was hopeless to try to build a life together. They separated and she returned to her home state months before his unit was sent overseas. His wife plans to divorce him, but not until after the war because of the allotment. Now he's hoping she'll agree to do it before then, but is reluctant to force the issue as they mutually agreed on this.

At this point, beads of perspiration were standing out on Bob's forehead as he added, "The thing that depresses me most is knowing I won't have the rights to be near my son often."

Bob said he was so disappointed in himself he didn't go out at all when he first came over to England and was almost a recluse. He also said he'd wanted to ask me out for ever so long but was afraid I wouldn't date him because he was married. As Bob talked I realized why Pop S. had approved our first date. You've never seen a man look happier than Bob after he'd talked it all out. I told him, as I sincerely believe, that what happened to him before was no concern of mine. We've all made mistakes far more serious than his. There was no reason we couldn't date and enjoy each other's company and when the war's finally over we can face serious decisions, if we both feel the same way.

As you must be gathering, you cannot file Bob with Joe as a mere "good date." (Incidentally, I filed Joe awhile ago as not such a good date.) I have wanted to write you about Bob for a long time now but waited, to be certain of my own feelings. I am sure that I am in love with him. There's never been any doubt in my mind, really. But old "Take It Easy Rosie" doesn't like jumping off the deep end. Bob was sure he wanted to marry me ages ago, and it infuriated him when I'd analyze his feelings and say, "Now, Bob, are you sure—very sure—you're not just lonesome?" We're both sure, very sure.

But we're both very much alike. I want to be married in Berkeley, California, and we want to meet each other's families and go to each other's homes before marrying. We want to return to our environments and be sure we're in our right minds! His family never thought his first marriage wise; his best friends told him his separation was the best thing that ever happened to him. We want to start out together with our families behind us.

And wait until you meet him! You'll love him, I'm positive. He's twenty-eight and from Indianapolis. His father works in the shops of the New York Central there. He has three brothers—a paratrooper officer in the Philippines, a Navy Seabee in Hawaii, one just graduating from high school—and his older sister, thirty, is happily married with two children. His family has always been a happy one and that's his goal—a warm home and family. As that's mine too, how can we lose?

He went to school in Indiana, plays golf, baseball, and basketball. Was captain of his high school basketball team. Has a lovely voice—only man I've ever known who can hum in my ear as we dance and have it sound right! (Yes, Sis, even better than your Willis.) He worked in Ohio before the war for a precision tool company. He was given the best territory in his district and before being drafted was their top salesman, making $350 a month, which is darn good for a man not yet twenty-five. His job awaits his return, or two others which have been offered by men with top steel companies in *Pittsburgh!* In his type of work every young man starts selling, but he's anxious to get into the office. He can't help being a success—just a successful type like Willis, Sis.

We've had oodles of fun these past few months. We've even played golf a couple of times—he usually plays in the 70s as he started caddying at ten in Indiana. The first time we played nine holes on a nearby course using borrowed clubs, I surprised myself with a gorgeous drive and par on the first hole (before falling apart later) and he says there's hope for me.

We're very much alike in disposition. He's the only man I've ever known who won't let me pull him around by the nose (and I hope that doesn't sound fatuous, but you know what I mean). And he's the only one I've ever known who can really make me angry. He says the same of me. We're both independent and stubborn, and we're good for each other. Bob's so charming that evidently girls have always chased him, and I don't know how to do that. If they don't want to come after me, to heck with them. Consequently, Bob has done more legwork than ever before in his life. Colonel M. asks me out often and a few others. Even though Bob knows I wouldn't go out with anyone else, it upsets him slightly and keeps him running after me. Despite it all, he says he never before knew what love is, and I'm sure I didn't. It's just as you said it would be, Mom—you know it.

He was drafted near the first draft—became a sergeant, then was sent to OCS and has come up quickly to major. When there's a difficult job to be done or a general and his division to be handled as they come through the Port, Bob is often handed the job. Right now he has been given a most challenging one as assistant coordinating officer for all troop movements in the Southampton area. Loading big ships is like moving a city. He'll be going to Scotland next month to gather information for loading the *Queens,* due to return to this, their home port, in the near future. We're so busy again we have a hard time even slipping in a date as our hours are very irregular. But we usually sit together at mess, with Tom and Ski or crew members if we can manage it.

As I know I've mentioned before, life here is without the superficial glamor it's so easy to find at home. This is a close-knit little world and you get to know the others, warts and all. You cannot escape this world for a day. When you have a date, there's only one place you can go dancing and only three things you can wear—and you've already worn them to death. Your everyday life is extremely limited by work, surroundings, and circumstances. Because of this you quickly go through the "frills" of knowing a new person and get down to essential qualities. It takes a very short time to find out whether you really enjoy a person or whether they affect you like the same phonograph record played over and over. I have never tired of having Bob around, not even for an instant. The fact that he loves me after months of seeing me in all kinds of weather, sometimes terribly tired and dirty, in the same drab combat clothes and with no variety of setting should prove something.

But I would just as soon the whole town doesn't know that Rosie's in love. The shock might be too much, especially for Bob B.'s mother who's always been good at jumping to conclusions! And don't tell the store, in case I want to work when I get home while Bob sees his divorce through and resumes his career. Only then will we be able to decide where our future together lies and make definite plans. Too, there's always the chance we may change our minds before the war is over and we're released to go home. Frankly, I think that's impossible. Bob's sure it's impossible, but there's no use having everyone "get their tea hot" (as they say over here) until we come home.

So you see, I've done what I swore I wouldn't do—fallen in love overseas. I deliberately went out of my way not to get too interested in anyone, but it didn't work. Bob says it's just his luck to have to come 3,000 miles to find me, and then I can't even cook. But, Mother, I told him you had an excellent cookbook on tap for me at home.

Mom dear, you know how you and I have always been about clothes? Sometimes we never find what we're looking for, but when we do we know it, even if it's the first thing we try on? That's how it is with Bob. I knew it. I know, too, that if all of you, my highly critical family, set out to select a husband for Rosie—if you could have found this R.J.N. from Indiana—you would have unanimously agreed on him.

I have to get back to work. I swiped an hour this morning to finish this as I've been wanting to tell you all this for ever so long.

All my love to the best family in the world,
Roses

P.S. Lest you think I've described him in too glowing terms, I have to tell you that after we got serious and I mentioned how impressed I was seeing him reading a church bulletin in the office, he burst into laughter and said, "That's the only church bulletin Mom ever sent me!"

❧

Journal   June 21, 1945

Now I can focus again on work and the war. Feel wonderful to get this letter off. Know I should have done it earlier. I can only hope family trusts my judgment as much as I do.

❧

June 29, 1945

Dearest ones,

It's started again. The round-the-clock work. We now have eighteen on the crew. This will have to be just a note. Your wonderful package came yesterday, Sis, and everything's perfect. The Elizabeth Arden collection was perfect. I smell like the original "Flower Mist," having just bathed and lathered myself in it.

Mom, I'm sending you a list of clothes I'd like real soon and thanks for offering to shop for me. Three rolls of 620 film arrived from you, Dad, and I'll try never to run out again. I so appreciate it.

Terribly tired so goodnight now, and oh, how much I love you all,

Roses

❧

July 5, 1945

Dearest ones,

Well, the deluge has come and are we ever busy! I'm grabbing a few minutes to write before having a crew meeting at 5:30 PM, and then we work all night. Bob leaves for Scotland in the morning, but if I'm lucky I'll get to see him for fifteen minutes at mess tonight. Otherwise I'll just have to wait three weeks until he returns. *C'est la guerre.*

My crew now numbers over twenty girls. Buddy came down from London to view our operations. On behalf of Mr. Eisner, the new head of Clubmobile (Mr. Mitchell has been sent to the continent), she made me a supervisor. Ski and Scud are to be captains under me. So you see we're big-time operators now.

I'm thrilled Ski and Scud can be captains as they're tireless workers and I wanted them to be promoted, as there's no way I can cover all operation areas and keep up with the crew and our myriad daily operations without assistance. I should tell you more about Scud, a Cape Codder from Hyannis where her family's lived for generations. She's a Duke graduate, calm, intelligent, and very observing. She's tall and slim, with lovely dark red hair, her features strong as if carved from New England granite, and she has a lovely smile—also a wonderful contralto voice. Best, she has a great deadpan wit, so we laugh a lot.

When I had lunch with J. Lester Eisner in London recently, it turned out he knows and likes Mr. Robert and Mr. James from our store, and had spent an evening with Mr. Robert at Adam Gimbel's last December. He thinks Ranso-hoffs the best run and most profitable store west of New York! Mr. Eisner is a director of the Allied store chain, which is all over the country and includes Marshs in Boston and the Bon Marché in Seattle. He's wealthy and quite nice. The fact that I'm on leave from the store seemed to really impress him, as he hasn't disputed one decision I've made and given me everything I've requested—from new trucks to brand-new serving equipment. Our whole operation now has to do with the transhipment of troops.

Right now an entire division is pouring back from the continent. They debark and load on trains, then we whip through feeding them coffee and dough-nuts as quickly as possible. Teams of girls go into a car as soon as it's loaded, the idea being to finish feeding them within two or three minutes of the time the Transportation Corps has loaded them. It's never been done that quickly before, but we devised a new system and managed to keep up. The other night they loaded a train in eleven minutes and we did it! Of course, from 11:30 PM until 5 AM the girls didn't stop running, and smiling, for a minute, and that's a little grueling. But it's worth the effort to see the guys wolf down the fresh hot dough-nuts and have the Port so pleased with our work.

Last night Ski was standing with me by the first train waiting for the first troops to debark when a voice behind us said, "Why don't you girls join the union and get some decent working hours?"

I said, "Maybe we should, but we like the work," when I spotted the stars on the man's cap and realized it was the division's commanding general. He talked for twenty minutes, friendly as could be, and today he came over to my table at mess to ask how we got along last night. Imagine—the informality of it all!

Must run. We've had several interruptions and it's time to go to the meet-ing. I'll write again as soon as possible. Oh! The golf balls and the darling combs arrived and thanks a million. Now, the first chance I get, Bob and I'll sneak out for nine holes of golf.

All my love to you and be home July 31st if you can. I've booked a tele-phone call home—6 AM from here on August 1st. Should reach you about 10 PM July 31st. Cable me if you're not going to be home and I'll rebook the call.

XXX
Roses

July 11, 1945

Dearest Family,

At this point we're all having difficulty telling day from night as we work such long and odd hours. Bob's been in Scotland for about a week. He just called a few minutes ago from Glasgow and he'll probably be there another week or so. He loves the work and is really looking forward to loading the *Queens*. We're so busy I now have well over twenty girls and they're all worn out. But they love it. Four turned down an assignment on the continent today as they want to stay here. For one thing the GIs appreciate the service so. Several have told me they've never seen girls work so hard, that one of us does more work in a single train operation than three girls do in a week on the continent. True or not, it does show they appreciate us being around at all hours to feed them and talk with them and do things for them.

At this time of year Southampton has a glamor about it. I realized again what a fascinating place it can be the other night. Several of us were sitting by the dock on the quayside waiting for a late shipload of troops. It was a beautifully clear evening, about 10:30, and there was a gorgeous sunset on the calm water. As the tremendous trooper pulled up Southampton Water crammed with our boys, the new girls with me were so excited they could hardly sit still. Little ugly tugs pushed and bumped the ship into position alongside us, and 3,500 guys started shouting greetings, and "Any coffee and doughnuts there, Red Cross?" The new girls were sold on Southampton.

Mother, I've been thinking of the clothes problem and I think I have the solution, if it's not too much bother to you. I'm happiest with clothes from Ransohoffs—the old school tie tradition, I guess. The best time to buy there is at the beginning of the season, when the merchandise is fresh. If you could tell Virginia, my former advertising boss, what I want she could tell you when to come over and look. She sees every bit of new merchandise as it arrives, for her prize-winning ads, and know she'd keep me in mind and show you what to choose from. That will save you getting a new saleswoman who doesn't know rayon from silk. I don't care about price (I have few chances to spend money here), but I'd love a few nice things for my morale. To start with: one knockout, smooth, and classy dress; one smart sports dress (from the second floor), and, if there are any dressy suits, good, if not, okay. I'm about ten pounds lighter than when I left home, so a size 10 is fine. It's late and tomorrow's a long day, so closing for now. Oh! Sunday was a gorgeous day and we had a break in operations from noon to 8 PM, so Scotty (Colonel M.) invited Tom, Ski, and me to go out on his boat. Bob is off in Scotland. He gets a bit miffed at Colonel M.'s attentions to me, so Scotty teases Bob by concentrating on being nice more than ever. I tried to refuse gracefully but was overridden by Tom and Ski, who said I needed the sun and should take a short break. My arm wasn't hard to twist as I was longing to swim and I love boats. I got tan as we went out by the Isle of Wight and swam from the boat. Matthews had one of his crew bring a rubber life raft and the four of us had a great time paddling in circles in that.

A girl swam out to the boat from the Isle of Wight and rested a few minutes aboard before swimming back. As she dove off the boat she said, "Cheerio, thanks for the use of your yacht." I suddenly realized that a boat with a four-man crew is above the dinghy class. Matthews and Tom grinned, and began discussing which one would have an apple stand after the war and which a peanut stand. But the luxury is nice while it lasts.

I love you *all so much,*
Roses

⚜

Journal   *July 11, 1945*

Still smiling at the experience Ruth, one of our brand new girls, had today. We sent some of our new crew to serve a shipload of guys going home on rotation, a happy and pleasant way to ease them into our work. I walked out on the dock to check on the operation and spotted Ruth laughing up at the guys crowding the rail having the time of her life, as were they. I told her we were glad to have her aboard and started to walk away when she called me back, "Oh, Rosie, look! Now they're even tossing off balloons, aren't they pretty?"

"They're not balloons, Ruth," I said, even before turning to watch the men enthusiastically throwing hundreds of inflated condoms into the air to drift down as the ship edged away from the pier. Her face turned bright red as I explained.

⚜

July 21, 1945

Dearest ones,

Some mail has finally arrived and am pleased no end that both my mother and sister think Bob sounds okay. Mom, don't worry about a thing. We wouldn't think of being married anywhere but home, and I'm so proud of Bob I can't wait for you all to meet him. I just had to tell you about him because I knew you'd be happy knowing I have such a wonderful companion with whom to share these months overseas. It may well be a couple of years before we can marry as when business falls off here in six or more months, the Port may be redeployed anywhere—including the CBI (China-Burma-India) theater and I may be sent scurrying in the other direction by the Red Cross. So much depends on how long it takes for all the other theaters of war to wind up.

Marty, I'm so glad you think Bob sounds right for me, and it was wonderful of you to send me that dress and hat. You must know I need clothes. Bob just returned from Glasgow and brought me two lovely sweater sets: a beige Shetland hand-knit slipover with matching cardigan and a beautiful gray set, lacy knit and very dressy. You'd love it. Now I need a couple of skirts I can wear them with. Mom, if you have a chance to shop I'd love a skirt from Roos Brothers campus shop, with a kick pleat, or pleated.

It's nice of you all to suggest that Bob settle in California. I've never mentioned where I want to live, as I think he should settle where his best opportunities lie. But I was thrilled a few weeks ago when he said he'd written his boss about the possibilities of working in their San Francisco office! I said, "But, Bob, I thought you wanted to live in Ohio, and how do you know you'd like the coast?"

He said, "I've always thought I'd like to live there. Besides, you love California, so it would be a shame if you'd have to leave it, and your family would miss you terribly." So you see, he thinks of everything.

Must get back to work. We're terribly busy. Bob's been back a week and we haven't had a date yet! I've either been working or had executives down from London to see the operations, and he's been put in charge of all loading coordination and has been working day and night too.

All my love,
Roses

～◦◦◦～

August 7, 1945

Dearest ones,

I can't tell you how *completely* lovely it was to hear your voices, Mom and Dad, when my telephone call went through. At times your voices came in waves, with here and there a word or two missing, but three times it was as though I were calling from Berkeley and your inflections sounded perfectly natural. It was indescribably wonderful and worth every second of the wait. Ski and I both got up at 5 AM here as I was curious to see if her call went through. She got it through about 7 AM but California took longer. I hope your night wasn't too sleepless waiting. What a marvel to talk, or shout, across oceans.

Oh, happy day! Yesterday your marvelous packages arrived and everything's just perfect. I love everything you sent. The black hat's adorable, the pink dress and gold dress both fit perfectly and look simply wonderful on me (on Ski too, as she was so excited she couldn't wait to try everything on). The shoes I'm crazy about and love the shade. In other words your selection was wonderful, Mom dear, and I don't think you can know how much they mean to me. I so appreciate the time and effort you've put into this.

(*Pause*) It's now Thursday and I'm on the London train. I was too tired to finish this the other night as I just had to get some sleep.

The past two days have been so breathtaking I can't fully realize what happened. First the atomic bomb and now Russia declares war on Japan. It looks as though Japan must fold soon, and that overjoys me. Frankly, the atomic bomb scares me to death. It certainly presages a new age, an interplanetary age, I'll bet. But it's such an awesome thing it passes my understanding. I agree with Tolstoy that the only way to stop war is to make it a completely fearsome, horrible undertaking—to remove all its trappings and glamor. If the atomic bomb doesn't do exactly that—in one day make obsolete armies of waving flags, blaring bands, and flattering uniforms and strip war down to its basic awfulness, expose its barbarity for all to see—then nothing can ever do it. Perhaps world peace, which we've never been able to attain through human reasoning, can be achieved through worldwide fear.

The great paradox of war is that, from my tiny and personal perspective, I've never had a more fulfilling (from the standpoint of being useful) or exciting period in my life. I wouldn't be anywhere else, given the choice. I'm completely at ease being here—yes, loving so many parts of this experience while absolutely loathing others. The horrible opening of the concentration camps from April on has only reconfirmed our commitment. The camps proved that, imperfect as we are, the cause we're giving our best years to is worth every ounce of our effort. I think most of those around me feel exactly as I do—from GIs to generals.

At any rate, unless Japan wishes to commit national hara-kiri, she must give up quickly. And that means in the foreseeable future I should be coming home to stay. Mr. Eisner was at Southampton Sunday and has taken my request for our girls (I now have a crew of thirty) to have continental leave to the commissioner. He agreed with all my suggestions, so plans are being made either for direct leave on the continent or for a rotation plan, whereby the girls would go over four at a time and work for a few weeks and see a little of the continent. Switzerland is being opened up as a leave center soon.

Right now we are swamped, the *Queen Mary* on its way, reputedly with the Duke and Duchess of Windsor aboard, and thousands of troops are coming and going night and day. Southampton has the reputation of being the best ARC operation over here. We never miss any man going through and the Army is so cooperative it's wonderful working under these conditions.

The GIs couldn't be more appreciative. At night we serve as many as ten trainloads—divisions coming from the continent for redeployment. They are fed in France in the morning, jammed on ships and from 8 or 9 PM on we give them piping hot coffee and fresh doughnuts, cigarettes, and chocolate bars *and* answer questions and suggest places for them to see and things to do here in England while they await shipment. They all say they've "never had it so good" before—as they eat five or six doughnuts and try to find a girl from their home state from among the fourteen to sixteen girls on a single operation.

Our GIs are funny and so proud of their "worldliness." Their gags change often but they all use the same ones the same week, it seems. The past few weeks it runs something like this:

"Hello, fraulein" (that's to let you know they've been in Germany), "can we fraternize here?" Or: " 'Allo, bébé" (if they're just back from France), followed by a few French phrases or German phrases.

I usually answer, "Say, chum, you'd better can that language because where you're going no one will be able to understand you at all."

And they whoop and holler and laugh at the guy who used the French or German, and then go into their "What state are you from?" routine.

The other night I was serving a compartment full of Mexican-looking GIs. Instead of the usual fraulein routine one of them shot a string of Spanish at me. I said, "What did you say?"

He said, "I said 'good evening and how are you?' in Spanish." So I answered in Spanish and told him I was fine and all the crew was fine and yes, it was indeed a nice evening. Well, the compartment became a bedlam. They all started in on me, and we had a lovely time. It seems they're U.S. Mexicans and come from Los Angeles.

Goodnight for this time. I'm on my way home after a very busy six hours at Headquarters. You know how I miss you and love you. Hope my flowers reach you for your wedding anniversary, which is almost here.

Roses

Chapter Sixteen

August 9, 1945
Friday night, 11:15 PM

Dearest Folks,

Just have to drop you a note, late as it is, to talk over all the tremendous news! The radio newsman in Paris is just now telling again how Japan has submitted a "surrender but keep Emperor" offer to Washington. It looks as though this war will be over within a day or two and I wonder if it wouldn't be wise to protect the Emperor, as all the Japanese revere him. Figurehead or no, he has always been Western in his thought and it's generally conceded that he was held virtual prisoner in his palace by the militarists who wished to start the war. Whatever the Allies decide, Japan has no choice—she's between the atom bomb and Soviet Russia! On a smaller scale, it looks as though life can return to a prewar pace within a year and Roses can return to California! So start the mint growing at the side of the house, Dad, and I'll be home for Mom's roast lamb feast.

Today was perfect all around. Your package with presents for everyone arrived today, Mother, and everything was perfect. I have on my beautiful pj's now and when I pulled out that package for Ski, she had tears in her eyes. She just loves her pink pajamas. Dad, the pen set is perfect as Shaeffer's has the best point, and I've been desperate since I lost my pen. The package for Bob and Tom was a huge success. They can't get fine soap like that here and they were so pleased you remembered them. Ski, Bob, and Tom send their thanks too—believe me, they were thrilled.

I'm terribly tired and the *Mary* arrives tomorrow with much ado, so I'd better get some sleep so I won't have circles under my eyes when I greet her—but I just had to tell you how I appreciate having the finest, most considerate parents in the world.

Goodnight now. I love you so, and will be home to prove it in about a year or less. Hurrah!

Roses

August 15, 1945
VJ day—9:25 AM

Dearest Family,

Just have a few minutes but had to drop you a line as from noon on I won't have a minute free until day after tomorrow. Not even time for sleep, I'm afraid.

Life is exciting in Southampton. The *Queen Mary* came "home" last Saturday. Scott (Colonel M.) took Ski and me out in his boat. We reached her just as she approached the Isle of Wight, circled her, and came back in to berth with her. The soldiers, sailors, congressmen and women, and Arabian royalty aboard all waved and called to us. It is nice to know the Director of Operations at times!

From noon today we load the 30th division aboard. They've already put huge division insignia on the sides of the ship, with a banner "OLD HICKORY" strung along the boat deck. These *Queens* are like cities. The advance party yesterday afternoon was over 1,200 men! And those are just mess and cleaning details. Bob and I worked out a special system of servicing the *Queen* which makes it possible for us to serve 500 men in four minutes and still be pleasant about it. Colonel K. complimented us on it at great length yesterday. We also hand out cigarettes, books, candy, and cards when the men start home.

Today is the first day of the victory celebration. The British have a two-day holiday but we, as usual on holidays, will be busier than ever. So I can't tell you how everyone is reacting, I haven't had time to observe. The Yanks are too busy to even get drunk. Everyone is so thankful this damn war is at last over, but personal feelings get mixed up with the joy. Tom drily observed at mess this morning that the colonels didn't look too overjoyed as they probably realize how soon they'd be returning to their old jobs at filling stations! Some very stupid men managed to become field grade officers in this man's army, and they do not look forward to being floorwalkers again. Most of the reaction is centered around the "How soon can I get home?"

Keep writing. All my love,

Roses

A.B. Dad, this pen is *wonderful*.

Wednesday, August 22, 1945

Dears,

Just a note to send home some snaps of the *Queen Mary*. I've had a lousy cold the past three days and don't feel too chipper yet, but wanted to send pictures along and let you see our commendation from Major General Hobbs. We are all thrilled, as generals usually aren't too lavish with their praise.

As we expected, many bigwigs appeared on the scene to see the *Mary* loaded. Mr. Eisner came down from London just in time to watch Admiral Stark

The *Liz* comes to berth in her home port of Southampton for the first time, 1945.

go aboard after reviewing a guard of honor of Royal Marines, Royal Navy, and Hussars. Stark was accompanied by several admirals, including the Lord High Admiral of the Royal Navy. Then Colonel Kiser called me over to meet General Strong, commandant of our UK base, and General Hobbs, commanding general of the 30th division. They kept complimenting me on the Red Cross setup. Said it was the finest they had ever seen and told me how much they appreciated all we'd done for them.

That night about 11:30 when we were waiting for the last two trains to arrive, General Hobbs came over to the pile of lumber we were sitting on in a corner of the loading shed, and sat down with us! For forty-five minutes he entertained us with his anecdotes and jokes. He was really a swell guy. It was rather dark in the shed and some of our GI and loading officer friends would hear us all laughing and slouch over to get in on the fun. You should have seen the looks on their faces when they saw the two-star general in the middle of a pile of lumber!

Anyway, our first *Queen* went well, and we're certainly busy again. The *Elizabeth* arrived a couple of days ago and we start packing her full tomorrow. So far this week the night crew hasn't finished before 4 in the morning as Le Havre is flooding us with divisions to be loaded on the big ships coming in. Our crew's happy as we're busy and everyone we work with has been very cooperative and appreciative.

Don't ask me about my reactions to VJ days. We were working the *Mary* for two and a half days straight. I heard there were crowds and bonfires and street dancing, but that's only hearsay. Everyone but the Red Cross and the planning section of Transportation had a three-day holiday. Personally, I'm glad we were working; it was more fun seeing the boys go home.

Have to run now and see about more billets for the girls. I'll write more in a day or two, as soon as I shake this cold.

All my love,
Roses

HEADQUARTERS 30TH INFANTRY DIVISION
A.P.O. 30, U.S. ARMY

Subject: Commendation of ARC Southampton Clubmobile.

To: Mr. Frederick A. Carroll, Commissioner, ARC Hqs.
USFET, A.P.C. 413, U.S. ARMY

1. It was just two days ago that I expressed to you my appreciation of the outstanding work done by the Tidworth Staging Area ARC during our stay at that post. Tonight, as we complete our loading aboard the *Queen Mary*, I know that it is very much in order that I call to your attention the inspiring service rendered to the personnel of this division by the ARC Southampton Clubmobile, and commend them for their soldierly devotion to duty.

2. Twenty-eight trains carried 30th Infantry Division personnel from Tidworth Staging Area to the pier, day and night, for a two-day period. Every train was met and an incredible quantity of coffee and doughnuts served by these women, despite the fact that many of them worked extremely long hours with very little rest and practically no sleep. There was no relaxation of vigor; no diminution of spirit. Had it not been for the fact that members of my staff saw the same women meet train after train, we could have believed that a new group came on duty every few hours.

3. To my mind, the Southampton Clubmobile women exemplify the spirit of the American Red Cross. The 30th Infantry Division will always remember them pleasantly and gratefully.

L. S. HOBBS
Major General, U.S. Army
Commanding

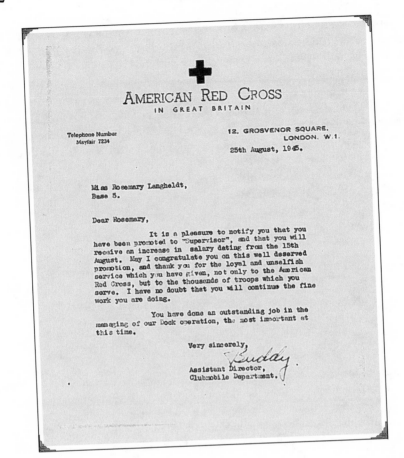

Miss Rosemary Langheldt,
Base 5.

Dear Rosemary,

It is a pleasure to notify you that you have been promoted to "Supervisor", and that you will receive an increase in salary dating from the 15th August. May I congratulate you on this well deserved promotion, and thank you for the loyal and unselfish service which you have given, not only to the American Red Cross, but to the thousands of troops which you serve. I have no doubt that you will continue the fine work you are doing.

You have done an outstanding job in the managing of our Dock operation, the most important at this time.

Very sincerely,

Buddy

Assistant Director,
Clubmobile Department.

London September 3, 1945
25 Old Bond Street (Elizabeth Arden's)

Dearest Family,

As I sit under the dryer at Arden's wondering how my new perm will turn out, I'll tell you all the exciting news of the past ten days. It's impossible for us to be busier, but daily we seem to be. Saturday night we had a "break" between big ships so had a dinner-dancing party at the Polygon and we all went formal. I wish you could have seen Bob's face when he called for me! My hair was just clean and the darling beaded comb set you sent me, Sis, went perfectly with my dress. The "Arsenic" sisters at Lordswood noticed us all come down the stairs and Mrs. Airey ran to get everyone else staying there to come see us. She took me aside to say, "My dear, you look like a queen," and I think she was sincere—if nearsighted.

Since I last wrote, the *Elizabeth* was in and left, with Colonel Jimmy Stewart onboard. It's exciting when the big ships dock here as so many notables show up and sailings have taken on lots of their prewar glamor. We all had midnight coffee and sandwiches aboard the *Liz*, between trains, and it's funny how possessive you feel about a ship you've once sailed on. I no sooner stepped onto R Deck and turned into the Officers Mess than the smells, the modernistic lighting, the table where I sat during the voyage all brought back forgotten memories.

The morning she sailed, Bob, Tom, Ski, and I went out on Colonel M.'s boat again and what a sight it was. We left on such short notice I had no camera, darn it! It was a heavenly day: 15,000 screaming GIs hung over the rails as the tugs pushed her into the Solent, *jet*-propelled RAF planes (the first I've ever seen) zoomed overhead in wonderful formations, flags and pennants flew, hundreds of tiny craft—from sailboats to seaplanes—tagged along, horns blaring, and it was generally breathtaking.

The *Mary's* in now. Scud and I happened to be on hand when she berthed and saw Secretary of State Stettinius and wife and three boys disembark and speak for the newsreels. Without doubt they're the handsomest family I have seen and we were certainly proud they are here representing America. Mr. Stettinius was superbly dressed, complete with tweed top coat; his slim, dark, and lovely wife had the smoothest black Persian lamb coat I've seen in fifteen months. Their three sons, immaculately clad and brushed with hats in hand, looked for all the world like steps in a ladder. You could tell they'd had a most efficient "curtain talk" from their mother or father as they were impeccable in their deportment during all the speeches.

Tom and Bob (Bob has 72 points as he's been in the Army five years) have both just been transferred to the 4th Traffic Regulation Group, on detached service to the 14th Port. They may be back in the United States by Christmas, as all men with 60 points and over are being put into the 4th Traffic Group and supposedly due for shipment within three months. Ski is going mad at the thought that Tom may beat her home and already rehearsing what she'll tell HQ to go home soon after he does.

Just about the time I've finished my service, Bob should be out of the Army and settled into his job with his affairs settled. So it looks as though things will work out well. You asked me about dates. By Christmas this Port should be through its big business and I'll probably be sent to Paris HQ until I can start back—sometime between April and June. A lot depends on how busy the ARC is and how much personnel they have to finish the job. I won't get a really good idea until Christmas or after.

I'm enclosing in a larger envelope a Certificate of Merit which Colonel K. awarded to Ski, Scud, Alice, and me, as we've been in the Port longest. One has never before been presented to a Red Cross girl in the ETO. We had our pictures taken with him amid much publicity. Colonel K. said he tried to get us a real decoration, but medals cannot be presented to ARC personnel. It was a nice gesture on the part of the Port and we were surely surprised when we were called to Port Headquarters. We're to get copies of the pictures they took, and if I ever do I'll send you one. Red Cross Headquarters was very surprised and pleased. You'd think we'd been awarded the Silver Star or something.

I was called to London the day after for an appointment with Mr. Palmer, the executive commissioner, to discuss a house the Army wanted to give me to use as a staff house. Everyone else has approached him to no avail and he's supposed to be a pretty tough customer, but he took Buddy and me to lunch at the Dorchester and insisted we have a rum cocktail before lunch, then proceeded to be affable about everything. Buddy had been telling me for weeks how hard he is to approach and she was simply amazed at his cordiality. When we arrived at the Dorchester in his Packard he told his chauffeur to return in an hour, but it was over two hours later when we finished lunch. I started back with the house deal okayed, leave on the continent pending, and new uniforms for the girls! So you see, the certificate came in handy.

We have such a large crew it's been necessary to take over a house for the extra girls. The Army "gave" me one for the duration and we're in the midst of repainting it. I wangled a PW detail to do the job. It's been quite a challenge furnishing it, but fun. I've spent quite a time in the ARC warehouse picking out everything from beds to curtain rods to a piano to silverware. We'll be able to billet about twenty-five girls in the house, and we're trying to do the complete job in two weeks. We're sandwiching this work in between our normal operations.

As you may have gathered, I'm on the train going back to Southampton and am jammed into a first-class compartment with two people reading over my shoulder.

Isn't it marvelous the whole war's over! I still can't quite realize it.

All my love to all of you.

XXXX
Roses

EUROPEAN THEATRE OF OPERATIONS
UNITED STATES ARMY
This
CERTIFICATE OF MERIT
IS AWARDED TO
ROSEMARY LANGHELDT
(American Red Cross, Clubmobile)
IN RECOGNITION OF CONSPICUOUSLY MERITORIUS AND
OUTSTANDING PERFORMANCE OF MILITARY DUTY

CITATION

For outstanding devotion to duty, loyalty, spirit of cooperation and general display of efficiency while servicing the Docks operated by the 14th Major

Port. For a period of twelve months Rosemary Langheldt has worked tirelessly, often under adverse conditions, in order that the combat and Ground Force troops en route to and arriving from the Continent could avail themselves of light refreshment upon entering the Dock area. Regardless of the long and strenuous hours involved, Rosemary Langheldt continued to discharge all duties in a manner which reflects much credit on her.

SHERMAN L. KISER
Colonel, TC
Commanding

❦

8 PM Saturday
September 22, 1945

Dearest Family,

Since I last wrote, Headquarters sent me a "saloon car," which is limey (as Tom says) for a sedan. It seems all supervisors are entitled to one. I was amazed but naturally I didn't return it. It's especially funny because the fellows have been teasing us about being big-time operators. I've been meaning to tell you that Colonel K. had a trailer built for us and provided another jeep to tow it, so we could use the contraption hauling doughnuts and coffee up and down the dock where the *Queens* load. It saves our crew pushing dollies up beside the trains. None of us mind pushing—Gad, I've been doing it for over fourteen months. On one occasion the Port Commander just happened to be observing and was shocked to calculate how many individual dolly trips a single girl made in a single night. He even had the jeep painted Red Cross gray.

Ever since, Tom and Bob and the other Port officers have been kidding us about it. They predicted that next Kiser would give us a sedan like the colonels have as we were so important. Bob's teased as much as the others with, "Well, after all, *rank has its privileges.*" So when my sedan was sent down from ARC Headquarters we decided to get even for all this R.H.I.P. nonsense. It's the tone of voice that gets me. Ski and Scud and I decided to make the most of this chance, and for a whole day I didn't tell them it was a Red Cross sedan. I said the Army had given it to us. They just about died!

Yesterday, Scud and I took the day off and got out of town. We drove to Lyndhurst in the New Forest for some antique shopping, and I'm happy to report the shops have much more stock than they did when so many Yanks were on the island. Then we drove on to Portsmouth, which is about the only place of any size in southern England I haven't seen. We stumbled on Portsmouth Castle, a lovely old castle dating from Roman times. We climbed all over the ruins, which overlook the sea.

We had tea at the Queens Hotel in Southsea, a popular watering place in the suburbs, while we decided whether to hunt up Dickens's birthplace or go to the Royal Navy Yard to see Nelson's flagship. HMS *Victory* won as we were nearer the naval yard. A British sailor took us all over the ship. I couldn't stand erect on any one of the very low decks. The men must have been crammed into the place to subsist on a diet of salt pork and salt beef and bread. Over 800 men on an 180-foot ship. The bread was baked and then stored in the aft part of one deck, where women also were stored! The brig was something unexpected. It was rather like a slit trench with a lid, where they confined a dozen or so men at a time. One of the lower decks was used for wounded. The floor was always painted red so the blood wouldn't stain the floor. It was here Lord Nelson died after Trafalgar. I don't see why they didn't all die much sooner, under those living conditions.

Goodnight. I love you and miss you but it won't be too long before I'll be seeing you. The longest part is behind us.

All my love,
Roses

≈≈≈

September 29, 1945

Dearest Family,

Bob and I have had long talks lately about the future as he's almost certain to go home by the end of the year. He has decided to return to the company he was with before as they want him back and his experience is there. He's been in the Army five years now, so he worries at times about his career being on hold for so long and his rustiness in his field. He's planning on taking any territory that is open to re-establish himself before considering any change. It's a challenge to do the intelligent thing to make up five years in the quickest way. I'm looking forward to the hurdles.

Today, after weeks of cold and rain, England enjoyed a really lovely day. After four hectic days of no more than five hours of sleep, we suddenly have a break and only two ships today. About ten of us have just enjoyed tea in the picturesque Lordswood drawing room. As usual, a *real* fire is crackling in the grate and we're lingering (what a luxury) and Sylvia Winsor, one of our newer crew members, is at the piano. Sylvia's from Boston and trained as a concert pianist, plays beautifully, Scud sings the same way, and it's wonderful to sit and listen. Even the staid older British types who often come to tea at Lordswood unbend a little when Sylvia sits down at the piano.

Tonight lots of us are going dancing at the Polygon and I shall wear one of my Ransohoff gowns. I'll let you know how it looks.

It's time to go to mess and then dress for my date. Please write, all of you.

Love, love, love—all of mine,
Roses

❧❧❧

Journal

September 30, 1945

Music hath charms—the Brits in residence have loosened up a bit! Mrs. Airey urged me to have the girls come anytime, as her guests so look forward to Miss Winsor's playing and Miss Scudder's singing! Now we actually converse at teatime—if you can call it that.

A little lady who barely nods whenever we enter the drawing room actually spoke to me. "You must like England much more than you do the United States, don't you?" Obviously she'd been worrying about the matter.

I evaded a direct answer and told her I loved my country but we all admire the historic traditions of this lovely land, the courage of its people, and the beauty of the countryside. Think she enjoyed our talk as she nods to me regularly now.

❧❧❧

October 2, 1945

Dears,

A real quickie as I just have a few minutes. Tomorrow Scud and I take off for Ireland and we hear travel conditions are none too good, but it should be fun and a brief change from our hectic pace. Buddy and London HQ are urging us to use our leave time now while we can.

It's strange, Mom, that you should suggest Bob and I have a photograph taken together, as we've been discussing it. I put the kibosh on it as I thought you might think it a little premature. But we have decided to go to London, if we can manage time off together, and have one taken. It looks as though Bob may possibly get orders home this month, or at least in the next two. In a way, I hate to go off to Ireland now, but he can't get leave and know I'll regret it if I pass up this opportunity. Especially as HQ is pushing it, a hint that the Red Cross picture will be changing soon.

At this point Bob and I are crossing our fingers and hoping he's not sent too awfully soon. In haste.

Love,
Roses

❧❧❧

Chapter Seventeen

October 13, 1945

Dearest ones,

The day Scud and I left for Ireland, the *Daily Express* carried a front-page story on the terrors of traveling to Ireland because of the chaos of the crowds shoving to make connections and book passage, and how it was a wonderful idea to stay in jolly England. Undaunted and totally unprepared, we set off. Correction. We carried K rations in case we were in danger of starving while standing in a queue. The trip proved a piece of cake! Belfast, Carrickfergus, Bray, Glendalough, the Vale of Avoca—and yes, we even got to Dublin.

In Ireland, there are horses everywhere. The big workhorses pull even more imposing wagons than we saw in Scotland. Belfast is not architecturally impressive as cities go, but pleasant. Immediately we were in a different world. Even in Northern Ireland, loyal to the Empire, the food is incomparably better than in England. For the first time in over a year I saw well-dressed businessmen and women dressed in clothes that had *chic* to them, even if they were a few seasons old. Everyone is so friendly and open.

We took a bus to Crawfordsburn to reach our lovely inn. Emerald Isle is right. I always think of countries by colors and Ireland is first of all green, although black is important too as the majority of dogs, cows, old ladies, and shawls are in black. And there are touches of red everywhere—in the scattered fuchsias, geraniums, and berries in the countryside.

Saturday morning we set off for Dublin. We gave our K rations to the maid and I told her we were going to Eire. "Have you been there?" she asked incredulously. "No," I said. "Do you *want* to go there?" I told her our arrangements were made. "Well," she said doubtfully, "ye'll find it a wild country."

What a difference we found in the atmosphere of our railroad compartment. The Irish talk your leg off, as we (Americans in general) are a novelty and every Irishman we ran into had relatives in the States. The most talkative Irishman on the trip to Dublin had a cousin in Mi*tch*igan and, God willin', he was going to Mitchigan to see him sometime.

The most wonderful feature of Dublin, outside of the food, is the plethora of horsedrawn cabs used instead of regular taxis. The cabs look like black body-by-Fisher carriages, but not quite so ornate and the cabbies are talkative, drunken, and thoroughly likeable.

It was a weird experience to find ourselves in a country almost totally unaffected by the war, with elegantly dressed women, smartly shod too—no wooden soles—and scads of great big, handsome, well-dressed Irishmen. It was fun too to be an attraction ourselves. Everywhere we went people stared at us. We'd hear them say "American Red Cross nurses," or some description, as we passed and they were all polite, friendly, and eager to be helpful.

Dublin's jammed with people of all nationalities, partly because of the food, partly because of the things unavailable over the border, and partly because it's the most cheerful and unwarlike place in Europe. Having no hotel reservation we had to take a room at a private boarding house in a suburb. We treated ourselves to tea at the Gresham, the nicest and most elegant hotel in Dublin. There, as everywhere in Eire, we saw priests galore and on the streets were many monks, shod only in simple sandals.

After tea, we hired a car with a handsome driver (lovely eyes and full of blarney) to drive us around the city—to Phoenix Park and all the public buildings, to the Abbey Theatre where Barry Fitzgerald and so many others began their acting careers. Along the way he told us of the revolution and where it had occurred. During the war, Phoenix Park has had acres torn up for peat (or turf), as fuel in Eire is a terrible problem, and he pointed out the wagons of peat blocks going by. Burning turf is halfway between burning paper and no fire at all.

The river Liffey which winds through the middle of the city is a quaint river but it has a tide that detracts from its charm and reminds me of the stinking east shore of San Francisco Bay. Most of the time it's lovely to walk or drive alongside and watch the Guinness Brewery tugs and barges forever poking up the river with barrels of stout for shipment to the waiting world. "My goodness, My Guinness," as the ads say. It's the largest brewery in the world.

Our first magnificent dinner in two years was immortalized at the Dolphin Hotel. This Dolphin is no relation to the Southampton hostelry of the same name. It's an old hotel with a restaurant in the tradition of San Francisco's older restaurants—or should that be vice versa? No phony atmosphere, exceptionally old and capable waiters in tails, clean tablecloths. For 8 shillings each (about $1.60) we had delicious charcoal-broiled steaks smothered in great big mushrooms, all the trimmings including french fries, and fresh pear and ice cream with whipped cream for dessert. What pigs we were!

That night we saw *The Plough and the Stars*, the Irish uprising story by Sean O'Casey, Eire's leading playwright. We topped the evening off with ice cream sundaes and hot fudge and a horse-cab ride back to our boarding house.

We decided we'd like to come home a new way and talked ourselves onto the Liverpool ship so we could cross the Irish Sea. Wow! Was that a mistake! We boarded ship at 6 PM and each got a bunk in cabins in the nether regions of the ship. The three other women sharing my cabin upchucked all night long. I tried to disassociate myself from the fetid and rancid atmosphere, as well as the violent rolling and pitching of the ship, by concentrating on trying to count the silverfish crawling all over the woodwork just above my head. I think it's safe to say at this point that I'm a good sailor, as practically everyone on the ship was sick. And I've crossed the Irish Sea in one of their worst storms in years. On landing, we had a glimpse of dirty old Liverpool, took another train ride down through the Midlands, and arrived safely back in Southampton. Very refreshed, rested, and ready to return to work.

All my love,
Roses

October 22, 1945

Dearest ones,

Each day now we hear more rumors on the situation here. We've sent five girls to the continent. Tomorrow I'll go to London and try and arrange for five to go this week and every week from now on. Except for a few trips of the *Mary*, maybe one of the *Europa* and some Liberty ships, I believe the rest of the deployment will be done from there. I don't think Headquarters will release me to go until the operation here is practically over, but things should wind up in the next month or so.

That suits me fine as I'd like to be sent to Germany, if there is work to be done. If not, I think I'll request having my thirty-day leave (due on arrival home from overseas service) on the continent, then ask to be sent home. Until now I've felt our work has been just as important as any we did a year ago, but I don't want to go to the continent for a country club assignment. I'd so love to come home but have to finish the job I started and I've no right to request passage home until the 112- and 80-point men are back in the States.

The other day when the *Mary* sailed, Lady Chesham (she was assistant personnel head in Clubmobiling a year ago) boarded, going home after six years, on a special Red Cross mission. She's a Philadelphian and a very charming woman. Buddy came down from London with her and we went aboard to see her off. She was in uniform and traveling incognito as Mrs. Chesham and we had a great talk before the ship sailed. I rushed down some extra K rations for her because the dining room is *sooooo* far from her cabin and she is not a good sailor, my deah.

As we were discussing ARC problems, a familiar and handsome profile appeared in the open door and smiled in greeting. I was trying to recall his name while Lady Chesham hugged him, before introducing us to her dear friend, Rex Harrison. He's a famous British movie actor—en route to Hollywood aboard the *Mary*. He's starred in some of the few good British movies I've seen while here, the Class A ones which usually also star James Mason or Deborah Kerr. It was a great pleasure to meet him and listen to Lady Chesham and him chat as old friends.

I'm back from London and a day has passed. We chopped some more heads and the crew is due for a gradual whittling-down. Things may close down sooner than I expected.

Must close and get to work. Mail situation terrible, do keep writing.

All my love to all of you,

Roses

✦✦✦

Journal

October 22, 1945

Lady Chesham's traveling on a secret mission which I can't write home about, but she was very open in discussing it. She is going to arrange for the adoption of babies born or to be born to a few of the girls. She explained with great sympathy some of the truly heartbreaking love affairs of wonderful individuals thrown together constantly and closely under the stress of war conditions, and of how easily admiration and close association can end in this not-intended result. She told me the people involved are often of the highest integrity and character. It's the most high-principled and innocent girl who gets caught up in the situation. Lady C.'s sure she'll have no problem finding families eager to adopt such a baby.

✦✦✦

October 27, 1945

Dearest Family,

The last three days I've been juggling our ARC commissioner, Mr. Bowles Rogers, back and forth between here and London. The *Mary's* been sitting out in the Solent off the Isle of Wight while we sit in town, both suffering from the effects of a 90-mile-an-hour gale and storm. Mines are popping up all over the place and the poor old *Queen* hasn't been able to dock for three days. Mr. Bowles Rogers arrives in his big limousine every day at high tide to meet two Red Cross bigwigs aboard the *Queen* and every day the ship is canceled and he returns to London, at least a two-hour drive. He's beginning to understand our operations better and appreciate the difficulties we face during bad weather. He's a nervous wreck at this point.

You asked about Ski and Tom, Mom. Yes, they're fine and going along in their usual way—either way up or way down! It's still much too early to decide about their marriage; heaven only knows if it will work. One thing is sure, they are very much in love. It may well be you'll meet them within the next year. I know they will feel perfectly at home with you, Mom and Dad, as our home and background fit into any part of the social scale and you are both astute enough in your estimates of character to immediately sense the realness, the genuineness, of Tom.

The gale still rages outside. All my love to both branches of my family, and thanks to the boys, dear Bing and Clipper, for their wonderful Christmas package which came today. Tell them I won't open it until the day.

Love, love, and more love,

Roses

P.S. I meant to tell you it looks as though Bob may get home in late November. Wouldn't that be marvelous? He's started two letters to you, but torn them up as he says they're too mushy! He's on his third now.

X

Roses

31 October '45

DEAR MR. AND MRS. LANGHELDT,

I've been such a terribly long time getting around to writing this letter. I don't know why I should be so timid either unless I may fall back on the questionable excuse that a young man writing his sweetheart's parents for the first time is just plain supposed to be timid. I hope that is true, is it? Perhaps after wading through this effort you'll suggest that I remain timid and in that event, I'll have to plead my case in person at a later date.

Who said this letter writing was so difficult? I'm beginning to feel better already!

Since Rosemary has already written you all about me I won't try to build myself up in this letter; rather, my primary purpose is to tell you that I love your daughter very, very much, and to get acquainted with you. Actually, what I've said above is a blundering feign, because what I'm really trying to ask is your permission to marry Rosemary, just as soon as we can get back to the States and arrange it. There! I said it and only had to rewrite it three or four times.

I wish I could put into words, so that you could understand, how much I love Rosemary. We've had ten wonderful months together and each day our love grows progressively stronger. If you could just see us together you'd know, because all of our friends tell us we're walking advertisements of "Love in Bloom" and "June in January." I can say honestly that I have never met anyone to compare to her and that I'll devote my life to her happiness.

I am on orders now to return to the States and must report to a staging area next month. With a little luck, I hope to be home for the New Year. Upon arrival I'll call you and tell you the latest news about Rosie. I guess she's just about the busiest person in our Port—never saw so much energy!

I see Colonel Stunston coming this way with a whole fistful of papers and I feel pretty sure they'll end up in my basket. I won't have the opportunity to meet you until Rosemary finishes her tour of duty and returns home. I am really looking forward, and am very anxious, to meet you and hope with all my heart it will be soon.

Sincerely,
Bob

London photograph of Rosie and Bob, taken in November 1945 before Bob sailed home.

HG. 14 Port APO 437
c/o Postmaster N.Y.

November 2, 1945

Dearest ones,

I have a surprise for you all. Bob and I whipped up to London one day and had our picture taken together in uniform. We went to Lesley's, which is supposedly a nice studio. Over here you can't have proofs—two poses, two prints for £3 3s! We held our breath, hoping against hope they wouldn't be terrible. We got them yesterday, and one is great. It's really better of me than it is of Bob as it's not full-face of Bob, but we're satisfied and I'll try and have them home for Christmas.

This last week the bubble burst! Bob received his orders. He's to report to a general hospital in Gloustershire, be attached there about a month, and sail home with that unit by early December. While he's a "medical administrative officer" (calling Dr. Kildare!) he'll be able to come down to see me at least a few times, if I'm here.

Yes, that's the other news. Between now and December I have recommended they cut the crew back to twelve, as the Port has had its biggest days. That means I'll be able to leave, but Buddy wants me to stay until December to break in a new supervisor. There are ten or twelve girls who don't want to go on to the continent, or who are married, so it's ideal. Write as usual as my mail will be forwarded when they move me, and I'll cable any APO change when the time comes.

You can't imagine how I hate having Bob go. We have such fun, we have so many common interests, we've done so many interesting things together, we so enjoy each other's company, it will be terrible to be separated. But I'm looking forward to seeing the continent and in a way glad that all of us will be separated within a few weeks of each other. It should be easier that way. As Tom's orders are due anytime, Ski is setting about getting "demobbed" herself to be home by January or thereabouts.

Monday, Scud and Luke (the charming and very able captain on Bob's staff) and I took a day off we have long planned together. Now that the picture's changing so rapidly we're all trying to squeeze in all the sightseeing we never had time for. It's lucky we did, as Bob's orders came through the next day. One of the colonels lent Bob his sedan and we drove to Bath.

It was a beautiful clear St. Luke's summer day (we Yanks would call it Indian summer). Rural England was at its loveliest, the leaves turning, the colors glorious. It's a fascinating city, and must have been since Roman times. The houses climb the hills in rows—straight or crooked, winding all over. Georgian architecture predominates in the center of town. We went through the Roman baths and drank the water but did not bathe in the springs. We walked and browsed through antique shops and laughed a lot.

Tuesday, Ski and Scud and I drove in my sedan to Newhaven, on the coast not far from Brighton. We had to investigate some cross-channel vessel movements for London Headquarters. As it was another perfect day (after last week's gales) we made it a pleasure trip too, and stopped at the cathedral town, Chichester (sneeze it out) and also in Arundel. Arundel Castle ranks with Warwick as perfection in castles. Set against a hill, it looks like something out of a fairy tale and is the seat of the Duke of Norfolk, who's also earl of Arundel.

I just found out that Bob won't have to report to the hospital tomorrow as he feared and received approval to be a week late reporting. He and Colonel Scherff and Colonel Matthews had orders cut for a trip to the continent next week, and we were afraid Bob wouldn't be able to make it. Now he can and they'll fly to Brussels and probably hit Oslo, Copenhagen, maybe Switzerland, Berlin, Venice, and Rome. I think it wonderful Bob will get such a trip before he comes home.

Have been adding to this all day, off and on, on the office typewriter. Gotta go now as the *Mary* is due to start loading. Bowles Rogers was here when the

Mary finally debarked Saturday. I watched, fascinated, because this is the first *Queen* which has brought back a majority of civilians. You should have seen the beautiful clothes, furs, and accessories coming down the gangway. Many Englishwomen and children were returning home and they certainly came laden with gifts, toys, and wonderful packages. It was like a glimpse into another world—a world of plenty.

My love to all of you, and tell my boys, Bing and Clipper, to start remembering me and to keep their paws crossed so I'll be home before too long.

Roses

November 5, 1945

Dears,

A short note as I'm cleaning out and "redding up" and you'll be receiving more pictures and books soon. Watch the papers and if you read that aircraft carriers are coming into Southampton more than once (four are due in around the 20th) you'll know I'm probably still here. If the carriers only make one trip then I'll be going on to the continent sooner. Our picture changes every day.

When Bob reported to his new CO in Gloustershire, the CO retracted his orders to go to the continent. The blunt colonel said, "Do you want to go to the continent or do you want to go home?" So Bob's now sitting around while his two buddies fly around the continent! But that's the Army. Bob is sure to be awaiting shipment for about six weeks. Last night when he called he told me the outfit will move down to Tidworth Staging Area, only a few miles from here, in a day or two so he and Jack will be able to come into Southampton often.

Have had a busy weekend with London brass visiting. I wish you could see our staff house, the one the Army loaned me, where seventeen of our crew live. Buddy said it was all right for the girls to have pets. She has two little white dogs who come to work with her—think they're "Westies," like white Scotties. But when I took Buddy into the staff house Sunday morning, I think her teeth almost fell out.

As we entered the house, two kittens chased each other into the living room; one of our newer girls was walking upstairs in her bathrobe, followed by her black poodle, Topsy—fourteen months old and very cute. Just at that moment Pim, a honey cocker spaniel, came tumbling downstairs with a black kitten close behind. At this point Sally Jackson appeared with a handful of fur called Shilling, a pup she had just bought for 5 shillings! The new housekeeper, not to be outdone, has a full-grown springer called Stinky.

Not present yesterday morning was Beth's German shepherd, Frog, a dog a GI left with her on the docks when he couldn't take him aboard ship. After three months, Frog is still looking for him. Every day he leaves the staff house and goes over to C18 and C19, two staging-area camps, sniffing at all incoming

GIs, trying to find his master. Also absent yesterday was Spot, another mascot a GI had to leave, complete with his own little Army coat and T/5 rating. June arranged passage for Spot through unofficial channels. I think he was surreptitiously loaded on the *Mary* yesterday. As you can gather, I don't ask unnecessary questions. His master is anxiously waiting for him on the other side.

Some days I think we do more dog business than coffee business.

This was to be just a note as there's lots to do today. No mail—how about some?

All my love,
Roses

November 15, 1945

Dearest ones,

A note because *soooo* much happening. Port plans changed and rechanged, the net result being that we'll be here until Christmas now as the *Europa*, *Mary*, *Enterprise*, *George Washington*, and several British carriers are all in or scheduled in shortly. We are having a work boom. Bob's unit was detached to Tidworth Staging Area and he's on detached service to the Port so he's here and working while awaiting shipment home—probably the first week in December. Ski is sailing on the *Mary* in December, as her request was granted, so she'll be home by Christmas. In other words, there's a delirium of work and changes and entertaining for those leaving, and constant uncertainty.

Thank goodness, this past week I managed to write a long letter to Bob B., in which I told him about my Bob. The only fly in the ointment is that I got a letter from him today and he's on his way home, so my letter will probably go all the way to the South Pacific and back. He may mention my Bob to you when he hears, but until that time you needn't say anything. I think my letter is tactful enough not to hurt him. I do hope so because I'd like us to remain the friends we've always been. Keep me posted if you see him.

Love,
Rosie

November 20, 1945

Dearest ones,

Exciting news is an experience Ski, Scud, and I had yesterday. It's certainly one of the highlights of our months in England. Remember I wrote you about driving through Arundel and falling in love with the castle? We decided to write the Duke of Norfolk a letter to tell him we wanted to see his old castle. We joked about it so much that a few mornings later as the three of us sat in the coffee kitchen office, we decided to have a contest to see who could write the best letter. Mine won and, half jokingly, we sent it. We had to call the town clerk to find out how to address the duke. We didn't know whether to just start off "Dear Duke," or what. He told me to start the letter off "My Lord Duke," and when I asked if I should begin the letter with capitals he was horror-stricken and hissed, "Oh *my*, yessss!"

Here's a copy of the letter that took so much time:

> Lordswood House
> Southampton, Hampshire
> November 5, 1945

My Lord Duke,

Last week while motoring to Newhaven on business we three American Red Cross girls passed through Arundel, and were enthralled by the beauty of Arundel Castle. It sparkled in the sunshine of a perfect St. Luke's summer morning like something out of a fairy tale. We all agreed that nowhere in this beautiful land is there a lovelier sight and Arundel, in an instant, became for us the symbol of England—ancient, enduring, and lovely.

Because we have been in England eighteen months and are scheduled to go home soon, we are writing to request permission to visit the grounds of Arundel Castle. If Your Grace is kind enough to grant our request, it will climax an unforgettable stay in England.

> Sincerely,

> Isabel Seaton Carver
> Harriet Scudder
> Rosemary Langheldt

While we were waiting to see if we'd hear back we were told the Duke of Norfolk is the highest ranked duke in England outside of the Royal Family. He's also head of the Catholic Church in England, Earl Marshal of England, and also Earl of Arundel, the oldest earldom in the country. So when we got back the enclosed reply, we were floored. Here it is, for the scrapbook:

> Arundel Castle
> 12th Nov. 1945

Madam,

The Duke of Norfolk desires me to thank you for your letter, and to arrange for you to see round the Castle when it may be convenient for you to come. Will you please let me know what date will suit you, and your friends.

I am, Madam,

Yours faithfully,

E. G. Harrison
Private Secretary

Any day this week or early next week would suit arrangements here.

Yesterday afternoon we returned to the castle. I can't adequately describe the beauty or the size of Arundel, but it covers 5 acres and dominates an entire hillside. It was a cold, crisp late autumn afternoon and between the inner and outer walls gardeners were burning leaves and the towers and turrets of the castle took our breath away. As we crossed the drawbridge over the moat, a lovely old man in striped trousers and black coat came towards us to welcome us. He's one of the old family retainers, having served the present duke and late duke for forty years. For over two hours he took us over the castle and we saw everything but the bedrooms.

We had boned up a bit on the history so were delighted when he led us up to the little room overlooking the main drawbridge, where Matilda petitioned Stephan not to storm the castle. We climbed up into the top of the round keep or tower (Saxon origin) and looked down on the old jousting grounds where the knights held their tourneys. Now there is a swimming pool in the middle of the jousting yard. In the center of the keep, the castle stronghold cellar, where all the valuables were kept during siege times, is still intact. From the top of the keep, Sussex Downs stretches away as far as you can see. It's a glorious sight.

All my life I've wanted to go through a real lived-in castle and this one certainly more than met my expectations. The first room we visited is the original castle's kitchen and it's still intact, although it's been there since 1086. It's not used now, but the present kitchen is a cosy little room about the size of the Opera House, where meals for a thousand at a time can be whipped up. The pots alone floored us, as there are copper pots from the size of an orange to the size of an oven.

The walls of the castle are about six feet thick. Castles, it seems, are drafty, due in part to the size of the chimneys and in part to old-fashioned construction, according to our guide. Yet we noticed how warm the building was without central heating and it's due to the thickness of the walls. Generally speaking, castles are rather dark inside because when they were built no one went in for wide windows, as they're too easy to shoot through.

The late duke spent most of his life strengthening, rebuilding, and improving his castle and it is truly magnificent. *Long*, low, vaulted hallways in every direction. The most beautiful furniture is found everywhere—Elizabethan, Chippendale chairs, Queen Anne pieces—each piece from each period perfectly preserved. On the walls hang portraits of former Dukes of Norfolk and Earls of

Arundel by the greatest painters: Van Dyke, Rembrandt, Sir Thomas Lawrence, Gainsborough. One small portrait of a duchess is valued at £60,000, or $240,000. There's a Turner, and even a Titian.

The present duke and duchess's portraits are at one end of a long gallery. He is thirty-seven and resembles the Duke of Windsor when he was young. She is blond and a typical English beauty. We were told she lives for dogs and horses. She is painted in a woolen sweater, a Scottish design running through it, with a Liberty scarf around her neck—looking oh so English country life and lovely—a strange contrast to the satin-clad women along the walls beside her.

The duke's private secretary, Mr. Harrison, joined us and took us into the duke's private chapel and then into the great banquet hall, which left me speechless. It's tremendously large, with a huge fireplace at either end. The floors are gorgeous, the walls paneled and hung with more portraits. Below them stand massive tapestry-covered chairs. A single one is worth a fortune.

The library is a long low affair with deep-red rugs and draperies, beautifully dark wood paneling, and thousands of leather-bound books. It also contains famous old pieces of armour and swords, the trunk of Anne Boleyn, and the steps Victoria and Albert had to use to get into their bed when they visited the duke. The beds are that high off the floor. Mr. Harrison mentioned what a costly thing it was to entertain royalty in the old days as everything had to be new for their use!

We gathered from the old retainer that he worshipped the late duke, who spent his life building churches and rebuilding Arundel, and that he had not too much to say about the present duke. And we don't think he quite approved of the duchess having her dogs all over the castle. And Mr. Harrison, when he joined us and began to talk about the castle, kept complaining about income taxes. Of course the scale is rather different from ours. Taxes for them, he explained, are 19 and 6 out of 20 shillings—which translated means you keep 10¢ out of $4. It's a wonder that they can keep up the castle at all and how much longer such an anachronism can survive a socialist government in England.

As you must have guessed, I loved Arundel Castle.

Back to reality. We're loading the *Mary* and I have to get to work. All my love to all of you. Next week we think we'll write the King, as we've always wondered how he lives too!!

Roses

Chapter Eighteen

November 22, 1945
Thanksgiving Day

Dearest Family,

Happy Thanksgiving! I've been wondering about what kind of centerpiece you have today, Mom. I've left the dock where we're loading the *Enterprise* to drop you a note. A big turkey dinner is scheduled at mess but we may be invited aboard the *Enterprise*.

Slight interruption, as in many interruptions!! It's now Sunday afternoon. Thanksgiving turned out to be a very busy day of troubleshooting, peacemaking, schedule-changing. Don't think you can imagine the complications of keeping soooo many girls happy, prompt, and on the ball.

Pop S. brought me some film from Switzerland, so I got to take movies of the *Enterprise* sailing and of the *Washington* tied up at the pier. Scott took some of us out on his boat the day the *Enterprise* sailed and we went over by the *Washington*, where seven or so assorted American and British admirals were having a soiree. The launch of the First Sea Lord of the Admiralty was alongside as our boat arrived and luckily enough Lord Cunningham was piped over the side just as we came on the scene. I was standing topside taking movies of him as he climbed into his launch. It pulled away passing about 6 feet from us and he smiled and waved. I was still taking pictures when our boat suddenly lunged. Luckily, three people grabbed me and saved me from going over the side, camera and all.

Ski is definitely sailing on the *Mary* around December 10th. Tom may be able to sail with her. Bob's unit has still not received word as to what ship they'll make, but I think he'll catch the *Europa* which is due to leave about the same time as the *Mary*.

Bob had a birthday on the 18th, his twenty-ninth and I arranged a birthday party for him over near Hythe, at Westcliff Hall. We had the PWs who staff our coffee kitchen make a lovely birthday cake; they enjoyed the change from making doughnuts. Everyone brought a silly present and Scott sent along two bottles of champagne from Germany. Bob was thrilled and we had a marvelous evening.

Westcliff Hall sits on estate-like grounds just across the Solent from Southampton and is the loveliest place I've been in England as far as service, accommodations, and food go. It's quite expensive, but Mrs. Rigden, who owns the place, seems to like us and arranges everything to perfection. We've all wondered where she gets the marvelous food, but are sure she stashed away a liquor and wine supply long before the war. It was Buddy and her English fiancé, George, who tipped us off about this prewar elegance available a few miles out of town. They, and her dogs, come down whenever they want a brief break from the stresses of London.

The first time we all went over there, there were several quality British types sitting around the drawing room as we came in from dinner. Sylvia was with Jack, so in a very short time found her way to the piano. After the cigars and liqueurs were passed everyone began to sing. We were trying hard to be "genteel" in our noisemaking so as not to annoy any of the guests and we all left before midnight.

When we went again on Bob's birthday we found over a dozen people sitting around waiting for us. The girls were served "Pink Ladies" cocktails, the men anything they chose. Sylvia played the piano and Scud sang. Charles, Mrs. Rigden's *maitre d'*, hovered and supervised the refilling of the glasses, and ushered us into the dining room when it was time to dine. The dinner was heavenly and we stuffed ourselves, savoring every bite.

When we returned to the drawing room after dinner, all of our top-drawer British acquaintances from the cocktail hour were already ensconced, waiting. Mrs. Rigden told me later she thought they'd never go to bed. Sylvia was called back to the piano and everyone sang and conversed. Jack acted the gracious Texan, delighting the ladies—especially a couple of old things with titles and diamonds. A haughty-looking Argentinian who spoke elegant Spanish sat in an ornate chair. I feared he was a Nazi but swallowed my distrust to try my Spanish on him, and discovered he's in England to buy planes. Had to admit he was fascinating, but at least a Fascist if not a Nazi, so ended the conversation.

Sylvia was playing every type of music. Bob and I always request "I'll Walk Alone," as we've loved that since we danced to it on our first date. An English clergyman walked over to the piano and began requesting some really old favorites. The "diamond lady," as Bob called the little old woman he was charming, turned to him and said, "There, he's spoiling everything, having her play all those old-fashioned pieces." After that we didn't worry about bothering anyone, as evidently they enjoyed it as much as we did.

All my love to you and how about some mail?

Roses

Thought long about telling the family more details of our Westcliff Hall party, but sanity prevailed. As they haven't yet laid eyes on their future son-in-law why worry them unnecessarily? I was feeling proud of our group as we bid goodnight to our drawing room friends and floated into the entrance hall for Charles to get our coats. Our behavior had been absolutely top drawer, even Tom hadn't uttered a swear word all evening. Just then a British woman wrapped in a sable coat walked in the front door with two miniature dachshunds on lead. Luke, Scud's date, always correct in behavior, demeanor, and performance of duty, dropped to his knees, ruining the razor-sharp press in his dress-pink uniform trousers.

"What are you doing?" Scud gasped.

"They're doxies, just like Mother's." Luke grinned up as if that explained everything. "Oh, hello you little . . ." and he started babbling to the dogs, nose to noses—in baby talk yet—the bejeweled owner smiling proudly down on the scene.

As Scud was persuading Luke to rise from the floor, I began to add things up. I had enjoyed one of those Pink Ladies, which taste like lemonade—no, two—Charles had refilled glasses without interrupting the conversation. I didn't have any scotch or bourbon or gin like the men. And I only took a sip of each wine at dinner then passed it on to Bob to finish. And I had accepted an Alexander when Charles passed the men cigars and port, sherry, or brandy after dinner. But I felt fine.

As we exited Westcliff Hall and paused to inhale the cold and freezing winter night air, I felt slightly light-headed for an instant. Bob, I noted proudly, opened the car doors for Scud and Luke and me with great courtesy before walking around to get into the driver's seat, totally in command. He started the engine, then revved it into reverse and backed out of our parking space right into the bumper of a car parked 20 feet behind us. It was only a little jolt but he didn't want to go look. So I insisted and accompanied him. Dark as it was we could see the Bentley or something expensive had good bumpers because there was no damage.

"I told you so," huffed the man I plan to marry, and marched back to the car.

The ride back to town is not one to dwell on. It involved Bob, the always careful driver, running an MP roadblock and being forced to stop. Having driven that far with all windows open at the firm suggestion of Scud and me, Bob again was in full command. The MP said he was going to report the major to the Provost Marshal and Bob said cordially, "Fine, he's our best friend. I'll talk to him myself."

That was a revelation to me as I thought they barely spoke, but Bob drove straight to the roadblock office to have a word with his lieutenant colonel friend. Thanks to open windows we were pretty well aired out by the time we went in with Bob to back up his explanation. I forget what it was but it sounded plausible, and not surprisingly, the Provost Marshal was cordial. We all know he's aware of the high regard the Port Commander has for the work of Bob and Luke. Even Scud and I have heard the scuttlebutt that they're two of Colonel K.'s fair-haired boys.

Scud and I agreed when we finally were deposited at Lordswood, this high living is too rich for our blood.

November 30, 1945

Dearest ones,

This morning some mail came, and not just a dribble—including two from Marty, one from you, one from Bob B. now back home, an announcement of Bettie's marriage to a tank captain she met in Germany. They were married in her hometown, Burlingame. Evidently Bob B. hasn't received the long explanatory letter I wrote him in the Pacific. But it should be coming back any day now so I'm bound to hear from him soon. I do appreciate your being so nice to him, Mom and Dad, when he came to see you. I hope he'll continue to feel welcome after he gets my letter.

The latest plans are these. Lots of work through the second or third week in December, so I'll be kept here until January 1st and then am being sent on to the continent. I'll let you know in plenty of time when my address changes. Poor Bob has been sitting around on detached service and just when his unit is set to go (they were supposed to sail on the *Mary* on December 9th), some unit is brought over from the continent with a higher point score and his unit is taken off the shipping list. He finds the hurry-up-and-wait period hard as he's eager to get back and get on with his career *and* plan for our future.

Ski is in London today to be cleared and then she'll be all set to sail on the *Mary*. She's starting to be excited about it at this point. Tom is still waiting to find out what's to happen to him. Both he and Bob are eligible for discharge on about every score—points and length of service. Both of them have put five years into this man's army.

Yesterday, Bob and Luke and Scud and I got a Wolsely sedan and went to Windsor Castle in our hearse, the sedan. We lingered in St. George's Chapel where King George V is entombed and Henry VIII, and where the Order of the Garter originated.

Eventually we walked down through town, lunched, and crossed the Thames to walk on through Eton. The first little boy I saw at Eton College (black suit and black silk topper, striped wool scarf dangling around his neck) startled me as he looked a character sprung from the pages of a favorite book. The boys seem to range from eight to eighteen, and their suits look exactly like dress suits would look if worn constantly by boys.

It was bitter cold and I wondered again that England never has had, and probably never will have, central heating. The best families send their children to schools like Eton or Winchester, and no attempt is made to heat any part of the buildings, other than with little coal grates. We walked through corridors and bleak, poorly lit classrooms which ooze with dampness and tradition and are filled with funny old desks with initials carved all over them. It's like high-class Dickens.

Back outside small boys with raw, red faces chapped by the cold, sniffly noses, and mittened hands clutching books and top hats hurry along, bracing into a frigid wind.

I have always loved tradition but am beginning to wonder if there can be too much of it. I'm thankful I've been privileged to live over here awhile instead of seeing this part of the world only through tourist eyes.

Suddenly I remember those wonderful *jet* planes flying over the Solent on VJ day, and the difference penicillin has made since the British discovered it, so maybe the cold education works pretty darn well!

Have to get to work, will write soon. Please, all of you, do the same.

Your little girl, Roses, in the land of the Rose—but not for long!

Berkeley, Calif.
December 1, 1945

Dear Bob,

We have heard or rather seen "Bob" so much that I feel that is undoubtedly the way to address you. From information in Rosemary's letter we were expecting to hear from you and we were glad to receive the type of letter we did. Rosemary had informed us of her feelings toward you and had summarized your background and qualities as she saw them. Needless to say her picture of you was one that any young man of high morals and excellent character would be proud of.

We, her parents, have learned to respect her judgement in her decisions in choosing the right path leading to a normal, happy and contented life. We do not think that, now where one of the most important steps in her life is to be taken by her, that she has lost the judgement or discernment heretofore shown and undoubtedly had found you to be a young man who possessed the morals, character and other attributes that a man of her choice must have, before she allowed herself to become so thoroughly acquainted with you and then allowed that deep love that you both profess, to develop.

Needless to say our daughter's happiness has always been paramount with us, because her being so brings that much more happiness to us. We are sorry that your acquaintanceship, friendship and love could not have developed where we could have seen and enjoyed it with you.

From what you both say, we have no doubt but that you both feel you are the right person, one for the other, and married will make a wonderful team. Before that comes to pass Mrs. Langheldt and I are looking forward to meeting you and adding our approval to that of our daughter, Rosemary.

Sincerely,

H. B. Langheldt

December 12, 1945

Dearest Family,

As the British say, "I've had it!" Bob sailed at noon on the aircraft carrier *Lake Champlain* and he'll be home for Christmas. Isn't that marvelous? He's planning on calling you, Mom and Dad, after he gets back to Indianapolis. As you can guess, I hated to have him go, even though we've both been hoping and praying for his turn to come. So many men have left the Port, and now we're busier than ever, so Bob loaded his own ship, then climbed aboard—still wearing his red and gold Transportation Corps armband. As the *Champlain* pulled away he called out that he is sharing good quarters amidship with a lieutenant colonel.

He gave me the most beautiful movie camera case as an early Christmas gift. It's black leather, velvet-lined, and has pockets for camera, rolls of extra film, exposure meter, and filters. Also a simply gorgeous Jacqmar scarf. I gave him a sterling silver cigarette case as he's never had one.

Ski sailed Sunday on the *Queen Mary* and should be home about Friday. She was of course given a choice cabin by the Port and I have movies of her waving from the porthole. Ski was sure full of mixed emotions. Tom won't be departing for about three weeks and, while excited at getting home for Christmas, she hated to leave Tom.

Scott (Colonel M.), Colonel Stunston, Jack, and General Strong also sailed on the *Mary*, so it was a gala occasion. General Strong was in command of UK Base (the whole United Kingdom), yet his cabin wasn't half as nice as Scott's and Stunston's. And Ski, instead of being with seventeen others, had one roommate. She remarked that all our cold months on the docks hadn't been in vain.

Please don't read this part of the letter in front of my dogs as I'm afraid they wouldn't understand. Do you remember how as a little girl I wanted a great big German police dog, and you always said we didn't have room for one? Well, my wish came true—for two weeks only, and he's an Alsatian (looks just like a German shepherd). It all began two nights ago when we were loading the first group on the *Champlain*. Bob came over from where he was working the next dock and said, "Rosie, you've got to come see a beautiful dog."

The dog turned out to be Duke, a huge and gorgeous Alsatian who sat waiting patiently at the gangplank for his master to come back for him. His GI owner had tried to smuggle him aboard but been ordered to board without him. My gosh, it would be simpler to hide a pony. Duke looked so pitiful I asked the Navy officers supervising the loading of their ship to get his master off so I could talk with him.

One Abraham Wilson soon rushed down the gangway, his eyes still red from the parting. He's a great big, bashful GI from New York and I've never seen a happier man when I promised him I'd somehow arrange passage for Duke on the next sailing of the *Queen*. Wilson—or Tex, as he said his buddies call him—teared up he was so grateful. Tex has had Duke over five months since picking him up in Germany.

Only after Tex reboarded did I realize what I'd committed myself to. Three men can't hold Duke, so all I could hope was that Duke would *want* to come with me. Fortunately, he took to me at once. He may even love me. He follows me around like a pup—I mean more like a pony. Tex said Duke always slept on a blanket in his room, so when I got me out to Lordswood House, about 2 AM after we'd finished work, I called him from the car. In my Hillman sedan he takes up all of the backseat and half of the front, giving—according to my friends—the general impression of Rosie and a wolf riding down the street. Standing in the backseat, his breath fogs up the windscreen (windshield in Yankee) while his wagging tail obscures the rearview window. Seriously, he's a match for Rin Tin Tin.

Somehow we galloped up to my room. I told you it's small, but now I realize it's tiny. I spread a blanket and, praise the Lord, when I said "Sit," he sat. When he lay down to sleep there was barely space for me to crawl over his prostrate form and into bed.

At 6:15, that's ayem, Duke decided we should get up and frisked over to put two paws on my bed. When I recovered my breath and stopped the water basin from shaking off the nightstand, I remembered that I had undertaken a nice little job for myself. Today he slept until 7:30 AM, and we get along smashingly. This morning I was airing him outside Lordswood and running at full speed while Duke walked slowly beside me. Suddenly he realized I was playing with him and, oh so gently, wrapped his jaws around my leg, then jumped up on me. On two legs he stands about a foot taller than I do, and I collapsed against a tree. I'm sure he adores me and he obeys like a dream, but just the same I'll probably be black and blue all over when he boards the *Queen*. And the damn *Queen* doesn't come in again until Dec. 24th. Why couldn't Tex have owned a Pekinese or a dachshund?

This morning when I went down to wave goodbye to Bob, Duke came too. He minds me so well I took a chance on taking him down as I thought maybe his master could see him from the deck of the ship. He did, and soon lots of Tex's buddies were calling to Duke. When Duke spotted Tex he trembled all over and whined and I thought for a minute he was going to jump into the water. I shouted up to tell them all how he was getting along. Tex was so glad to know things were okay he threw me down his favorite snapshots of Duke, taken in Germany when he was a puppy.

At this moment my temporary (thank goodness!) dog lies asleep at my feet. Really, he's wonderful and I wouldn't miss this experience for the world. We've made all his sailing arrangements—only thing is, he'll probably need two kennels.

Now! A fanfare at this point, please. I've saved the best until last as I knew you wouldn't read the rest of the letter if I wrote it first. Rosie is being presented to their Majesties, the King and Queen, at a tea at Buckingham Palace next Tuesday, December 18. It seems royalty wished to thank the American Red

Cross for their work, so about 150 of the longtime workers from all over England have been invited to tea. I am one of those (please bow) and so is Scud.

Imagine! I don't know quite whether to practice curtsies or to rush out and buy three white feathers for my hair. Since the news arrived, the British are treating us with a new deference. You'd think I was going to heaven.

Oops! Right now Duke (the dog) wants to go. He hasn't told me where yet, but I don't like to argue with him.

All my love to my commoner parents, from your commoner (but not for long) daughter. Also, a gracious toss of the head to my sister and brother-in-law. I love you all, so very much. And, of course, my undying love to Bing and Clipper, small and gentle souls that they are.

XXXXXX OOOOOOOOOO
Roses

Journal   *December 12, 1945*

What a lovable distraction Duke has been today, a lifesaver—all that's kept my heart from breaking. I took Duke to the docks when I went to say goodbye to Bob as I didn't dare leave him unsupervised at Lordswood House. The weather this morning matched my mood. It was absolutely miserable. A steady drizzle was falling, it was bitter cold, and wisps of foggy steam rose off the water to mix with the falling drizzle.

There was almost no time for a farewell, which is probably just as well. Bob and I are long past words now. We're glad he's finally on his way home to be discharged, to plan his, and our, future and work out the divorce details. But each day we've grown more miserable at parting. We know the sooner he's home, the sooner we can begin our life together. But it's terrible not knowing how long it will take.

Bob stood waiting beside the ship gangway as we drove up, authorized as the loading officer to board ship last. We joined in the laughter and shouting of hundreds of jubilant GIs leaning over the decks, as Tex and his GI pals yelled down at Duke. Finally, Bob and I walked toward the end of the dock until the drizzly mist obscured us enough to hold each other one last time, and whisper again the hopes and promises we've so often whispered before.

In only moments the ship's whistle blew and we had to hurry back for Bob to board. Duke and I stood together, me laughing and waving as the tears pouring down my cheeks mixed with the rain while the tugs slowly nudged the Lake Champlain out from the docks and into the mists of Southampton Water.

Duke and I wandered to the end of the dock to watch until the Champlain disappeared into the fog. I made no effort to wipe away the tears as the weather only added to the sense of loss that filled my heart.

Duke finally lost patience and dragged me back into the day, into work, into reality.

Chapter Nineteen

December 17, 1945

Dearest ones,

What a five days it's been! I planned to repack to be ready to move (to help fill up my time now that Bob's gone) and have been swamped in work—ordering Christmas packages and supplies for the GIs, preparing the January forecast on ship loadings for HQ, and holding general meetings for the crew regarding Christmas and future plans.

Not to mention caring for Duke. Every day he seems to love me more and I'm trying to get him in A-1 shape for his master. He eats about 3 pounds of raw meat daily. I'm now on very good terms with the Port mess officer, having discovered that when I ask for a few scraps, Duke's presence beside me is very effective. I brush him and feed him cod liver oil and he should look gorgeous when he sails on the *Mary*. I won't look half as good standing on the docks.

The other reason I haven't written sooner is I received a cable from Bob B.! It depressed me terribly and I realized I should have followed my instinct and just continued my infrequent friendly letters and waited until I got home to talk things over with him. I felt positive that by that time he'd be in love with someone else. Obviously, my letter to him brought the matter to a head. But for him to cable, now that he's back home, that he loves me, wants to marry me, and will call soon, *after* reading my letter, was upsetting.

Yesterday at 0600 he did phone me, as though he could change my mind long distance! Mrs. Airey knocked on my door, shouting about the Le Havre operator calling. Alarmed and half awake, I rushed down to the main entrance to pick up the phone, anticipating bad news from home. His voice came in waves, faded out completely, then came in clear for a moment before fading away again. I feared something had happened to the *Champlain* after sailing. Groggy with sleep, I didn't know which Bob was calling.

Through the static I shouted, "Bob? Bob who?" By this time half of Lordswood House was peering down at me, enjoying every word. Having to shout, "But Bob, I don't *love* you. We've always just been friends, *you know that*. I had no idea you feel *this* way" didn't help the situation. I couldn't hear him more than a few seconds at a time and I'm sure he couldn't hear much of what I said. It might have been funny if it hadn't been sad. The only thing I'm certain of is that it was the most exciting early morning Lordswood House residents have enjoyed for ages.

I honestly feel it's Bob B.'s pride that's hurt more than anything else and he wants me more now that he knows someone else does too.

Tonight we have only one ship, then we're going to start decorating the huge Christmas tree we had Art, one of our mechanics, cut down and put up in the game room. It's about nine feet high and still has the little pine cones on it. We're planning a big Christmas party here for the crew and all our friends in the Port and it should be lots of fun.

You can't know how I'd love to spend Christmas at home, as we always have. But this should be the last one away from the best family in the world. Have a real merry one—for me, too, because although you won't be able to see me I'll be there, all day, opening packages and eating turkey legs and olives and leaving all the celery to Sis.

Goodnight and Merry Christmas.

Love,
Roses

P.S. 11:30 PM. My hair is clean, my nails lovely. I am ready to go to Buckingham Palace. Everyone here at Lordswood (the British) is overcome with awe at the grandeur of it all. The Misses Needham and Airey (*Arsenic and Old Lace*) are in a complete dither. I expect them to die of joy any minute, for we are going to see the *King!!*

✿

December 19, 1945

Dearest ones,

Yesterday was the day. Rosie was presented at court. I'm sending you the invitation for a prominent place in my scrapbook.

Scud and I arrived in London about noon in complete Class A uniform, formal dress consisting of black uniform and top coat, a white blouse, white gloves, and white scarf. Our shoes and bag were polished to perfection.

On entering Headquarters we found approximately 150 others in exactly the same condition. They had come from all over England, Scotland, and Northern Ireland, from all the Red Cross establishments. Most of us were Americans but there were a few Britishers who have been working very hard for the American Red Cross throughout the war.

About three o'clock we had a meeting in the commissioner's office and we all listened, fascinated, as he told us such weird bits of information as, "The women will all curtsy when they are presented to the Queen. Not necessarily a deep curtsy, but as you take her hand, you look her in the eye and curtsy." He explained that as Americans we weren't required to curtsy but implied strongly that it was the only mannerly thing to do.

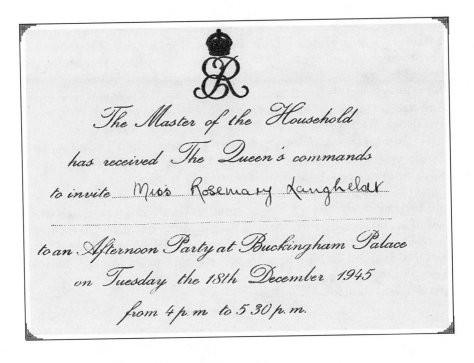

The Master of the Household

has received The Queen's commands

to invite   Miss Rosemary Laughelar

to an Afternoon Party at Buckingham Palace

on Tuesday the 18th December 1945

from 4 p.m to 5.30 p.m.

The second enlightening point was, "You do not speak to royalty until spoken to. When addressed, you say "Ma'am" here and there in the conversation. If by any chance you wish to attract her attention, you say "Your Majesty."

At this point in the proceedings all of us made mental notes not to attract her attention. Then the commissioner said, "The men do not curtsy. The men simply click their heels together and bow stiffly from the waist." The men didn't seem to think that was as simple as our commissioner implied. For the next fifteen minutes 150 of us made curtsies or clicked our heels and "Ma'amed" all over the commissioner's office. Executing a curtsy in narrow uniform skirts while extending your right hand and keeping your head up and smiling, we discovered, is one of life's less simple tasks.

It was a strange frame of mind in which our motor procession started off for Buckingham Palace. I drove Buddy's sedan over as she went in Lady Chesham's sedan since she had just arrived back on the *Queen Elizabeth* in time for the party. It was a tremendous thrill for me to sit in the driver's seat, follow along in the long procession of cars, and sweep (there is no other word) through the imposing front gates of Buckingham Palace, then between the open gates on the facade of the palace and on into the interior courtyard.

Footmen—fascinatingly dressed staff of some kind—helped us out of our cars and up some marble steps and into the foyer. Two red-waistcoated, gold top-hatted men opened the foyer doors and Brother!! we were in the palace!

And what a beautiful palace. The foyer had lovely red carpeting and white marble walls with gold trim illuminated with diffused lighting. It was like walking into a dream world. On our right a Guards string band was playing. First we went into a library where we left our top coats and handbags and took a last glance at ourselves in the mirror to be sure we had a white glove on the left hand and carried our right-hand glove. We also carried cards with our names inscribed on them.

In her uniform Lady Chesham was as smart-looking as ever. As we passed back through the foyer to the reception room where we were to wait, she admitted, "I always have the most intense desire to sit down the minute I get within a mile of royalty and that you can never do, unless they do. In fact, Princess Margaret Rose is forever poking Elizabeth to sit down at royal functions as she gets so tired of standing."

I know I must have been staring as we walked the length of a great hall towards a reception room. The Grand Hall was very long with buffet tables set the length of it with the most beautiful china and silver and food I've ever seen. There seemed to be a flunkie every two feet ready to serve us after our presentations. Rare, dainty pink begonias in silver pots decorated the tables.

We waited in a lovely large reception room, very high-ceilinged, with tremendous portraits of Victoria and Albert on the wall, and the date 1855 on the ceiling. Suddenly the high, wide double doors at the end of the salon swung open, the Lord Chamberlain appeared in the doorway, and our presentations began.

Up until the very moment I reached the threshold I was viewing the whole thing with a delighted but detached air. The Lord Chamberlain took my name card from me. Scud tells me the Lord Chamberlain called out my name in a loud voice, pronouncing it perfectly, but I wouldn't know. I have no recollection of hearing it at all.

I do remember going through the opened doors and being struck dumb by the sight of the whole Royal Family—the King, the Queen, Princess Elizabeth, and Princess Margaret Rose. Just like that. They were such a beautiful family group I almost felt dizzy, and all perfectly lovely looking. The Queen had invited us and our instructions had focused on how to address her, so Scud and I hadn't expected the whole family.

As I took the King's hand and curtsied he smiled and said, "How do you do." I did not know exactly how to respond although I was sure it wasn't "Ma'am," so I just said "How do you do," back at him and passed on to the Queen and curtsied and went through a curtsy for each of the Princesses.

They each greeted me so graciously, sincerely is the word, that I think I floated out of the room into the Grand Hall. In a few seconds I came to again and there was Scud standing beside me with just as silly an expression on her face as I must have had on mine. I have never before been so completely carried away by an experience.

After we recovered our equilibrium we returned to the doorway to watch the others come out. One by one, without exception, they floated out on a little pink cloud, with the darndest expressions on their faces.

Looking back in at the Royal Family, I began to register a few details. They are so lovely looking it's hard to focus on anything but their faces. They all have exceptionally high color and wonderfully direct eyes. The King is short—about an inch taller than me when I have on heels. He wore his Admiral's uniform and is he ever attractive! The perfect face for coins.

The Queen wore a black velvet dress, street length, and the most beautiful ropes of pearls I have ever seen, with an emerald clasp—and a silver fox piece thrown over her shoulders.

Although Princess Elizabeth is inclined to be a little heavyset, I have seldom seen a more beautiful face. Photographs don't begin to do her justice. She wore a red dress, peplum style, and awful elbow-length gloves (white), black shoes (hideous—look like the pointed-toe jobs Pinet displays in their Bond Street windows). Still, she was perfectly lovely. That's when I decided the Royal Family cultivate such radiant and overwhelming personalities in carrying out their royal duties, what they wear is completely unimportant.

Princess Margaret Rose was all in baby blue with shoes to match. She has tremendously large eyes and looked rather pale, as this was her first public appearance since she had her appendix out three weeks ago. She wasn't supposed to be present, but she wanted to see the Americans.

Besides Mr. Winant, our ambassador, and Secretary Forrestal, the King was backed by his equerries, including his aide, a group captain RAF pilot who is a handsome and famous Battle of Britain hero.

About then Scud and I felt the need of some tea. The beautiful table seemed to stretch over 100 yards down the Grand Hall. I had one cup of tea and only one of the fascinating little petit four tea cakes. For once in my life I was too interested to eat. Ladies-in-waiting and the King's men, all distinguished-looking and wearing civilian attire, floated about being charming. Some Lord offered to get Scud another cup of tea—the table was all of 3 feet away—and she let him.

Old New Englander Scud identified far more of the blue bloods than I would have been able to, which was very helpful. By the time she pointed out Princess Alice and the Duchess of Marlborough in Red Cross uniform and Mrs. Biddle in American Red Cross uniform, and we chatted with Lady Spencer from the west of Scotland, the receiving line was over in the next room and the Royal Family came into the Grand Hall.

Before I knew what was happening, the Queen had drifted over to us and started chatting. I completely forgot my "Ma'am" as she was so gracious and charming Scud and I found ourselves talking completely naturally. She asked us how long we had been over, what we did, how we liked it, and we were discussing the changing morale of the troops since the fighting has been over before I realized what was happening.

She has a completely engaging way of talking with you for a few minutes, then, somehow, rather dismissing you with a gracious nod of her head and turning to a new group. It sounds a little abrupt but really it's an art, and the only way she is able to circulate through a large group.

As we were recovering from this encounter the lady-in-waiting to the Princesses caught my arm and introduced us again to them. Then Princess Margaret Rose quietly signaled her and left, as she was feeling weak by this time. Elizabeth has all her mother's graciousness plus her own good looks, but how I would love to see another designer dress her.

Somehow we got to talking about trucks (lorries to her), as she had to learn to drive them for the WAFs, and we agreed Bedfords are hard to handle. She is most eager to come to Canada and the United States and added, "There is really so very much to do and see in the world that one wonders how one is ever going to be able to do it all, doesn't one?" One surely does! Seriously, from her it sounded natural and good.

Eventually we found ourselves with the King. Mr. Bowles Rogers, our commissioner, introduced us again. He is really something—the King, I mean! He stammers only slightly, but makes you feel at home instantly. Our conversation ran something like this:

The King asked, "Have you all (meaning Scud, Buddy, and me) been here all the time?"

Everyone but Buddy said yes but she said, "No, sir, I spent some time on the continent in France."

The King smiled and said, "You like it much better here, of course."

"Naturally," said Buddy.

"I am often glad," said the King, "that there's some water between us. And, too, it saved us a great deal of trouble in 1940, didn't it?"

I was very much relieved to find out that the King has his opinions. I'm betting he's doing everything in his power to influence Prime Minister Attlee at this point.

All of this was occurring while the Guards were playing selected American airs with British verve. For the first few strains I didn't quite recognize "Way Down upon the Swanee River." And a darling little old man kept coming around in black knee-breeches-and-coat livery with a gorgeous Georgian silver cigarette box in one hand and a silver candle-like lighter in the other.

After exactly one and a half hours of this dreamlike world, the Royal Family seemed, as though by magic, to find themselves together at the entrance of the Grand Hall. There was a sudden hush and the Guards struck up "God Save the King" while everybody got goosebumps. Then Queen Elizabeth said in a clear voice, "Goodbye," and they disappeared through the high doors, which closed behind them.

Love from your still awed daughter,
Rosie

Journal   December 18, 1945

Although the train's almost back into the mist, fog, and cold of reality, both of us remain enchanted with our experience. We agree we've never seen anything quite like it, and that we've changed our thinking about the Royal Family being parasites on the public purse. I've never seen a group work a crowd better—skillfully drifting from group to group to converse with everyone. How they manage to show up day after day, year after year, at all the official functions demanded of them—dressed to the nines, standing for hours at a time, yet remain cordial and welcoming and expressing sincere interest in everyone present—seems to me the hardest job in the world. It sounds glamorous, but after seeing them at work, it's obvious they are devoted to their duty and obligations. Despite Blitz, buzz bombs, and V-2s, they never left their post in the heart of the storm.

Know I'll be rooting for them from whatever corner of the world I end up in. I think we all need a little enchantment and glamor in our leaders and a little fairy tale stuff in our lives. Under the magnifying glass of a watching world, this Royal Family has managed to cheer their subjects through the Blitz and bombings and discharge their duties and royal responsibilities with courage and character. I say cheers!

                                                December 26, 1945
                                                Happy Boxing Day!

Dearest ones,

Christmas is over and the one thing I'm sure of at this point is that this is my last Christmas away from home, which makes me happier than you can imagine. All day yesterday I was mentally following you through the day and thinking of you, wondering if Bob got through to you, how your tree looked, all sorts of things. Lots of mail arrived Christmas Eve, which was lovely, and I got a cable from my Bob on the 23rd, and he's finally back to Indiana. I do hope you'll write to him from time to time as know he'd love to hear.

Sunday night the 23rd, we all (the twenty-five now left on the crew) gave a Christmas party at Lordswood House for all our friends—in the Port and out of the Port, anywhere in fact. It was to be just an open house, and we had decorated a big tree. We finagled special liquor rations from the Officers Mess so we could serve punch. Beth Cole, one of our Southern belles, cabled home for the recipe for a Plantation Punch and it was some recipe! From the *Augusta* we corraled several crates of oranges to use in the punch, which also contained gin and vermouth and soda water.

We hadn't planned a formal open house but we all decided to dress formally for the boys, as they always see us in Clubmobile uniforms. The effect was breathtaking—or maybe it was the punch! They all seemed thrilled to see long dresses again and the party started off an instant success. We expected maybe fifty would come but by golly it turned out to be more like 175! We used the huge game room at Lordswood and it was crammed full with every rank in the Army from buck private to full colonel, plus Navy men of all ranks and descriptions. Even a couple of RAF boyfriends showed up.

We had all kinds of food: shrimps and fish spreads and anchovies and all sorts of dainties the girls had asked family to send from home, and cake the PWs had made. Everyone ate themselves sick. Sylvia played the piano, we all sang and no one was the least bit out of order. Buddy brought George, her fiancé, down from London with her and they had a wonderful time. Everybody was having such fun it was 2:30 before I finally got the last ones to go home. I was worried as to how the Misses Needham and Airey would react to such a big party, but they were thrilled to death with all the uniforms and wanted to know where we had met such nice people!

Christmas Eve day we were busy working and wrapping packages to give our British help. We distributed 3,000 packages to the boys waiting in the C areas to go home. They queued up for miles in pouring rain at the C18 marshaling area to get their Red Cross parcels. We stuck little Christmas decorations on the doughnuts and brought extra Christmas candy and caramels to give away. We also helped the 82nd Airborne boys at Tidworth decorate their camp as they aren't going home until the *Mary* sails on the 29th and didn't have any Christmas packages or decorations.

During the day some of us went shopping for 5 shilling gifts to put in each other's stockings at Lordswood on Christmas Eve. I'd give almost anything to have you all go Christmas shopping over here for just one hour. It is so tragic I wanted to cry. They have no decorations to speak of and the merchandise is dreadful. I don't see how the poorer people can give anything at all. I didn't see one thing you would even consider giving to charity for less than a pound. Their Woolworth's hasn't a thing that our 5 and 10 would handle, and saddest of all, there are no trimmings, bright wrappings, or strings or stickers. In our Red Cross shipment containing supplies for Christmas arrangements, there are lots of packages of red and green tissue paper and red ribbon and stickers. Our British help kept thinking of excuses to go into the storeroom and I'd find them in there just staring at all the bright Christmas wrapping.

Unofficially, we gave them lots of trimmings after we had taken care of all our Red Cross decorations. They were so thrilled it was pitiful. They've been through such a long war and I wonder if the country can ever recover. All of their best merchandise is exported and internally the country's so hamstrung with red tape that no one, we hear, can open up a small business or produce little things to sell. It's a shame they can't have a better Christmas after all they've gone through.

Mr. and Mrs. Harris, the very nice couple who run our doughnut factory here, gave me a sterling silver cross on a chain for Christmas. They've always kind of liked me. I gave them a bottle of sherry which I wangled through the mess. They were so grateful. Mom dear, when I opened packages Christmas Eve and saw that gorgeous big fruitcake I decided to give it to them too. I wish you could have seen their faces. Fruitcake is like gold to the British and rarer. They both had tears in their eyes and Mrs. Harris said, "Oh, Rosie, this will just make Christmas."

For Christmas Eve I'd been roped into going to the Port celebration with Lieutenant Colonel Bannister, the Deputy Port Commander, who's been dating a lovely British girl for over a year. Doreen went home for Christmas and he was obliged to attend, so asked me to go with him as he knew Bob had left. Luckily, Scud and Luke went with us so it made an enjoyable evening.

When we got home about midnight, all of the girls at Lordswood came down to the tea room and we sat in front of the fire and opened our presents from home and the silly gifts in our Christmas stockings. I've been away so long you've become experts at sending exactly the right gifts overseas. Ginny opened a present and moaned, "Now *why* does Mother send me things here that she never would have dreamed of getting for me at home?" She'd just opened a gruesome mixture of liver paste and onions and olives and pig's feet. So thank you all for your wonderful taste! Bob B. sent me a nice little gold compact. It was 3 AM before I collapsed into bed.

Christmas morning Pat, Alice, Scud, Sylvia, and I had breakfast at Lordswood before work. When Duke and I came down to breakfast, Pat was convulsed with laughter. She told us she'd hung a stocking over the fireplace for Gordon, an officer she's dating, before going to bed as he was coming to open his silly presents on Christmas. When Pat came down to breakfast, little Mrs. Airey came rushing in and said, "Isn't it wonderful! Father Christmas has paid us a visit and left a stocking for my Gordon!"

Mrs. Airey's son Gordon is a young man in the RAF stationed in Alexandria, Egypt, and the only way we had heard of him at all was when he sent "all the American girls" a Christmas card! Pat was speechless but finally managed to say, "Yes, isn't it?" before Mrs. Airey went raving out the door.

Alice and I were firm. "You have to tell her, Pat." At which point Mrs. Airey came back in with our breakfasts, simply tickled to death because Father Christmas had paid her Gordon a visit. Alice and I exchanged a look, then began agreeing with her. She was too excited to disillusion, so after breakfast we rushed upstairs to wrap some more gifts for Pat's Gordon!

Both Miss Needham and Mrs. Airey were delighted with your remembrance, Mom. We had given them a bottle of wine and one of gin (they love a nip) and a box full of our rations and cigarettes. They were almost overcome. They just couldn't get over the gifts. So many people are niggardly givers over here. Every landlord seems to begrudge doing anything for you (it being an old English custom—*see* Dickens, Charles), and the *Arsenic and Old Lace* sisters are the same. Not deliberately malicious, just traditionally so. The British know little of generous living—except for some of the top-drawer set—and it's beyond them to have people want to do little things for them. The sisters were so overcome they went around with big tears of happiness in their eyes, wringing their hands. That's a sign of emotion—great joy or great sorrow—as in when one of us dares turn a light on before 6 PM at night because we can't see, something that just isn't done you know, even though it gets dark by 4:30 in winter.

After work Christmas morning I was duty-bound to the second part of Colonel Bannister's invitation, the Port Christmas dinner. The turkey proved to be perfect, so tender and good, I stuffed. At the party they screened *Going My Way*, a lovely Christmas Day movie. Then we all sat in front of the fire and listened to shortwave programs from home. As we enjoyed Christmas music in a room garlanded with beautiful English holly hanging under a huge red parachute draping the entire ceiling, I realized everyone in the room was thinking of home and not the party.

Duke enjoyed Christmas tremendously. Honestly, he's the most beautiful and intelligent large dog I've ever known. If I ever can afford a big dog I wish for nothing better than Duke. He's now an American citizen, as I got his papers today and he's all set to sail on the *Mary* (with Tom on the 29th). Already I have Tom's promise to exercise him daily while crossing. Talk about first-class travel! The latest on shipping dogs is that you pay for them by their size. Strictly *entre nous*, Lieutenant Rosenthal in the Transportation Office is arranging Duke's passage as Duke's master couldn't afford it. Don't tell too many people or there will be a Congressional investigation! However, I'll get a dog home, illicitly or legally, as we all think it's a shame so many have to remain behind. Thank goodness I don't have to pay, as a dog much smaller than Duke cost $130 and Duke would cost a small fortune if Cunard Lines knew how he eats. Am so grateful to Lieutenant Rosenthal for offering to pay his passage.

Boxing Day, almost over, is a really big day in the UK. Did I tell you it started centuries ago when the day after Christmas the nobles went around to the butcher and tradesmen and their villagers to distribute presents? Consequently, on Boxing Day the ordinary people usually had nicer gifts than on Christmas Day. They still look forward to the day eagerly. It's a complete holiday—no trams, no newspapers, no nothing—but we Yanks have been busy loading the *Wasp*.

Goodnight to all my best loved ones. We're on the homestretch now—Paris in January and home, I hope, within six months. How does that sound to you? And here's the poem Alice (our cute reddish blond from Topeka, a radio station reporter and soap actress—wrote to put in with her stocking gift of a tiny model of the *Queen Elizabeth*). She's a very talented person, but then I keep telling you what a wonderful crew I have.

All my love,
Roses

Alice's Christmas Poem
Christmas Stocking December 1945
To Rosie

May I give to you this souvenir
To recall to you in a future year
Long nights spent slaving on the docks—
Feet encased in numerous socks,

Hands grown numb, noses red—
Long johns under, hoods on head.

The ships came in, the ships sailed out;
We served the men as they stood about.
Coffee and donuts, our steady diet—
But with them we stymied many a riot.
We made them laugh, we made them smile;
We made them gripe, and forget the "heil."

From these ships and men we learned a lot—
Some of it good, some of it rot.
But down on those docks we saw our boys
As they really are—full of noise,
Full of jokes, full of bad, full of good;
Living war as Americans would;

Living each day for all it's worth;
Giving each man his wealth of birth;
Hating war but doing his job,
For no one has the right to rob
Peace and good will from any other.

We learned to call each human "brother";
We learned to laugh from deep inside;
We learned that petty thoughts must hide;
We learned in S'oton on the docks
To take our hearts from out their locks,
And follow true the age-old trend
Of knowing everyone as friend.

—Alice

CERTIFICATE OF HEALTH

26 Dec 1945

THIS IS TO CERTIFY:
That one German Shepherd DOG, Male , AGE 1 year 5 mos.
NAME Duke OWNED BY 1st Lt. Myron Rosenthal 01945474
and Mascot of Shipment No. RE7442S has been examined by me this
date and found to be free from any acute infectious and contagious
canine disease.

JOHN A. UTTERBACK
CAPT. V.C.
PORT VETERINARIAN
14th MAJOR PORT
U.S. ARMY

P.S. Sudden sad news. Mrs. Airey just got a telegram that her only son Gordon had been killed in an accident. He was due home on leave in two months. Poor little lady. She keeps saying there's nothing left to live for. We're all glad we let her think the stocking was for her Gordon, and that she had a wonderful Christmas before getting this dreadful news.

Chapter Twenty

December 29, 1945

Dearest Family,

Right now, I'm desolate. Duke went home on the Mary today. I put him aboard late yesterday afternoon and took him up to the kennels myself, the ship's butcher following along behind. Duke seemed to sense he was going and was halfway eager to get aboard. But when he realized I wasn't staying with him, he looked as though he would die. I felt the same way, as he's been my consolation and support during this lonesome time since Bob left. I tried not to get too attached to him during the past two weeks, but he has too much personality and intelligence for me to maintain an aloof attitude. Everyone in the Port got a big kick out of the way he followed me around, right at my heels.

The other day I left him in the operations hut in Hut City while I went to mess. I was in the middle of dessert when in he bounded, tickled to death at finding me. Everyone laughed as he's so big he almost knocked over the tables. I couldn't help noticing how some of our brave officers scattered as he came bounding in. I scolded him all the way back to Hut 9, but he was real pleased with himself.

Tom left yesterday on the Mary also, thrilled to be going home to Ski, and will arrive back on his birthday. Isn't that great? He's planning to check on Duke and walk him daily on the top deck outside the kennels. He and I had only a short time together and despite our happy talk of future reunions it was hard to leave Tom and Duke aboard and walk off that ship. I have not heard from Bob yet, except his arrival cable, but I don't think it's possible to expect mail for a few more days as it's very slow. Bob B.'s came in good time, but it was sent special delivery and special handling, too.

Have to get to work. Write soon again, I'll be waiting to hear.

All my love to all of you,
Roses

Journal   *December 29, 1945*

Mom and Dad sure have come through in keeping relationships running as usual and I keep pushing more on their shoulders to fend off until I get home. Guess I'm feeling a little end-of-the-year depressed, as everyone most dear to me is gone, down to and including old Duke. Know I can't expect to get letters or hear much from Bob until he's out of the Army and a civilian again, but it's mighty lonesome out tonight.

Feeling guilty, too, as I haven't told Mother and Dad that his divorce isn't in the works yet and I'm sure they're hoping it's already accomplished. Bob's ex-wife didn't even answer his requests to go ahead with it. That's the first thing, after getting discharged and contacting his company, he has to get started. I can't fault her for not starting divorce proceedings when I stop to think about it—her allotment is a good one and there are custody agreements to be discussed and arranged. But she could have answered. So who knows how long it will all take?

WESTERN UNION
CABLEGRAM

RECEIVED AT 26 OXFORD STREET, SOUTHAMPTON
SO 7/30 INDIANAPOLIS, IND   18 29/1115 AM

ROSEMARY LANGHELDT
LORDSWOOD HOUSE
NR SOUTHAMPTON HANTS ENGLAND

HAPPY NEW YEAR DARLING   I LOVE YOU   BOB

Journal   *December 31, 1945*

What a relief to know Bob's back in Indiana! Had to laugh when I got his wire as it's proof of what he says about his fellow Hoosiers. He told me once his mom can squeeze more news on a postcard than most people can get into a letter. "Rosie," he said, "Hoosiers don't chew their cabbage twice." Now if only his letters catch up, I'll get a few details. Can't wait for the mail to come.

January 2, 1946, 11:30 PM

Dearest ones,

Have just returned from London where I took up my plans for revamping the operation. Hold your hats—Tuesday, Scud, Pat, Alice, and I report to London for assignment on the continent! At long last. We'll go to Paris first and will try for a Germany assignment. I'll cable you at the right time to change my APO number.

I'm sending almost all my civilian clothes home because if we're sent into Germany only uniforms are allowed and even in France I won't be dating so won't need many off-duty clothes.

Gosh, it's cold. Old winter is starting—14 degrees above zero, clear and bitter cold and damp and bone-freezing, too. Frost everywhere. I'm glad to be going as I'd rather spend a winter in the high and dry Alps than another one in Southampton.

Goodnight. I love you oodles.

Roses

January 4, 1946, 10:15 PM

Dears,

Today I went to London on business to finish the reorganization and Buddy burst out of the commissioner's meeting with the news that all of the Red Cross in Great Britain is closing by the 20th of the month. I don't have to stay to close the base, thank goodness, and the four of us are still going on to the continent, but everyone else must go home. I was tempted to turn in my suit and go home too, but I have a tremendous urge to see the continent and the effects of war for at least a short time, as I certainly won't be able to come back soon.

Sis, when the picture of Bob and me comes, just be honest and say, "This man is Marliss's future uncle." Everyone may as well get used to the idea now.

Millions of things to do so probably can't write often. I love you all so much, please keep writing, often. Goodnight, I love you.

Roses

Journal   *January 5, 1946*

What a day brightener to know Duke made it. Hope he likes Brooklyn!

WESTERN UNION
CABLEGRAM

920 FLUSHING NY   19 5 1946 JAN 5 PM 7 53

NLT ROSEMARY LANGHELDT
ARC 44244 CARE AMERICAN RED CROSS
APO 413 LDN

RECEIVED DUKE PERFECT CONDITION   THANKS   TEX WILSON

January 6, 1946

Dearest ones,

Sent you a cable this morning so know you'll be using APO 887 from now on.

Got my first letter from Bob yesterday. He wrote it just as the *Lake Champlain* was berthing in New York. He said he was seasick every inch of the way and I believe it, as his letter sounded like he had written it with one hand across his mouth. Poor guy. He wasn't too sure he'd get home for Christmas either, as they have to wait to be discharged. He thought they'd go to Fort Dix first. I've been worrying, as the storms on the Atlantic have been terrible these past weeks.

Yesterday I saw Mrs. Roosevelt debark from the *Elizabeth* and speak for the newsreels. I was shocked. She looked so worn and tired and old and gentle I felt awfully sorry for her. It had never occurred to me that she would grieve for her husband as they led such independent lives, but she looked as though she had experienced great sorrow.

Gotta keep going. Goodnight, God bless.

I love you sooooo much,
Your Rosie

✦

January 12, 1946
10 Charles Street, London
10:20 AM

Dearest ones,

Here we are in London, where we will be until next Tuesday when we sail from Newhaven to Dieppe, arriving in Paris Wednesday afternoon. We're all cleared—that means our papers are in order and we're full of shots. Had a flu shot and tetanus booster Tuesday and felt very dopey for two days. I get such decided reactions to those darn things. Don't mind having them but they do make me sick.

Such fun for the first time in eighteen months to have no responsibility. Alice, Scud, and Pat are great traveling companions, all being equipped with the most important requisite—a sense of humor. We've laughed often since our arrival at Waterloo Station, when we had so much luggage we had to have a lorry drive us to Charles Street (a footlocker, two duffle bags, a suitcase, and musette bag *each*).

Night before last we saw a movie, a British epic colossal spectacle *Caesar and Cleopatra*, with Claude Rains and Vivien Leigh, in technicolor. Take my word for it and don't go. It is stupid and sententious and generally dull. The George Bernard Shaw wit is not worth the torture of the rest of the movie.

Yesterday we went through the Tower of London, and later had tea at the Dorchester. Arabs are all over the place as the UNO conference opened yesterday. Probably a great many of the same delegates you saw in San Francisco. We went to the Savoy Theatre to see Robert Morley and Wendy Hiller in *The First Gentleman*, the story of the Prince Regent who became George IV. The costumes and staging were magnificent, particularly Morley as the fat, gouty, dissolute, egomaniac Prince Regent. A wonderful company. I've always thought the clothes of the Regency period ugly, but they are beautiful when you actually see them on people. Wendy Hiller played in *Pygmalion*, remember?

We are the last four girls to go to the continent. Buddy got special permission from the commissioner for us, as 1,000 ARC personnel are being sent home from here, whether or not they wish to go. We are exceptions because of the jobs we did at Southampton. I won't be surprised to be sent home any time after arriving, but I'll get to see some of the continent and still get home this spring. Isn't that wonderful?

We have to go to Headquarters so will close.

I love you all,
Roses

January 13, 1946, 12:10 PM
10 Charles St., London

Dearest ones,

Sis, I'm thrilled at your news. I think it's marvelous that you're having another baby. Naturally I hope the baby can be a Rosemary, as your intention to name her after me if it's a girl is wonderfully flattering. So you must know I'm thrilled, and highly honored, to know "she" may be a namesake. And I'm so glad you liked Bob's voice when he called, Mom, and that you liked the picture. You'll all love him, I know. Bob is going to see his boss this week about his job, and particularly what territory he'll have. I'll let you know as soon as he does.

Yesterday we had a marvelous afternoon in the National Art Gallery on Trafalgar Square and last night yet another play. Will write again before we cross the channel.

I love you all,
Roses

Tuesday, January 15, 1946
10 Charles Street, London W.

Dearest ones,

Tonight we leave for Paris and we're all repacking before checking out. Thank goodness the store gave me a Val-Pak! Everyone has been pulling and tugging and sitting on their suitcases so they'll close. It's so easy to pack a Val-Pak I finish way ahead of everyone else, which makes them exceedingly bitter.

Sunday morning we went to services in Westminster Abbey and were seated in Poet's Corner. We could see the dean well as he gave an excellent sermon on the UNO and world peace. I so wish you could hear the organ, Mom, it's beautiful. They're putting the stained glass windows back in and they're gorgeous.

Scud and Ginny arrived back from Southampton yesterday, where they went to see Luke and Chuck one more time before they leave. They traveled on a nonstop train that didn't even stop at Waterloo—it ran right into the bumpers at the end of the platform. Papers said today forty people were injured. Scud and Ginny were thrown to the floor, bruised and dazed. But they rushed through the confusion of bloody injured people to queue up for a taxi! They were still dazed when they arrived at Charles Street, but recovered in time for lunch.

The other girls are finally packed, so we're off to get our bags checked and report to Headquarters. I love you all, you know how much, and I'll write you from Paris.

Roses

Part Five

The Journey Towards Home

When the Japanese signed the surrender documents on the deck of the USS *Missouri* in August 1945, the news was flashed around the world and the celebrations went on for days.

But there was much still to be done before normality could set in. The European continent faced the devastating aftermath of war. With the liberation of the concentration camps we heard that hundreds of thousands of refugees and displaced persons of all nationalities were on the move. Many of them, penniless and starving, didn't know if they had home or family to return to.

The Allied Army of Occupation began its efforts to restore government and a semblance of order in the ruined and impoverished German cities and countryside.

And, with the advent of world peace, all of our thoughts turned homeward.

Chapter Twenty-One

Hôtel de Nouailles, Paris
6:30 PM, January 18, 1946

Dearest Family,

Tuesday night the four of us left Charles Street, for assignment in France or Germany and traveling with Ginny, Kay, and Sally, three of our Southampton girls going over on leave. We were laughing hysterically by the time we arrived at Victoria Station as we were crammed on a Chevie 1½-ton truck with not only all our luggage, but two Red Cross men going over, the driver and a porter! The luggage alone scarcely fit in the truck, so how eleven people squeezed aboard is a miracle. Buddy and George came down to see us off, which was very nice of them. The train ride to Newhaven was fun, as we had a compartment to ourselves and the night was gorgeously clear with an almost full moon.

At 11:30 PM we arrived at the ship and the queues began. It was terribly cold so I had on my overcoat and liner, a wool scarf, fleece-lined boots, and fur-lined gloves, with my camera cases, purse, and full musette bag dangling from my shoulders. Other than that all I was carrying was my bulging Val-Pak, which weighed a ton. What a struggle! We had to queue up to show our orders, to turn in our tickets, to be given sandwiches, to change our pounds into francs, to go through customs—all in different lines.

I was fascinated because I have never seen such a conglomeration of people. In the military queue were enlisted men and officers from the United States, Great Britain, Canada, Poland, France, and Russia. The civilian queue was the truly exotic one, looking like the perfect cast for a Sidney Greenstreet, Peter Lorre, Charles Boyer Class A mystery: Swiss and English and American and Dutch; DPs (displaced persons), peasants and big shots; a gorgeous blond Frenchwoman in Persian lamb and a gray cloud-effect hat, traveling with a Frenchman so ugly, including his thick-lensed glasses, that he was almost good-looking. It was a crowd featuring pipes, lorgnettes, black seal collars on men's overcoats, berets, and homburgs.

Our seven finally boarded the *Isle of Guernsey*, a British major having nobly carried my Val-Pak up the gangway. We had to queue up for bunks outside the

229

purser's office, there being more passengers than bunks. We were lucky and assigned to a large room with thirty others. Bunks stood two deep all over the room.

Each had a pillow and gray blankets. Soon our "cabin" was a raucous hubbub complete with seven languages and as many crying babies. At which point we decided to retire. One look at the john and washroom, still dirty and reeking from the last crossing, convinced us we couldn't wash. We all just lay down and threw our blankets over us. You know me, I can sleep anywhere and was proceeding to prove the point when a man suddenly prodded me. He and the matron were trying to open the porthole at my head to let air into the cabin. I looked out when the icy breezes started blowing in to see it was a heavenly night with the moon and stars making the water look almost green.

The *Guernsey* made it to Dieppe by 10:30 AM, but several of our girls had been sick on the crossing and felt weak. The train sat in the station from 10:30 until 2:30 PM, so we had lunch in the diner looking out on the stone walls of Dieppe. The lunch was so much better than the food available this past week in London. The waiters rushed around, knocking themselves out to please us, and the fish had a lovely mushroom sauce and wine to wash it down with.

Now that the franc has been devalued (Fr 120 to the dollar), money means nothing, but cigarettes are priceless. An excellent tip for a meal is a cigarette! They say a carton is worth $150 in Germany, a package worth Fr 500 or more in France.

Our train ride from Dieppe to Paris was very comfortable and we stopped at a few small towns en route to Paris, some badly bombed, and the open country is full of craters. We've been told there's not enough to do in most villages and that people just stand around, still gripped by postwar inertia and detachment. As we watched the passing countryside, a lovely scene would be jarringly interrupted by sudden reminders of the war. Everyone was preoccupied with memories of the troops we served who passed this way.

We arrived at the Gare St. Lazare in Paris at 6 PM. We were met by a Red Cross woman and taken to the Nouailles, a hotel used for Red Cross women only, just off the Place de l'Opéra. Our rooms are centrally heated with a bathroom and bathtub, and bidets!

We were instructed to report in to Headquarters Friday, so had the next day free. We quickly washed up and walked to the nearest Red Cross mess, La Potinière, right up the street. La Potinière is lovely, with red drapes and golden lights, positively the most glamorous place imaginable after England. As it's Red Cross there's no charge, no money involved. And the food, not boiled but cooked and seasoned, food with *flavor*, is served with wine or any beverage you wish.

We simply made pigs of ourselves and then, revived by the food, decided to explore. It's hard to describe the impact we all felt when we emerged from the Métro to see the Eiffel Tower standing out against the moon and stars. By that hour, it was freezing cold, but a nice *dry* wintry cold and crystal clear. We stood right under the enormous tower and looked first towards the Military School (l'Ecole Militaire) and then across the Seine to the Trocadero Palace. The scene was breathtakingly lovely.

On Thursday our group started doing Paris. We walked to the church of the Madeleine then down the rue Royale, with all its wonderful shop windows, to the Place de la Concorde, where Marie Antoinette was beheaded. History seems to hang over every street in this city. For the first time since I left home I longed to buy things—perfumes, silver, jewelry, leather, lingerie, blouses—as they're displayed everywhere. It's hard to see a scarcity at all, or war damage. The obvious shortages are food (the French tell us they eat poorly), taxis and autos, and tobacco. Beautifully dressed people everywhere but not a cigarette butt in sight. They are snatched up by respectable people before they hit the ground. The shoes are not of good quality but stylish and how I wish I had just one of the pairs of nylons I've seen adorning the legs of the women on the streets.

All seven of us took the Red Cross tour of Paris. As you can see from the enclosed picture we were with a bunch of GIs and it was a picnic. We covered the whole city sketchily and since have decided to do some of the places again on our own—the Louvre, the palaces, the Arc de Triomphe, rue de la Paix and Champs Elysées and Montmartre—everything we can squeeze in.

Napoleon's Tomb fascinated me. It is awesome it's so large. I found myself thinking that if Hitler had won the war and survived he would be installed in similar, or grosser, splendor. Those two were so alike it irks me to see Napoleon, as ruthless as Hitler, accorded grandeur on such a scale. Frankly, I don't like French splendor much—it's too flamboyant and garish. They put everything but feathers on their buildings. Napoleon's Tomb is imposing, but I was more emotionally moved by many of the buildings and shrines in England.

The one exception is Notre Dame. I was forced to admit that the great cathedrals of England have an equal. Notre Dame is so huge, yet centered, as it dominates its perfect placement on the island. The first sight of it is overwhelming and the facade and the windows are as marvelous as we'd heard.

This morning we were up at the crack of dawn because we wanted to get in one more tour before reporting to Headquarters. Nobly, we did without breakfast in bed—they serve hot cocoa or coffee and continental rolls at the hotel, but we went to mess to eat. All we got was fresh oranges (ho hum), fresh eggs (are you listenin'?), lovely rolls or croissants, and coffee. Then off we went to the catacombs, which was a long way even by Métro.

At the catacomb office we rounded up a little man who spoke no English and he lighted a lamp and off we went. He opened up a vaultlike door and led the way down, the seven of us trailing behind. It was one of the weirdest, most uncanny walks I've ever taken. The passages are hewn out of solid rock and zigzag all over, occasionally sloping downwards, sometimes dripping water.

We passed carvings removed from walls of castles, made by prisoners kept there during the French-Spanish war. When we had walked until I felt sure we were at the gates of hell and would never find our way out, we came to a big door with a French inscription—so French, so dramatic—STOP! Here Is the Empire of the Dead. And in we went to wander among the 6 million skeletons, stacked neatly and with macabre artistry, bone upon bone, row upon row—20 meters thick—for miles. We were told Roman Catholics cannot destroy bones so, as Paris grew in the seventeenth century, they began storing them in the catacombs.

The bone piles are stacked in different groups: one for those beheaded on the guillotine during the Revolution, one for Protestant rebellers, one for monks, one for nuns. What got to me as we viewed thousands of meticulously arranged bones were the signs, mostly in French or Latin, tacked beneath a skull and crossbone symbol or in front of a few thousand bones—all poems of death.

One started in French, "Thusly must pass from this World, All Grace, Beauty and unusual talents" and ended "and so, to where I am, come swiftly on." I can't remember the rest but that was enough. Another admonished, "Live as though each day were your last on earth." We came out a different passage and had to walk eight blocks to get back to our starting point.

Revived by the cold air, we reported in to Headquarters. Scud, Pat, Alice, and I are to leave Monday night for Germany. We'll arrive at Wiesbaden Tuesday morning, which is where Clubmobile Headquarters are located, and be given our assignments from there.

After lunch we took the ARC bus tour to Versailles. For four hours (my aching feet!) we trekked through room after room filled with gold and glass and crystal and paintings, all Louis XIV style—with nine or ten different kinds of marble in one pillar and every inch of every room decorated. It left me cold, except for the gorgeous Gobelin tapestries and needlepoint. Scud said it best, "You can certainly see why there was a revolution, Rosie."

I've enjoyed every minute of it, but do you wonder my feet and legs and back ache? It's 12:30 AM and we're off again at 0730. Glad I have you, my family, up to date. I must write Bob now. I love you so and how I wish you all could be with me,

Roses

Hôtel de Nouailles, Paris
Monday, late, January 21, 1946

Dearest ones,

Saturday I had a dream of a day in Paris shopping. The windows of the stores are beautifully done. I enjoyed a spending spree that will last me a long time and loved the time to myself. I bought some handmade lingerie, one three-piece white set and a pale blue slip. I'm having a pink blouse made and think you'll love it, a blouse to wear with my trousseau suit. If I decide to marry in a suit, this will complement it nicely. It has lovely sleeves. The price was Fr 4,000, or $35 U.S., and I couldn't duplicate it at home for any price.

You should see the stores and the merchandise. I got so homesick for Ransohoffs I almost cried. The salesgirls were very courteous, even though many work draped in heavy fur coats as there's no heat in the stores. My basic French served me well—just well enough to buy without paying any coupons as "coupon" is a word neither the salesgirls nor Rosie seemed able to find in their French-English vocabulary.

This morning we again walked along the Seine and through the open-air markets and stalls. As we'd gotten tickets for l'Opéra we arranged to leave for Wiesbaden Tuesday instead of today. We'd exchanged most of our francs for German marks, and I regretted being almost out of francs when I spotted a stall of incredibly old maps, hung by clothespins for display. All of the Western Hemisphere drawn by famous old cartographers in the fifteenth and sixteenth century (with geographic proportions and features completely out of position)—they fascinated me. They were dirt cheap to buy and I'll treasure them always.

We had boxes at l'Opéra for *Romeo and Juliet*. I loved the Opera House. Debussy said the outside looked like a railroad station and the inside like a Turkish bath, and he wasn't too far wrong. The red draperies and gold trims, the boxes paneled in rich red material, the lobby with its famous staircase and marble and gold and crystal—all seemed fitting and exciting, right for Paris. The opera itself was fine, with lovely scenery and lighting and a magnificent ballet scene in the second scene of the fourth act.

It's off to Germany tomorrow and the last chapters in this adventure. Hope we don't lose touch en route so please do keep writing. I love you all so much and will write as soon as I can,

Roses

Chapter Twenty-Two

Limburg, Germany
11:30 AM, January 27, 1946

Dearest ones,

Pat and Alice and Scud and I took the sleeper to Frankfurt from Paris. It was a German train, Dad, taken over by the Army. The diner is run as a mess and the sleeping cars are compartments with two berths. Following long-established family custom I spent lots of the night looking out the window. Only this time I was not waiting to see the Mississippi, but the buses, tanks, and guns—and war damage. It was depressing.

Our arrival in Frankfurt even more so. The great station is a bombed-out shell of its former grandeur, packed with all ranks of all the services, queuing up for tickets to Berlin and Munich and Mulhouse and Paris. Germans of all ages fought to carry our luggage for a few cigarettes. We waited awhile outside the station to be picked up by the Red Cross for the drive to Wiesbaden Red Cross Headquarters. The devastation, the rubble, the jagged skeletons of buildings stabbing skyward were chilling reminders of the effects of war. I kept thinking how easily this could have happened to San Francisco if the Axis had not been stopped.

Wiesbaden, once an international spa and resort area because of its mineral waters and not being too far from Frankfurt, is also a wreck. They were very nice to us at Headquarters and Alice, Pat, and I were assigned to the Third Army section out of Munich while Scud had to leave immediately for a temporary 7th Army assignment at Buschlag. She's been promised a transfer to our area soon.

While we waited around for assignments, we called Lil in Limburg to say hello. Know I've told you about our wonderful Lil from Brooklyn, who left Southampton with Kari, and Lil's little cocker spaniel pup, Brother. Lil's now a field captain and arranged for me to come spend this weekend with her before I take the sleeper to Munich Monday night. Today Scud surprised us with a brief visit here at Limburg, driving in from Buschlag to share the good news that she'll be transferred to this area within a week or so. Then Alice and Pat called from Munich to tell us we are *all* to be assigned to the Munich area. After all

Kari, Rosie, Lil, and Brother, Limburg, Germany, January 1946.

this time overseas, we've learned to live on rumors and hopes so perhaps our luck will hold awhile longer and we can stay together.

In just three days I've noticed one major problem with the Allied occupation. The replacement troops, individually, are mostly sweet boys of nineteen or twenty-one, just adolescents cut loose from home for the first time, drinking themselves to death on cognac, each one with his German "laundress." So many of them are drunk when they should be sober, mean when they could be understanding, soft when they should be firm. They haven't the vaguest notion of the importance of their actions.

Here at Lil's base the GIs flock around all the time and love Lil and Kari and the Red Cross girls. They treat us like queens—or sisters, or mothers—but it breaks my heart to see them ruining their lives and the world's future at the same time. For example, yesterday morning they were really upset because they had to turn out in full battle dress for a "Tally Ho." This is a house search for weapons and Nazis, and this part of Germany is full of both. It was a dry run, a practice turnout, and they were mad and groused about how foolish they looked standing around acting like soldiers. They were afraid the Germans would laugh at them. These young replacement troops seem to have no idea of the Nazi record—of what the German nation did to deserve this rigid supervision.

Military government, from what I hear from Lil and the ones who have been here these past months, is made up of "mystery and mistresses." Everything is accomplished through dealing—a carton of cigarettes is worth $150 in Berlin. Barter and dealings seem the only way of getting anything done. All GIs have "cash books" designed to help check on the money sent home and to stop black marketeering. Instead, a GI will give $100 to another GI (who hasn't sent away money so has an available cash book) to send home for him. Just 100 percent profit and an easy way to escape suspicion and beat the system.

There are so few troops around that anything could happen and everyone fears it's going to eventually. This morning Lil and I drove over to Weilburg on business and passed through three villages. Not a single soldier is stationed in any of these towns and the people could be making atomic bombs for all we, the Allies, know. Lil, I was pleased to see, is very accomplished at working with the townspeople. She orders what her installation needs and they spring to fill her requests. I was impressed at the cooperation and complimented her on her German.

"Rosie, I don't use German. I give them instructions in Yiddish. It's much more effective in getting things done. Call it my revenge, a little reminder of the horrors they allowed to happen in this country."

In our rounds today I noticed that all Germans dress up in their best clothes to go to church. You should see the difference between weekday and Sunday Germany. On Sunday, good shoes and good clothes are worn. I realize that Germans dressed well while their satellite captives, in rags, furnished them with slave labor.

I'm well, the living conditions here are luxurious—for us—despite war devastation surrounding us. It's not too comfortable a feeling.

All my love,
Roses

Journal   *January 27, 1946*

Have just retired to my room in this villa-like mansion that is the Red Cross staff house to enjoy a little time alone, feeling grateful Lil insisted I needn't show up at her dugout tonight. She said I should relax and get ready to hop into action Monday. I've already written Bob and the family and am glad I didn't tell them about my drive to Limburg from Wiesbaden.

Limburg's about fifty miles (or kilometers?) from Wiesbaden and Lil got permission for me to come by arranging for me to drive up an extra vehicle for use at her base. I volunteered eagerly, exuding confidence at my driving ability, and was given a crude map marked to show the autobahn entrance and where to turn off, then taken outside to find the vehicle. I couldn't believe it when I was handed the keys to an old Mercedes convertible, parked in icy slush on the street. Low-slung and racy despite its faded paint job and mud spatters, it also sported a filthy canvas top. Isinglass side curtains, cracked and opaque, were rigged in place to ward off the weather. But it was a Mercedes convertible, the kind I've only seen in romantic movies starring Marlene Dietrich (or was it Ingrid Bergman?), a car I've always longed to drive. Delighted, I tore back into Headquarters to get some rags to wipe the snow and ice off the windshield and the isinglass side curtains.

It took awhile to start the engine but I finally succeeded, consulted my map, and got to the first turn, using the throttle all the way. About then reality hit me. "Here I am, after all of five hours in Germany, trying to keep an old German car running as I search for an autobahn going to a place I never knew existed, driving through a bombed city with almost no direction signs and the few I see I can't decipher as I speak absolutely no German. What am I doing? How do I ask directions if I get lost or the car quits? How can I find a phone if I need one? Will any of the hostile passersby, bundled up and scowling as they brace against an icy wind, answer if I have to ask 'Limburg, ya?' with a silly smirk? Or will they spit in my face?"

My relief was huge when I finally found the autobahn. Hitler's one great contribution to civilization, all four lanes of it, stretched ahead in graceful curves. The broad lanes were empty except for an occasional vintage vehicle and I seemed to have it all to myself, as few Germans have cars, or fuel to drive them. As I got Marlene (our family always names cars) going on the swoops, my confidence increased and I moved to the inside lane, looking for the play areas and fruit trees Hitler planted in the middle strips when he built these highways "for his people to enjoy." And for his invading troops to move swiftly over, a reason he neglected to mention at the time. Marlene was perking on most cylinders by now and I was enjoying the drive.

I'd been told Limburg had both a German and a U.S. Army sign at the turnoff and felt sure Limburg must be spelled the same way in either German or English. Suddenly Marlene started to slip to the right as I drove into a long curve. I turned into the slide as I'd learned to do in England and shifted down a notch, but obviously I was driving on solid ice. Slowly and steadily the car drifted across lanes towards the right edge of the autobahn and there was nothing I could do about it. Just as I ran out of sliding room and praying time the road straightened out. I was shaking all over but didn't dare brake the car. One straight mile ahead the Limburg sign beckoned. Did I ever hug Lil and Kari when I finally arrived!

⚜

Dachau, 11:30 AM
Thursday, January 31, 1946

Dearest ones,

Bet this is one place you never expected your daughter to be—in a concentration camp. Actually, I'm not in it. We Red Cross are billeted just outside the side gate of Dachau, adjacent to the railroad tracks, on the ground floor of one of the houses SS officers lived in. We eat most of our meals inside the camp, right next to the place all those Russian DPs and PWs who didn't want to be repatriated tried to commit suicide the other day. Our troops realize the Allies have to return all displaced and captured Russians because of the pact we made with Stalin. But it's hard to comprehend the fear that would cause someone to prefer suicide over forced repatriation. They all agree it was the bloodiest sight they've ever seen and are still talking about it.

Monday morning Lil, Kari, and Brother drove me back into town on the worst ice I've experienced. The autobahn was just impossible. We almost slid off into two canyons even though Lil's an expert, experienced driver. Somehow we made it and I picked up my travel orders for Munich.

Happy day! There were fifteen letters waiting and I again feel connected to the world I know and love. I sat down and read them all before doing a thing about getting to Munich.

Slight pause! It's now past midnight five days later as I've been busy ever since this letter was interrupted. I'm dead tired and have too much to tell you to start. I work at the Karlsfield Dugout and have spent most of my time there getting into the Club routine.

Got two letters from Bob today (hooray!). I love you all, and am working to do my job so I can come home at exactly the right moment—which I hope is soon.

Will write more details next letter.

Love,
Roses

Midnight in Dachau
Tuesday, February 5, 1946

Dearest ones,

It's late but I'll write until my eyes close as I want to fill you in on my actual journey to Dachau. I left Wiesbaden in a Jerry-driven truck with all my luggage. The German driver sped to Frankfurt, with me consigning my soul to heaven all the way as he was a horrible driver who completely ignored the icy conditions. Somehow we made it to Frankfurt Station, which was still packed with servicemen of all nations.

I had a reservation on the Munich train but didn't expect to find a full colonel in my sleeping compartment for two. Just a slight error and I hastened to leave as he outranked me slightly. While sitting on my Val-Pak at the end of the car waiting for the Mitropa conductor to find me another room, a chicken colonel suddenly stopped to stare at me, then said, "So this is what my daughter's been going through in the Red Cross!"

"Oh, this is sheer luxury, sir," I replied. He stayed to entertain me until I was given another compartment, this time with a girl civilian working at the Nuremberg trials.

In true Red Cross tradition, no one met me in Munich, but I managed with cigarette tips and no German to check all my luggage and found the Hotel Excelsior, where I breakfasted. It's just across the street from the wreck of the Munich station. Finally made contact with Headquarters and was assigned to Dachau, about 17 kilometers from Munich. Louise, one of the Red Cross Club girls, drove me out, so I had time to try and absorb the sight of a city blown to bits. A light blanket of snow softened only a little the ugliness of burned-out building skeletons and rubble-strewn streets. All I could think of was how beautiful Munich must have been.

Soon after we left Munich behind, Louise pointed out a quaint Bavarian town climbing the hills to the left—the village of Dachau, she said—just before she turned right towards the camp, which sits only a few minutes down a level road. Dachau's main entrance is impressive, as its setting is almost parklike. Above the gates an imperial German eagle sits, still, with wings spread and talons clutching a swastika. Most Nazi insignias have been replaced by American flags and division pennants, but Nazi credos haven't been removed from many places. The entrance grille gate proclaims in wrought-iron lettering, *Arbeit Macht Frei* ("Work Makes One Free"), a favorite Nazi credo. We circled around to arrive at the side gates.

Know I've told you that we live in former SS guards' quarters. I share a room with a Red Cross Club girl who works different hours, so I have yet to talk to her for more than a few minutes. The whole place seems to have a black cloud over it—or perhaps it's the lingering insect spray odor of the DDT used to erase a typhus epidemic raging when the camp was freed. It gives me the willies to have to stay in a room and, especially, to sleep in a bed long used by SS guards or Waffen SS young zealots. I can't get it out of my mind.

It also takes effort to go to bed at night, as the orderly work here is done by DPs. Ours, named Ladislaus, strips my bed completely each morning, neatly folding up the blankets and sheets at the foot. This is the Hungarian way, and as he speaks no English, no one has succeeded in getting him to leave the beds made up between sheet launderings. I've tried pantomine, smiles, demonstrations, cigarette tips, but he just stares blankly at me and strips the bed each day. When I pile in at night, after remaking the bed, the rough Army blankets itch my skin. Always have thought I could sleep anywhere, but this is the most uncomfortable bed I've ever graced. The bed is a lumpy straw ticking mattress laid on a wooden base, so every time I move I sound like a horse chewing hay while pushing open a rusty gate.

The bathroom adjacent to our room is adequate, but I detest using a bathtub the SS used. I'm working on my attitude, but still find it loathsome. The bathtub is very plain, with a geyser heater attached to the wall above the tub faucets. The water heats quickly, but I simply can't bring myself to linger or soak.

Polish guards live in nearby billets and many Poles and other DPs come into our dugouts all the time. As you probably know, Dad, Dachau was Hitler's first

concentration camp, built back in the 1930s, where he sent thousands of dissenters of all nationalities and where countless slave laborers ended up. Some
were captured or drafted for labor so many years ago they walk around like zom-
bies. Many no longer know if they have any relative still living, I'm told, or any
family to return to. It's obvious they have lost all hope or joy in life.

I hadn't realized before that Dachau led the way in testing Hitler's race theories. The horror started here, even Heinrich Himmler trained here. The
thought is haunting and a pall clings to the area, at least for me. Especially as on
a sunny day I see all too clearly the quaintly Bavarian town of Dachau, not a
mile away, picturesquely climbing up the hills with the houses and apartments,
crosses and beet-shaped domes of churches glistening in the sun.

As far as I'm concerned, there's no way anyone in the town could have been
unaware of the smoke rising into the air from the chimneys of the crematorium
at the camp, and the smells drifting up with the black smoke. There's no way
they could avoid seeing work parties of skeletal prisoners in striped prison garb
filing along the roads around the camp. They must have seen the guards prod
them like animals, and shoot them or leave them beside the road if they dropped
on the way.

Even more depressing, as I try to fall asleep on my straw ticking, is the
thought that the German citizens I've seen in town, almost without exception,
look neat and tidy, plump and polite. Worse, they look like relatives of our family or friends of the family. They could be almost anyone I've seen in the States
or England or Canada. They are polite, correct is the word, some more than
civil. I can understand the resentment of any proud people after defeat in war.
But how, I keep asking myself, could this happen in a country that has produced
so much of beauty and worth to civilization? How could these villagers keep
silent? How could they not realize the paranoia and hate behind Hitler? Maybe
it's not the ticking in the mattress that keeps me awake.

I keep thinking about the genetic tests, the horrible medical experiments
and the extermination theories to purge the pure Aryans of Jews, Gypsies, and
political dissenters. The other larger camps designed to exterminate millions of
human beings developed only because of the experiments and training initiated
at Dachau. This is where the horror was learned, and perfected.

The fact that habitual criminals also were sent here along with thousands of
Jews and Gypsies and other non-Aryans—*plus* politicians, religious sect believ-
ers, freethinkers, Catholic priests from Poland, homosexuals—leads to a lot of
distrust of the DPs working around the camp. Our guys feel many of them are
criminals who worked more than willingly with the SS to execute Nazi orders.
Some of the Polish prisoners are reputed to have been especially zealous in
carrying out Nazi orders to obtain special privileges as *capos*, sub-bosses under
the SS. Others, of course, were simply slave laborers imported from all over
Europe as Hitler took over their countries, but at this point no one seems able to
tell the difference, so distrust is widespread.

The DPs wear GI garb and the first day or so I failed to notice their "flashes" (a patch designating origin, nationality, or status) and began to talk with them before realizing most don't speak English. But it's easy now for me to recognize the homeless and displaced. Even in GI garb, they're completely un-American in look and behavior—not open and friendly, like our guys. Most are gaunt of face with deep circles around haunted eyes and sullen expressions. No humor or laughter. Years of Nazi subjugation and exploitation have erased all expression from their faces and all expectations from their lives.

We eat at the Army Dachau mess just inside the side gates and a short walk from our quarters. Takes no more than three or four minutes. But as we have to pass the crematory near the railroad tracks en route, it's not a lovely way to start the day. So far all I've managed is a quick peek in the doorway at the first little anteroom where a table is piled with a collection of eyeglasses, shoes, and human hair. Every day I promise myself I'll make time to go through, but know I'll have to work up to it.

The mess is clean and German PWs wait on tables. I've never seen a more interesting collection of Aryan types, almost all of them handsome, blue-eyed, blond young men still proudly wearing their uniforms and caps as well as PW insignia. They're young Waffen SS types, serving our troops with a friendly smile. It makes me want to throw up as many of our young replacement troops are buying the Nazi line. They haven't a clue that these SS boys are the ones Hitler brought up through the German youth movement and instilled with his philosophy. These are the young Germans who dreamed of becoming Waffen Luffe members and were taught to tattle, even on their parents, if they wanted to be selected. I can't forget that a year ago they were willingly participating in prisoner torture and executions, with probably as much efficiency as they now serve meals to our troops.

Most of our replacement troops seem unaware of what these Hitler kids did. Right now the PWs have adjusted well to waiting on table as they wait to be sorted out for war crimes. They're making the most of this opportunity, by hard work and charm and efficiency, to ensure they'll be forgotten once the war crime trials are over and their records lost in the shuffle of DPs and the trials.

I'm working at the Karlsfield Dugout, the Red Cross Club on the road to Munich. It's next to the Karlsfield Ordnance Depot, a permanent installation and part of a ten-year building plan for the occupation. The dugout is luxurious. Called the Alpine Village, it is decorated in Bavarian manner and has a snack bar and all sorts of facilities for our guys to use, including a theater right next door. Knew it would be hard for me to switch to Club work as all my experience has been in Clubmobile, but I don't mind the change of pace as the dugout is a great listening post.

Luck once again has been with me, as there is wonderful morale among the troops, a welcome change after sensing the hostile atmosphere around Frankfurt. Most of the GIs I've met are specialists and there's no officer-GI antagonism or rank-pulling. Although a GI Club, all grades and ranks come in, mingle, and get along. So it's pleasant—I certainly can't call it work to listen and talk to the guys, play cards and checkers with them, sit with them in the movies, then listen to German orchestras and SS bands playing as we enjoy coffee and ice cream after the special movies each night. The Club is open from 10 AM to 10 PM and we're shorthanded this week so I'm working full-time.

The other night Lee, a young GI about twenty, drove me back to Dachau and invited me to look at his horses. He's in charge of the stables and had talked about the horses all evening. They're *gorgeous* high-spirited prize specimens appropriated by the Nazis from the Vienna Riding School for the use of SS officers at the camp. I spent forty minutes being personally introduced to thirty beautiful horses. Lee expected it. Now he and his sidekick Johnny, a GI working cowboy from Wyoming, want to teach me to ride. They have two skilled German PW Olympic trainers who manage the horses. It will be nice to learn, providing there's time.

If I can accept the atmosphere of Dachau, I can enjoy the work and put in my time until I take my leave and come home. I think the two will occur almost simultaneously. I'm glad to be in Third Army territory, too, as I have more confidence in its administration from what I've already seen. General Patton believed in setting up recreational activities to keep the GIs on the ball and troop morale as high as possible. So while there's much that's depressing here, there's much that's encouraging.

I'm so tired I must go to sleep. Goodnight. I love you all *so*.

Roses.

❦

Sunday night, Dachau
February 10, 1946

Dearest Family,

The mail situation remains lousy. Three letters from Bob got through, but so out of sequence it's hard to know much more about our plans than before. It's maddening to get so little mail and have it so scrambled. He misses me as much as I miss him. His divorce should be final in March and he's now taking a review course at his firm's home office in Massachusetts. I hope this week's mail will clear up where he'll be sent and if it will be possible for him to come west and marry me at home. We both prefer that option but realize he can't jeopardize his career by requesting time off too soon.

I've had a big job dumped on me by the Clubmobile head. It will last through the middle of March. The Third Army is holding basketball championships at Jubilee Hall in Munich from February 20 through March 17. General Truscott, commander of the Third Army, wants the Red Cross to serve coffee and doughnuts to at least 3,000 people each afternoon and night during the championships. Headquarters decided I was the one to coordinate the installation of kitchens, booths, and equipment, order cups and supplies, oversee the German help who will make the coffee, and schedule the twelve ARC girls for serving. I'll do this in the extra time from my Karlsfield job. I quickly requested Scud be sent down from 7th Army to help me organize the work. She should arrive any day now and boy, do I need her!

Gotta stop as I must write Bob.

Love,
Rosie

Journal   *February 10, 1946*

Just sent off a long letter to Bob about having dinner at the Dachau apartment of an American couple who came to Germany for a visit and got caught here when the war broke out. If I hadn't put so much mush in the letter I could have had Bob send the letter on home.

Jack, a GI technician and machinist, works with Fred, the American who got caught here with his wife Greta when war broke out. They are both originally from Brooklyn, so have a lot in common. Jack's dating my roommate, a Club girl from south Texas I barely know as we work different hours and only cross in passing. So I was quite surprised when she asked me to take her place and go to the dinner with him, as she had to work a Red Cross tour. I agreed, thinking it a chance to learn more about the feelings of the town residents about all the horror that had gone on so near them. I hoped it would help me gain perspective, perhaps even restore my peace of mind, which has been so missing these weeks in Germany.

The evening started out like old home week. Jack and I arrived at the apartment in a jeep loaded with gifts he'd rounded up—butter, coffee, sugar, flour, wines, a cake made by PWs, and the PX supplies I contributed: my liquor rations and a carton of cigarettes. Fred and Greta, plump and middle-aged, greeted us warmly and ushered us into a typically Bavarian apartment, complete with a window-boxed balcony looking out over part of the town and towards the concentration camp in the distance.

During dinner (American-style pot roast, Greta assured us) served in the dining room on their best lace tablecloth set with Rosenthal china, I concentrated on listening, only touched my lips to the wine when toasts to a quick return to the good old U.S.A. were made, and cautioned myself to hold off on direct questions. They came to spend the summer of 1938 in Germany, Fred said, and enjoyed it so much they stayed on for the winter. Yes, they had been very impressed with the new Germany. The cleanliness, the order, the efficiency. The new autobahns with play areas for picnicking, the Volkswagens (a nice little car people could afford), young children in uniformed groups hiking over the beautiful countryside, singing as they marched, the value of the German mark after the terrible inflation that followed the Great War. They simply waited too long to apply to return to the States, and then the war caught them.

Fueled by liberal pourings of wine and the drinks they enjoyed before, during, and after dinner, our hosts became expansive. I sipped coffee, sympathized with their plight, and asked an occasional tactful question while my mind raced with real questions: What new glories of the Third Reich was Hitler celebrating in 1938? Didn't you have any idea of what was happening in Dachau or of the Nazis' plan of an Aryan future for the world?

Once they trusted me to be a sympathetic listener, the truth spilled out. Right now it seems too big a load for my heart to hold, especially as I feel guilty for leading them on. Finally I got answers so honest they made me sick.

Yes, they had considered becoming Germans again, which is why they stayed on another year. During the war Fred worked a lathe at a small Messerschmidt plant in town, making airplane parts and screws. Yes, there were camp inmates who worked at the plant, hundreds, but they were dirty and sick and not very efficient. They often slumped over their work and the guards dragged them away. They didn't last long. Nazi troopers rode them hard—even the Germans, Fred complained. That's why it was hard to help one Dachau inmate who worked alongside him and was smart and efficient. But he grew weaker each day. Fred liked the poor bastard and felt so sorry for him he himself risked being caught to slip the man an occasional apple or half a sandwich from his own lunch. He had to be very careful, as it was dangerous. He'd put half a sandwich on his machine then slide it down for the guy to pick up. He could only do that maybe once a week when guards weren't hovering, or he would have been arrested by the SS. The man didn't last long anyway, Fred sighed. One day he was just gone.

Trying to change the subject, Greta asked about my Red Cross duties, then told me about her work for the German Red Cross. Said she sewed and made bandages for the wounded—even prisoners, she added proudly—with other women of the town at the home of the camp commandant. His wife gathered the town ladies right in her lovely house to do the work.

I gasped in surprise and it came out. "You knew her?" Greta jumped up and led me out to the balcony to point out a nearby rooftop.

"See, the house is very near, Rosie. She is a dear friend and a fine lady. Although," she added, frowning, "she's not there now. I can't imagine where they've taken her, or why, as she's a real nice person."

My guard came down. I had to know. "What about her lamps? Did you see them?"

"Oh, the whole house is lovely. Why do you ask?"

We stood in the cold on that balcony and I told her as calmly as I could manage that the commandant's wife was reported to use lamps with shades made from the finest skin of executed camp inmates. The word around the camp was that prisoners with especially fine skin were sent to be exterminated more quickly.

She was absolutely unbelieving and led me back in to have her husband confirm that this was a lie, that it couldn't be so. He did, of course, and I didn't believe a word. That's when I told Jack it was very late, and I'd like a drink now before we had to return to camp. I joined them in a brandy from crystal snifters. It kept me from crying for the whole human race and gave me courage to ask about the last days. The rest of the story flooded out.

Things only got worse when Hitler's plans failed and the war turned bad, Fred explained, his eyes tearing up. He and Greta realized they'd been misled, but there was nothing he could do. We had to understand how it had been, with food supplies running out, increasing bombings, and the final indignity, when, after U.S. troops took over the camp, General Eisenhower ordered all the local citizens to go through the camp. They were forced to help load all the corpses strewn over the camp on wagons. They even had to remove rotting corpses from freight cars sitting at the side gate of the camp. The cars had remained locked in the station for three days after arriving from Buchenwald because the SS fled before the rapidly approaching U.S. troops. The townspeople were ordered to pull the loaded wagons back to town and up a hill, then help dig a pit so the corpses could be buried in the town park that was to become a monument.

"I tried to explain that we were American citizens," Fred almost sobbed. "That we were here against our will and not Nazis, that we had no idea conditions were so bad in the camp. But nobody listened and we had to do it. But what could we have done? We had no choice and had to make the best of things. It's been very hard."

It was past midnight and I knew more than I was prepared to hear. I stood up to remind everyone that I had to be in Munich in the morning and dragged Jack away from his friends. On the short ride back to camp, he rambled on about poor Fred and Greta and all they'd been through. I did manage a polite goodnight before jumping out of the jeep and running into my quarters. Then I threw up.

Chapter Twenty-Three

Dachau
February 11, 1946

Dearest ones,

Scud is here and I've never seen a girl happier to arrive anywhere. Buschlag is full of dissension for many reasons, with a nasty undercurrent everywhere. The Army unit in Buschlag moved out, but the Red Cross girls stayed on in their billets as they were centrally located for Clubmobiling. Scud tells me the telephone wires to the house were cut twice and they received threatening phone calls—just "Beware" in a guttural German voice.

The end of March should see me set to go home and get to the States sometime in April. Yes, that's right. I'm planning to resign right after my leave. Think you'll agree that's the right time to return, as it will be spring and Bob will be settled in his job. Oh, you know all the reasons. I'm thrilled just thinking of it. Won't it be marvelous to be together again?

Goodnight, I love you all.

XXXX
Roses

Journal   *Dachau, February 11, 1946*

It's such a joy to have Scud around. She's a real antidote for the depressed feelings that keep threatening to overwhelm me here at camp. I've felt like a yo-yo ever since entering Germany, my emotions changing from one minute to the next.

When mail arrives I'm happier than I've ever been just looking ahead to the future. Bob's love shining through his letters makes my spirits soar. I see again his bright blue eyes, that wry and knowing smile, and find myself humming our song, "Please walk alone, and send your love and your kisses to guide me, 'til you're walking beside me." And letters from Sis and my family are a real tonic—newsy, upbeat, caring, full of the normal. I smile just thinking of their joy when they finally get to meet Bob and know him as I do—and realize why I chose him. They've never mentioned it but surely

Rosie and Scud, Dachau, February 1946.

they sometimes wonder if I've been swept into an unlikely romance because of the war. I can hardly wait to bring him home.

But in between these high spots, the horror of Dachau, the lingering Nazi attitudes of most of the people, their fear of and obedience to orders after years of living in the Third Reich, the whole enigma of this ruined country make it hard for me to keep giving everyone that sincere Red Cross smile. So often I feel like weeping. Once in a while I do.

⁂

Journal   February 16, 1946

Working with Germans in setting up Red Cross services in the Deutsches Museum is a real eye-opener. Today I had to fire one of the Germans as he's been stealing small amounts of our flour and sugar supplies—a small sack or so at a time, some butter, some eggs. Three Germans reported his thefts and I confronted him. His English is poor, but other German workers vied to curry my favor by translating.

I feel sure he was honest in the story he told. He's an architect, one of those most involved in building the Deutsches Museum, this great temple to Nazi glory. His demeanor is that of an educated man, a man of dignity, his story that he only stole supplies for his wife and children because of their hunger. He showed me their pictures, with tears in his eyes. He is one of the most efficient German workers here. Of course I let him go but, having bought his family story, didn't turn him over for prosecution. I keep reviewing that decision. Was I gullible?

What stuns me is how eagerly other German workers grab my arm to report infractions and carry tales about each other. Since starting this job, it's been an almost daily occurrence. Scud and I keep wondering if a nation of tattletales is the result of years of living under a dictator. It's not an endearing quality to an American.

≈≈✦≈≈

Hotel Excelsior (what's left of it, that is)
Munich, Tuesday, February 19, 1946, 10 PM

Dears,

The days slip by too rapidly with this Munich job, the Dachau work still requiring time plus trying to write to you and Bob.

We've moved into "town" temporarily to supervise the Red Cross part of the games and the girls (twenty German frauleins, six German men, two GIs, eight ARC girls) and supplies needed to serve thousands daily and nightly. Billed as The European Theater Basketball Tournament, it is to be held at Jubilee Hall, which is actually the Congress Hall of Munich's famous Deutsches Museum, site of many famous Nazi meetings. Allied bombing destroyed much of the hall but it's been rebuilt to provide a pavilion for the championships. Lieutenant General Truscott, commanding the Third Army, pushed through this temporary restoration to provide a competition site for Allied teams from all over Europe—the 1st Infantry, 78th Infantry, 3rd Infantry, 508th Parachute Infantry Regiment, the Bremerhaven Navy Base. The list goes on. And to provide wholesome entertainment for the occupation troops.

I'm sending along this cable from Bob because it's so exciting. He's to be sent to Chicago! Imagine your younger daughter, Rosie, living right where all trains meet, a perfect stopover for all of you. I'm thrilled for Bob, as Chicago, he says, is a darn good territory for a sales representative. Eventually we may end up on the West Coast, as Bob wants that too. I was surprised he was assigned so quickly because I thought he'd have to be in Massachusetts longer. His letter yesterday was full of good news. His boss called him in to say he'd been reconsidering the salary arrangement and decided Bob ought to have $25 more a month to begin. He also told him to include all travel expenses in his expense account. After five years away in the Army he starts out with a good salary ($225 a month) plus expenses, plus a car, plus commissions. It's not what he made in the Army but it's a start towards a career—I don't think it will take him long to get crackin', as the Brits say.

I am already looking forward to being home in April, won't that be perfect? Sis, maybe I'll get home in time to go north with Mom and help deliver *Rosemary*, if you're still determined to have a girl so you can name her after me.

Goodnight. I love you all. Can you believe it? I'll be twenty-seven on Friday!

Roses

≈≈✦≈≈

Journal

Munich, February 19, 1946

What an amazing week this is turning out to be. I came up to Headquarters to get my marching orders, then checked into the Excelsior ahead of Scud as she had to be at the dugout until tonight. The facade of the hotel doesn't look bad compared to the ruined buildings all around and the rubble, some piles two stories high, stacked neatly off the street in the bombed-out areas. The entrance has cracked panes of glass taped together, but a doorman is on duty, making it seem almost normal. The help is polite, correct is the word, dressed in well-worn black jackets with a grayish tinge, as though sprinkled with rubble dust. There is an elevator with an operator. When the elevator door opened, my jaw dropped as he's a dead ringer for Hitler, mustache and all.

Our room is bare but neat and I was glad to have time to unpack and bathe before Scud arrived. The porter had indicated a door down the hall as the bathroom—or at least I thought that's what he pointed out. Once unpacked I walked to the bathroom door and pulled it open. A blast of freezing air and snowflakes hit me in the face and I stared out at snow swirling down a sheer dropoff to heaped rubble three stories below. Luckily, I was juggling pajamas, robe, towel, and toilet articles so hadn't rushed through the door. Obviously one section of the hotel had been bombed away entirely.

I slammed the door and leaned against it, in shock as I realized I had almost stepped out into space. Then cautiously I explored the hall further until I found the right door into a damaged but large room with big tub and hot water. As I soaked I mulled over the possibility of that door to nowhere being a Nazi booby trap. About then I became aware of whispering, or was it chuckles? I looked up and around the room and spotted rough little peepholes in the wall. Casually, I hoped, I reached for my towel, rose dripping from the tub, and threw on my robe to flee back to my room, almost in panic. I dried off in the room, after struggling unsuccessfully to lock my door from the inside.

Sure was relieved when Scudder finally showed up and I had a chance to fill her in on the facts of life in the Hotel Excelsior.

WESTERN UNION

MCH47/17 INDIANAPOLIS ING 17 17
NLT ROSEMARY LANGHELDT
ARC CLUBMOBILE 3RD ARMY
APO 403 MUNICH

HAPPY BIRTHDAY DARLING   I LOVE YOU   BOB

February 23, 1946—11:30 PM

Dearest ones,

Last night Scud made me drive out to Dachau with her after we finished work to walk in on a big surprise party for me—Pat and Alice down from Töging, all the

GI stable boys, all the crew, two beautiful and luscious birthday cakes made by the PWs, champagne, and candlelight. What a lovely surprise!

Today, I received two long letters from Bob. The Chicago job is a big opportunity, he'll have his own territory and the chance to advance more rapidly. So off we go to Chicago! Bob's very eager for us to get married (who *isn't?*) and hopes I can come in March. I can't make that because of this Munich job, but sometime in April looks possible. Yippee! Bob wants me to stop in Chicago and go to Indianapolis with him to meet his folks and decide on a date to get married.

Then I'll fly home with time to get organized and maybe even go to Seattle for the arrival of Marty's new baby. Won't it be nice, me living in Chicago where you can get to us so easily? After being separated by thousands of miles for so long, Chicago will be like being in the next room—with the door always open.

Goodnight. It's terribly late and I must write Bob and tell him he's wonderful.

All my love—XXXXX—WRITE OFTEN
Roses

❦

Journal   *February 23, 1996*

This is worth foregoing ten minutes of sleep as I'll smile all night remembering Bob's report on his weekend trip to Moosup to see Tom and Ski and meet her family. He was greeted warmly and they had packs of fun. He loved them all and is tickled pink at the way Tom's adjusting to the New England lifestyle. Tom keeps the family in stitches, calls Ski's dad "Father Seaton," and even wore a matching outfit to male members of the clan. I gather New England weekends-in-the-country these days call for gray flannel slacks and tweed jacket, with a knit tie, of course. Tom's entering the University of Kentucky soon to finish his college degree, hooray!

❦

Munich
Wed. night, February 27, 1946

Dearest ones,

Tonight I have something special. Living at the Excelsior we eat at the Officers Mess here at the hotel. A meal at this transient mess is the best way possible to observe first-hand a cross-section of postwar problems. We sit with all ranks in all services and tonight we were introduced to a Dutch army colonel. Colonel Vorenkamp is a Smith professor of art who heads the Netherlands Art Mission, here to sort out Dutch art from all the treasures looted by the Nazis. He's a short man with a heart-shaped face, the nicest man you can imagine. He invited us to come over to the huge and still intact Nazi Finance Building, where the art is stored, to see his work.

We were thrilled, as it is next to impossible to get into that building because there are millions, rather billions, of dollars worth of art cached there. Naturally, we arrived on the dot of 2, the time he suggested. This building is the only unharmed one in the largest Nazi square in Munich. It was here that the sixteen bodies of the Nazis executed in the *Putsch* were enshrined by Hitler. The Finance Building is just around the corner from the rubble heap that is all that remains of the Brown House, where Hitler worked.

Colonel Vorenkamp first showed us some of the articles to be returned to the Netherlands. He's been working since last September and is just finishing the identification of the Felix Mannheimer collection. In one large room were gorgeous objets d'art such as I've never seen anywhere, smaller ones literally heaped on tables for sorting. We also saw positive abortions (as we say in the retail trade): solid gold camels with ruby eyes, worth a fortune if you could stand them collecting dust; a small gold pair of scissors overdecorated with pearls; precious objects of Cellini mixed in with all sorts of figurines, vases, bowls, cups, and religious objects. All are so encrusted with rubies, pearls, sapphires, emeralds, and diamonds it is impossible to fathom the wealth involved. One set of six rock crystal bowls and goblets trimmed with gold and jewels is valued at over a half million dollars.

The vast building is loaded, literally, with art objects, the smaller ones packed in wicker baskets (then dumped in heaps on tables for sorting). The detective work involved in identifying and separating collections is voluminous and demanding. Missions from each of the Allies work together in the building, cooperating to reclaim their own collections.

The Nazis seized the entire Mannheimer collection when they invaded Holland. They even removed the paneling and ceiling from the Mannheimer home. The collection is actually worth $11 million. Hitler offered $7 million from captured Dutch funds. He cached the collection in a monastery in Bavaria, after trumping up charges to have all the monks removed to make room for the collection.

There has never been such an aggregation of art in one place before. We're so fortunate to see it before it's shipped back to all the countries the Nazis looted. Barbara Hutton was due to visit yesterday too, but we didn't wait to see her arrive. We were too engrossed tagging along after the colonel as he took us into room after room, floor after floor, loaded with treasures.

In one storage area thousands of paintings are racked up—Rubens, Titian, El Greco, Van Gogh, Holbein, Cézanne, Rembrandt, Velasquez. Mention any great name in painting and there are examples. The colonel told us fascinating stories about some of them. Velasquez's *Portrait of an Amsterdam Burgomeister*, for example, bought the lives of twenty-six Jews. The art collector who owned it gave it to Hitler in exchange for twenty-six passports to Switzerland for his family. Now it will be returned to him. Such sweet justice *finally*.

Yesterday was our day off so we squeezed in the ARC tour of Munich to see where everything had been. No joke. "Those are the walls of the eleventh-century church, world famous as the oldest church in Munich." Or, the guide pointing to a heap of chimneys and rubble, "This was the Gestapo headquarters of all Germany." Munich was bombed sixty-nine times and some people will never forget it—like the little old lady of about eighty who stuck her tongue out at us when she spotted our American Red Cross jeep. Who could?

Goodnight. I love you all,

Roses

✿

Journal   February 27, 1946

The old lady who stuck out her tongue and thumbed her nose at us (that I didn't mention in my letter) is haunting me. I stopped the jeep to let her cross the street near the Deutsches Museum and Scud and I were admiring her trim, black-clad figure and her tidily arranged white hair as she pulled along a battered child's wagon piled with salvage. She was walking, tiny but erect, when she glanced over to see the American insignia on our jeep and reacted with anger.

Scud and I smiled and waved at her, agreeing that she might be any of our older relatives if war had shattered our country. The woman's reaction is exactly how some of our better-loved relatives might react to conquerors of the United States. We're betting the proud little lady probably ignored Hitler, too, as just another crazy politician. We'll always wonder.

✿

Munich
February 28, 1946

Dearest Family,

Today's been a wonderfully springlike day and my heart is so happy as Bob wrote he's trying to get time off to come west to be married. I hadn't asked him, as I know he doesn't have time off coming so soon after starting back to work. For him to suggest it makes me very happy, as you know how I'd love to be married in Berkeley, at home.

Scud and I have laughed a lot about war's absurdities. Today, for example. The Burgobraukellar, where Hitler started his party and where he came every year to make a speech on the anniversary of the party's founding, is now a Red Cross Club. Every morning Rosie or Scud jeeps over to this Nazi holy of holies to pick up 3,000 doughnuts for the boys at Jubilee Hall! The big barnlike hall where the bomb exploded during the party rally (it was meant for Hitler and would have killed him if he hadn't left early) has now been turned into a basketball court by the Yanks.

Isn't it strange that almost all of my recollection of these historic places will forever be tied up with coffee and doughnuts?

Goodnight. I love you so.

Roses

Munich
March 3, 1946

Dearest ones,

You asked about a ring, Mom. No, I haven't an engagement ring yet as I didn't want Bob to buy one here. Even though diamonds are cheaper in England, there's a terrific tax on them and we didn't have time to select one anyway. When he left he gave me the gold class ring he always wears. It was given him when he was president of the senior class and he prizes it sentimentally. I've worn it ever since as it helps me get out of dating gracefully. I've already tried to talk him into skipping an engagement ring, as I'd hate a cheap one and I don't want him to spend too much getting a good one. I'd just as soon wait until we're successful. Mom, these things are so unimportant. As the Germans say, "It's igal," either way and I don't want him to be extravagant now but he's like you and keeps mentioning it.

Yesterday I talked to the head of the Clubmobile department who was very nice and urged me to stay on. Said the Red Cross is cutting overseas personnel from 2,800 to 800 immediately, but they want to keep the outstanding people. I thanked her for the compliment and told her I wanted to go home and be married. She agreed that is a good reason and we figured out this: as soon as the ETO basketball championships are over, Scud, Pat, Alice, and I are off on the Rome-Swiss tour, which is ten days plus travel time. The day after we get back, I'll start on the other week's leave due me, probably to Denmark. Then I come back to pick up my luggage and report in to Paris on *April 15th* for shipment home. How long it will be from Paris to New York I don't know, but it shouldn't be an undue delay. I may arrive home with Sis's new baby, so please tell me Marty's due date quick!

Keep writing for goodness' sake. I'll cable you when it's time to stop.

I love you all sooo much.
Roses

Munich, 1:30 PM
March 4, 1946

Dearest ones,

Mom, no, I'm not in the least worried about Bob's future as I haven't a doubt in the world as to his ability. Neither will you when you meet him as he's wonderfully capable and ambitious. I've told you all the details because we were trying to figure out all the angles. As to my working or not working, that's unimportant at this point. I *loved* my career and certainly will resume it when the time is right. Right now, the important thing is for Bob and me to get married and started on our life together. Never fear, we'll have packs of fun doing anything at all as long as we're together.

His letter today was full of enthusiasm for his new job and his boss. I'd live under a bridge with Bob and love it, if we had to, and we may be doing exactly that. Bob is spending every spare moment, following every lead, and all apartment houses have waiting lists of over one hundred. The wives of the other men in the office are searching too, so with this much time surely something will turn up. Bob says the company has a brand new car ordered for him, as soon as cars start rolling off the production lines.

Must close. Tonight the big banquet is being held for all the basketball players, with General Truscott present to hand out the trophies. We're all going to sit with our favorite teams.

All my love,
Rosie

Hotel Excelsior, Munich
March 8, 1946

Dearest ones,

Scud and I attended the basketball banquet for division team winners with our team and had a steak (oh so small) and champagne. After the banquet and speeches we got about thirty GIs together and took them over to the Burgobraukellar mardi gras celebration. If only Hitler could have seen the originating spot of his beloved Nazi Party, its very birthplace, jammed with GIs on the carousel, dancing and testing their weight, having their fortunes told, and throwing baseballs at cans.

Tuesday, still between series, Scud and I drove to Töging to see Pat and Alice, stayed overnight there, then we all drove to Berchtesgaden by way of Austria. We talked our way in and out of the international border as we wanted to see Salzburg, whose beauty can't be exaggerated. Luck was with us, as we saw it on a gorgeously clear day, the Castle Hohensalzburg overshadowing the whole town. The streets are so narrow our jeep could scarcely pass through some of them. We hurried on to Berchtesgaden, also breathtakingly beautiful.

The town was blanketed in snow and the colorful houses with murals and stone-dotted roofs sparkled in the sunshine. Our big thrill was yet to come when we were billeted in the Berchtesgadenerhof, one of the finest hotels in Germany, where Hitler's staff stayed when they came to visit him. Pat and I had a huge double room with a 7-foot long bed, single mattresses set in a double frame. And, of course, those wonderful down comforters. The rose rugs, draperies, and furniture were lovely and our balcony opened onto the terrace. From the balcony the Watzmann seemed a stone's throw. It's a magnificent mountain.

In a happy frame of mind we jeeped off to Hitler's Retreat—the Berghof and the Eagle's Nest. On such a lovely day we failed to consider that the mountain roads were still nearly impassable. One-half hour of front-wheel driving and

Ruins of Hitler's hideout at Berchtesgaden, March 1946.

View from the Berghof, March 1946.

many a sweat later we stalled on a 6-foot-wide, 90-degree-angle road. Somehow we turned the jeep around. I put blankets under the wheels, had the girls get out of the way, and skidded the jeep around to face down. Whew! We left it beside an alpine house below.

Undaunted, we decided to climb the rest of the way on foot. This proved especially difficult as we were dressed in Class A uniforms but luckily wore our topcoats, scarves, mittens, and fleece-lined boots.

Two hours later we had the panting, gasping reward of standing at what had been the huge window of Hitler's Berghof and surveying the breathtaking view of the mountains and all that remains of the ruins of Goering, Goebbels, and

Bormann's neighboring homes. In the dark tunnel leading to the lift to the Eagle's Nest, people (mostly GIs) have initialed their names everywhere. In one spot, splashed in white paint against a blackened wall is the plea, "Oh God, give us back our Fuehrer." It's signed by the Hitler Youth Movement. I took pictures of everything, before we all slipped back down the mountain (much easier) to our jeep.

Mom, this Berchtesgaden Hotel sticker is to add to the collection on your suitcase.

All my love,
Roses

Munich, March 14, 1946, 10:45 PM

Dearest ones,

Just heard from Bob that he has a room in Oak Park, Illinois, so at least he's not sleeping in the street. He's contacting every source for an apartment. If the housing doesn't improve, my cooking may prove adequate. I'm a whiz at cooking eggs on rocks or pigs in saddles around a campfire in the high Sierras, as you well know. The problem is, we won't be camping in the high Sierras.

This week has been busy with the European basketball championships and the odds and ends I'm trying to get done so I can move fast when the time comes. The First Division Team (Third Army champions) have adopted Scud and me. They're a nice clean-cut bunch, have two former Illinois Whiz Kids on the team. Scud's been dating one of the players, a tall, handsome corporal. The other night Van, the corporal, begged me to come along with them to the GI nightclub here, "The American Way," with Montgomery, who wanted a date with me. When I found out Montgomery is nineteen I agreed to go and he is the nicest little (6 feet, 1 inch) boy from the Philadelphia Main Line. He's very handsome and very shy. We had a fun evening, dancing and eating ice cream, until 9:30 when the team had to get back to quarters. The team took us back to the Excelsior in style in the team bus. They're sweet kids, Grandma said, dropping her knitting.

I love you all soooo much and just think, I'll soon be home.

All my love,
Roses

Munich, March 15, 1946 11:15 PM

Dears—

We've had a sudden and extensive change of plans. Our orders were suddenly canceled for the Swiss-Rome tour. There's some billeting trouble in Rome and rumors that the pope is not well and has canceled audiences. We're all disappointed, especially about Rome. The Bavarian alp country seems a charming Switzerland without watches so that loss is easy to face. But I did want to see Rome—not enough, however, to wait around another month instead of coming home.

In the midst of our disappointment we were told we could go on the Denmark tour, leaving tomorrow night. Isn't that marvelous? Maybe we can talk our way into Sweden, we're already discussing that. It should be lots of fun with Scud, Alice, and Pat.

This change could mean I can start home earlier in April than I hoped as I may be sent into Paris soon after the conclusion of the trip.

I'll write often on the trip. Right now I must pack—but quick!

Goodnight. All my love to all of you,

Roses

Chapter Twenty-Four

Dearest ones,

Here we are in Denmark, country of castles. It took awhile to get here because Germany's a very large country. It's a constant surprise sightseeing in Germany using Scud's *Satchell Guide of Europe*, published in 1938. The guide states that Frankfurt Central Station is the finest station in Europe. You should see it now—no roof, not many walls, just remnants.

At 6 AM we arrived in Bremen and after checking into the leave center had the day to see the city. Although terribly bombed in strategic areas, much of the central part looks better off than other German cities I've seen. We wandered along the Weser River, had ice cream sundaes at the PX, dutifully saw Bremen Cathedral. It left me cold—very uninteresting and forbidding.

Our evening was spent processing (Army term) for the tour, changing money, and getting lots of information, most of which seems to be dire warnings. I'm enclosing the one on VD for your edification, and tossing some others, which also added considerably to our knowledge of the ways of the world:

HEADQUARTERS BREMEN PORT COMMAND
APO 751

To All Troops Going to Denmark

The average VD rate for American troops returning from Denmark is 204.04 per 1000 per year.

This rate is considerably higher than the overall enclave rate.

The Danish Government is doing its utmost to control VD, but all troops entering Denmark are urged to remember that the VD menace is great.

If you find you have VD on reaching Denmark report promptly to a medical dispensary.

If while in Denmark you choose to be promiscuous, remember
  a. Army prophylaxis
  b. Get her name and address.

ARTHUR J. RICKER
Captain MC
BPC VD Control Officer

We arrived at our hotel here in time for a late lunch and each had a bottle of milk at our places! Thick, creamy pasteurized milk. If you wonder what I'm doing in Denmark, the answer is drinking milk. My teeth feel better already.

Aside from the fact that this old wooden hotel is on a fjord instead of an inlet and that everyone looks Danish, I can't believe I'm here. We took a walk after lunch and it reminded Scud of Cape Cod and me of Carmel on a foggy, drippy, relaxing kind of day. We love being near the sea again. Tomorrow we go on to Copenhagen, our pockets full of kronen in case we feel like shopping.

All my love, foggedly and relaxedly—the four of us seem always to be tired!

Roses

❦

Copenhagen, March 24, 1946, 8 PM

Dearest ones,

After five days of Copenhagen I am sitting in our hotel room, stuffed and happy, listening to the lovely Rathaus chimes strike the hour and trying to rally my satiated brains enough to tell you about these past days.

Wednesday we left Kollund and took the train from Padborg to Copenhagen, an all-day trip that includes ferrying via a boat train to the island Copenhagen sits on. We arrived in Copenhagen about 4:30 and I felt happy just walking through the railroad station to our buses. The station is clean and light, with beautiful woodwork, so unlike any I've seen these past two years. The city is beautifully maintained and many of the buildings are modern. Not garish modern but a quiet, more livable modern with lots of space, many windows. The period buildings are most impressive, with centuries-old copper roofs glowing green in the sun. Here variety blends well, providing character without shabbiness.

The shops are wonderful and when I think back on Copenhagen I will always remember *food*—gorgeous cuts of meat, milk—at least a bottle a meal—creme puffs, more milk, ice cream sundaes, milk, ice cream (*creamy* delicious ice cream), whipped cream—gobs of it on everything—and naturally, Danish pastries every time we stop for breath. I will forever recall the four of us eating, sightseeing and eating, just eating. We've all gained pounds.

We took a day tour up the coast to Frederiksborg Castle. One-time residence of the Danish kings, it's a museum now and we climbed all over it and gave it a high rating. We lunched in Elsinore, Hamlet's hometown, then went on to Kronberg Castle. We even paced the ramparts on a suitably foggy day, looking for Hamlet's father's ghost. Sweden, just two and a half miles across the channel, of course, remained invisible.

Friday evening we arrived early for dinner at a famous seafood restaurant on Copenhagen's marvelous working canal. Krog's, world-famous for its lobster, looks as though it's always been there—with clean tables and white cloths, waiters in traditional garb, black coats, white shirts, and aprons and towel. Pat and Scud took so long eating lobster we had to rush to the Royal Theatre for the ballet.

We were barely seated when the packed house hushed and King Christian X and his Queen entered the royal box. The King fell from his horse and injured his leg during the German occupation so had to be wheeled to his box. This was their first public appearance since the liberation of Denmark. The house went wild and stood to applaud in tribute to their stubborn courage during the long occupation, as they nodded graciously all around.

I'm afraid I've had it, as the British say. All the castles, palaces, and tours of these past days are starting to blur and run together. But I'll not forget us all walking into another impressive room to stare in surprise at a wall filled with portraits of modern European royalty. The two largest were of Victoria and her consort, Albert. Grouped around were the other royal families—Kaiser Wilhelm, Nicholas and Alexandra, the deposed monarchs of Greece and Spain and the Balkans. The family resemblances are striking as they were all related. It made us wonder if some of the wars of this century began as family quarrels that got out of hand.

Tomorrow's our last day here. We've enjoyed every minute, but I can hardly wait to get the long trip back to Munich over with and see how soon I'll be starting home. I have a feeling that before you receive this I will have cabled you that I've started—hurrah!

Goodnight, I love you all,

Roses

❧

Copenhagen
March 26, 1946

Dears,

I've so much to bring home it's a worry. The girls have kidded all week about giving me a Copenhagen kitchen shower as there's fascinating new stuff in the shops. They said it's high time I learned to cook and relished the idea of me struggling with kitchen utensils on the long return to Munich. I hoped they were joking. Tonight I found out they weren't and ended up with a big clunky Danish eggbeater, tools, spatulas, *and* a wooden and pottery condiment set to match the Danish salad plates I bought. It is darling, much too attractive to leave, but very heavy—just as they planned. They sat around giggling and making snide remarks even as I struggled to cram more into my already overloaded Val-Pak. Who else has friends like these?

I've had a terminal case of sea-level hair so today I got a permanent at the Elizabeth Arden Salon. I tried to explain to the Danish girl to take it easy on the heat. She was lovely but spoke not a word of English. The only Danish I've learned this week is *Tak*, which means thank you, and *Trysk* and *Traack*, signs appearing on swinging doors. One means push and one pull and I'm always doing the wrong one. You can see that the permanent wave girl and I didn't have a very extensive conversation. But, happy day, I got a nice wave and am ready to come home.

Must pack. I'll write when I can. Imagine! I'm almost on my way and I'm thrilled to death. I love you all and soon I'll be *home*.

Roses

Chapter Twenty-Five

WESTERN UNION

1946 MAR 29 PM 3

VLT THE LANGHELDTS
BERKELEY (CALIF)

STOP WRITING   LEAVE APRIL SECOND FOR PARIS TO CLEAR
WILL CABLE SAILING DATE   HAPPY BIRTHDAY MOTHER DEAR
LOVE   ROSES

Dachau, Saturday
March 30, 1946—3 PM

Dearest ones,

Yesterday I cabled you the unbelievable news—I'm coming home. I've been rushing around packing and doing the million things there are to do and not believing for a minute I'm actually coming. I keep pinching myself. Tuesday evening, the 2nd, I take the night train to Frankfurt. The morning of the 3rd I'll be in Wiesbaden to clear and see Lil and Kari for a few hours. Probably the 3rd or 4th I'll clear again, perhaps from Paris, then go on to Le Havre. I won't have the exact sailing date until I arrive in Paris but will cable when it's confirmed.

Once in New York, and I can hardly believe I'm saying this, I'll call you as soon as I get to a hotel. I'll have to spend two or three days there clearing for the last time. May have time to touch base with Ski and Tom in Moosup and Aunt Stella and family in Pittsburgh. Bob will meet me in Chicago to go visit his family in Indianapolis. Won't decide times definitely until I arrive in New York. Know once I land I'll have a great urge to rush home, with only a stop in Chicago for Bob and his family.

Lots of mail was waiting for me yesterday, including your two letters, Mom, mentioning Dad's letter to me about how you scattered Clipper's ashes over the backyard. I haven't gotten Dad's letter yet but so regret the loss of one of the boys. I've been looking forward to seeing the dogs for a long time as they're such an important part of my dreams of home. Clippie certainly had a long, lovely life though, didn't he?

We'll take stock of the new-baby situation when I arrive in New York. Mom, if you're in Seattle for the birth of Marty's baby, I can return to Berkeley, pick up Dad, and we'll go to Seattle for ringside seats for the event. We'll work it out.

Isn't spring the perfect time to come back? Suddenly it's heavenly weather here, and has been all the way from Copenhagen. The snow has disappeared from the ground, the grass is coming up new and green. I'll be in Paris when the chestnuts are in bloom. I'll call Jean Sherman to reserve us a table at a sidewalk cafe under a blooming tree—for the 15 minutes I'll probably have free while clearing!

When Jean came through Southampton last year, lugging her guitar, she looked the same as when we first met in our teens, with that Dutch-cut black and lustrous hair, flawless skin and teeth, and lovely eyes and smile. She was en route to the continent to join a Red Cross entertainment unit. We promised to meet at a sidewalk cafe. Now perhaps we can!

Happy birthday, Mom. All my love. Here I come!

Rosie

Journal   *April 2, 1946—Night train to Frankfurt*

I sit here staring out the window, sad at leaving Scud and Pat and Alice, wondering when we'll meet again. In the midst of my joy at going home I'm feeling desolate at this special time ending. I've been so busy with my plans I forgot about the necessary good-byes, and I've always hated them. We swore to get together, no matter how far apart, to keep in touch no matter where we all end up. Our banter was light, but my voice wasn't the only one that cracked as they laughed me onto the train, lugging the extra heavy bundle of Copenhagen shower gifts. We all realize this time never will come again.

I'm sure Alice will resume her radio work in St. Louis after she finishes her tour of duty. Pat and Scud are footloose and well matched. They'll stay as long as there's work to be done. Both share wry wit, a zest for life, great intellectual curiosity. I can't see them hurrying back to careers they can resume anytime. But I do see us managing to meet from time to time in odd convenient places when we can arrange it, and taking up in the middle of a sentence. I pray life turns out that way—for wartime friendships made when the world is upside down are like no others in the world.

Normandie Hotel, Paris
Midnight Sunday, April 7, 1946

Dears,

A tiny note as I'm dead tired and on my last sheet of paper. Dope is, we go to Le Havre Wednesday and if lucky should sail within two or three days.

I turned down a leave in Switzerland and also one to Nice and Cannes, both surprisingly easy to refuse as I feel like a soaked-up blotter at this point, oversaturated with experiences. Besides, taking my leave time would delay sailing about three weeks, so Bob will just have to bring me back in about twenty years. I've discovered that, once packed and all mail stops, the United States looks more inviting than anywhere else in the world. More important, I don't feel it fair to ask Bob to wait for me forever and I'd like to get back before Sis's new baby arrives.

I've seen Jean Sherman and her French friend, Charlotte. They made Paris in the spring even more memorable than it's reputed to be. Will try to report when I scrounge more paper. Have been knocking myself out seeing all I can squeeze in before clearing Wednesday—today it was a day tour to Fountainbleau with a busload of servicemen.

I'm so excited at the thought of home.

> All my love,
> Rosie

❦

Journal   The Ritz, Place Vendôme, Paris
                                                        April 9, 1946

What a way to wind up an unforgettable week in Paris! I was requested to move to the Ritz, right here in the heart of the city—this hotel famous for Chanel and its bar, a hotel I've read about all my life. I still haven't a clue why I was chosen but it's probably because the Normandie's crammed full and I'm traveling alone.

While waiting for my room to be ready, I summoned courage to seat myself at a small window table in the bar. I started to order a Coke, but the waiter hovered, pencil poised, and under the pressure of his gaze an Alexander was the only slightly exotic drink I could think of. I sipped it slowly, basking in the atmosphere as I conjured up images of Fitzgerald and Hemingway and Chanel, and tried to remember if Balzac and Dumas wrote about the venerable Place Vendôme right next door.

When I was shown to my room I wanted to cry because Bob isn't here with me. Even this great bed is a masterpiece, says she, reclining on it for her second night of lonely luxury. It's been heaven to have time for myself in Paris, freed of Red Cross responsibilities. Time to wander the Seine, to browse bookstalls and bookshops, to explore the fine shops and couturiers clustered in this area, to pick up mementos for relatives and friends who've so faithfully written even when I didn't often answer, to meet Jean at sidewalk cafes when she had a free hour or two.

One morning, fog still rising off the Seine, we had coffee and croissants at Les Deux Magots; one afternoon we sipped aperitifs on the Champs—sun filtering down on us through a chestnut tree!—and watched Paris pass our table: shoppers, cyclists, couples leading dogs, rickety taxis tooting loudly to clear their way. One night we dined at Prunier's because, as Jean pointed out, "Rosie, you can't leave Paris without eating there, it's an experience." The duck didn't live up to expectations but the check sure did, so we split it.

One night Jean and her French friend, Charlotte, invited me to hear Edith Piaf sing, for the first time since war's end. The theater was jammed and the crowd enthusiastic as a full orchestra swung into big-band versions of the jazz standards and popular music of our generation, our war. And then Piaf walked quietly on stage, as though trying to slip in unnoticed. The packed house went wild with applause and shouts. She stood center stage to accept the tribute, wraithlike in a little black dress that seemed to reflect the grayish pallor of her skin, her only jewelry a single strand of pearls. Pale, reed-thin, and emaciated in the spotlight, she looked in danger of being blown away by the acclaim.

Finally, she signaled the orchestra, the audience quieted, and she began to sing. Her deep, vibrating voice poured out across the footlights. It seemed impossible such a voice could come from such a body. When she sang "La Vie en Rose" and "J'Attendrai," she bent one leg to beat her left hand on her thigh, as though forcing that marvelously strong and compelling voice out of her body, her very guts. The audience couldn't get enough of her and didn't want to let her go. Her performance was a triumph.

Afterwards, too energized to want the evening to be over, Charlotte insisted I must see her apartment so we all went back to her place, near the Place de l'Etoile. We walked into a small, dimly lit room, and a tiny woman half lounging on a daybed with a blanket draped around her shoulders, sat up. Her face was pale and gaunt, her hair dark, but her large and strikingly blue eyes radiated vitality as she smiled in greeting.

"Ah, Rosie. This is Fania," said Charlotte. "Fania and I got to know Jean when she joined the ARC entertainment unit we worked in last year."

In the intimacy of that dimly lit, cold apartment, warmed by a glass of wine, we laughed as I learned about their Red Cross experiences together. Jean admitted their friendship didn't get off to a very good start. While she was in Paris on a break last November, Red Cross Headquarters ordered her off to be company manager of Fania and Charlotte's group. It was the fourth such company Jean had worked in and she was furious.

Charlotte said the first time she saw Jean she looked like a thundercloud and the whole cast wondered what kind of Red Cross shrew they were stuck with.

It seems that Charlotte is terrific with torch songs, Jean great on her guitar, and Fania was pianist for all the acts. They worked Red Cross Clubs in Paris as well as the cigarette circuit in Normandy (so called because the camps and troop movement areas are named for popular brands of cigarettes, like Camp Lucky Strike and Camp Hit Parade).

Jean added, "The biggest crowd we ever had was 19,000. What a time it was."

Eventually I asked about the German occupation, as Jean had mentioned earlier that Charlotte worked in the French Resistance. Charlotte gestured in that unique Parisian way and shrugged. "Eh, who knows, Rosie? My luck held." She's a mezzo-soprano who before the war specialized in French and German lieder and during the occupation got by with nightclub jobs, but her hours of work were irregular and long. She let her Resistance group hold their weekly meetings in her apartment despite the risk, even if she had to go to work. She always carried with her false ID cards and ration tickets for resisters in hiding, and yes, she narrowly missed being arrested and deported.

Charlotte shrugged again. "But compared to Fania, I suffered nothing. She's still recovering from the typhus she had when Auschwitz was liberated."

"You were there?" I blurted out. Fania slipped the blanket from one shoulder and held up her arm so I could see the dark numbers tattooed on her pale skin. Fania said she was a member of the Birkenau women's orchestra and got into it only on a fluke—she knew the words to and managed to sing, "Un Bel Di," at the demand of a German officer who created the camp orchestra to play for official Nazis when they toured the concentration camp.

Fania's knowledge of Madame Butterfly and of opera generally, her lovely voice, and musical skills saved her from almost certain death in Birkenau-Auschwitz. Her job was to arrange the music, play the piano, and sing. The orchestra played each day as the internees were herded and flogged off to work and when they returned. They also played for gatherings of Nazi leaders, the orchestra dressed in finery retrieved from suitcases seized from arriving internees before they were sent off to the showers. Despite the horror of the life, she rearranged some beloved Jewish songs into marches, and the orchestra mixed them in with other marches they played as the labor details marched off each day—their small signal of encouragement to the internees. "The stupid guards especially enjoyed 'Josef, Josef' and often requested it," Fania said. In the last days, as the Allies approached the camp, the Nazi Brass panicked and fled leaving chaos behind. By the time the British liberated the camp, Fania lay half dead with typhus in her filthy bunk. She remembers with love the red-headed British soldier who scooped her up in his arms to carry her out of the barracks, tears running down his freckled cheeks. "Someday I'll write the story," she said. "The world has to know."

That evening in Paris was overwhelming, in every sense of the word. . . .*

---

*Author's note: Charlotte Euvrard later moved to the United States, married John Stuart Hyde, and was awarded the "Chevalier de l'Ordre National de Mérite" (National Order of Merit) by the French government after the Games of the XXIII Olympiad in Los Angeles, to honor her services to France from the Resistance.

Fania Fénelon Perla later did write down her story, "Sursis pour l'Orchestre," which was made into the film Playing for Time, starring Vanessa Redgrave.

Camp Philip Morris, Le Havre
11 PM, April 15, 1946

Dears,

A last note before sailing. It's gorgeous weather, a full moon tonight and stars all over the sky. The *General Muir* is supposed to take seven or eight days to cross in good weather, so let's hope it continues lovely. These past days we've soaked up sun to remove our pallor, gone to on-post movies at night, and spent time with servicemen thrilled or worried about returning to real life and eager to discuss their hopes and problems.

Today we visited the French brides' section to see the nursery. The Army's taking splendid care of the babies, adorable and of all hues, and we watched the brides learn to make introductions properly at the special ARC class for brides. The women ran the gamut from beautiful and elegant to healthy and wholesome to very ill at ease and uncomfortable, from farm girls to city girls. A few looked, shall we say, worldly—far too worldly. There are bound to be culture shocks for them and the American grooms awaiting them.

I must get a lot of sleep tonight, my last in the ETO. I'll be telephoning you *next week*—happy, happy day!

All my love,
Roses

WESTERN UNION

VLT THE LANGHELDTS   1946 APR 15 PM 12:15
BERKELEY (CALIF)

SAIL APRIL SIXTEENTH ABOARD GENERAL MUIR   WILL CALL
FROM NEW YORK   ALL MY LOVE   ROSES

Chapter Twenty-Six

Aboard USNT *General Muir*
Thursday, April 18, 1946—3 PM

Dearest ones,

We sailed Tuesday at 7 PM. As we climbed out of the trucks at the Le Havre docks and filed to the ship, wooden arrows stuck in a pile of rubble pointed towards our various destinations, as in New York 3400 Miles, San Francisco 7900 Miles. Texas, of course, was painted in huge letters, twice the size of all the other places listed.

Right now I'm bundled up and perched topside as this Navy troopship rolls and pitches, and how I love it. The weather changed the day after we left port and two-thirds of the troops and Red Cross aboard have been sick, including my bunkmate. Roberta's a charming Easterner who was a Red Cross Clubmobile supervisor on the continent, so we have lots in common. She's in the bunk beside mine but rarely leaves it. She said she crossed the ocean a lot before the war and learned to survive by taking several good books to read and remaining flat in her bunk. All she'll let me bring her back from mess are crackers and a banana or applesauce, but we have some great bunk conversations when her stomach's not upset. More often one glance at her pale face is a signal to leave her to books or naps until the storms pass.

I've been enjoying this marvelous Navy food, lonesome at the dining table most of the time, especially when it's so rough the tables are set with false tops, holes cut in them to anchor the china and cups so they don't fly off when the ship pitches. This is a neat ship although it acts like a cork on the water. As I write, it's rough and getting rougher. There are about 1,600 aboard, over half of them seasick, so the rest of us have lots of room.

I keep marveling at the contrast between the trip over on the *Liz* and this trip back. Then we were all jammed together, mixing and socializing every minute, 16,000 of us off to help save the world. Now 1,600 of us rattle around the ship. We've done our jobs and are again individuals heading home. We have nothing left to prove. Relaxed instead of spit and polish, no one feeling the need to make points. All ranks mix and there's a minimum of procedure and protocol among the technicians, officers, enlisted men, special forces, Army nurses, military government people, Red Cross men and women—you name it. All focused on our own plans. Everyone's pleasant but sort of politely detached, thinking of the future, thinking civilian.

It might take about two weeks after we dock to get home and I won't be able to tell you everything over the phone when we land. I've avoided sitting in at the bridge tables of the hardy souls aboard. As you know, I enjoy bridge but these games go on night and day and far too seriously.

We're headed south and in a day or two should be in the tropics. With luck we'll dock the 24th. I still can't believe I'm coming home. I keep telling myself and the fact keeps slipping away from me.

I'll be phoning you, said she casually.

All my love,
Roses

Journal   *Sunday, April 21, 1946*

Contrary to our expectations we've sure not found any tropical breezes this trip. On one of the stormiest days an officer on the bridge spotted me on a side deck, clinging to the rail with one arm while trying to take a movie of the enormous waves breaking over the bow. He rushed down to order me below—before I washed overboard, he said. Did I realize this was the worst storm of the year and the waves coming over the bow often crested at 30 feet over the bridge? No, I didn't and yes, I now did. I apologized, as he graciously escorted me inside.

The weather's finally moderated and at last we're on the home stretch. When the public address system announced we will dock Wednesday, excitement raced through the ship. And through me as I realized our separation is almost over—all those long months of being apart, of waiting for letters, of uncertainty. No longer need I push thoughts of Bob out of my mind to concentrate on getting through another day, another week, another month alone. Now I'm counting the days with joy, and gratitude.

As though on cue it was announced church services would be held on deck this morning. The foredeck soon was jammed, all the folding chairs filled, and the overflow crowd draped all over the superstructure, lifeboats, and even parts of the rigging. Most everyone turned up in Class A uniform and most women wore scarves instead of caps to preserve hairdos already being fussed over. It was like a dress rehearsal for a wedding—fun but serious and important.

Sun broke through the high clouds as hymnals were passed around. The hymns chosen were old ones many of us have known so long we'd forgotten we know them. We all tackled "Onward, Christian Soldiers" in full voice and tears unexpectedly filled my eyes as I suddenly remembered singing it in Sunday school. Singing the words was like hearing them for the first time and I again felt so thankful, to be returning from instead of marching off to war. The Navy chaplain, in white vestments for the service, gave a brief sermon on brotherhood, and on the necessity of working as hard in peace to maintain it as we had in war, to prevent future ones.

All day since I find myself smiling as my thoughts turn to Bob and random memories surface to delight me, so many of them. His blue, blue eyes (can they possibly be as blue as I remember?), those eyes that twinkle with amusement as quickly as they glow with love and understanding, with tenderness. And his wonderful sense of humor, that way his wry quick smile makes a corner of his mouth turn up and his eyebrows crinkle when he's teasing or making some outrageous statement to liven up a party. And always, the spark between us when we're together, whether we're dancing, romancing, or just standing side by side in a crowded room. I glow just thinking about it.

About then I made myself try to think of drawbacks (as Mom would put it) just to be sure I'm not a hopeless romantic, but I didn't get far. Annoying, yes—he has that Midwestern tendency to put ketchup on everything and to salt and pepper a meal before tasting it, which I tell him is an insult to the cook. OK, so I'll keep lots of ketchup around—at least until I learn to cook decently. I can live with that. And he's firm in his opinions—no, stubborn is the word. But so am I—at least as stubborn. From the beginning I knew I couldn't change him and, this is the miracle, I didn't try to, I don't want to—for the first time in my life. When I realized that, I knew I was in love. Also a first for me.

I've seen his command presence under pressure as a man among men, and know he measures up. He's a leader and he certainly has character. As Tom Carver said to me once, intending it as a great compliment, "Bob's no ass-kisser or bullshitter." He gives an honest opinion, no matter how frank his answer. He doesn't feel a need to impress, and consequently he does. Especially me, hopelessly happy looking forward to a life with that man. Our love from the first has been overwhelming, the sense of rightness when we're together has been there from the start.

And today I realized again how much I've loved this whole experience since the day I left home—all the funny, terrible, exciting, frustrating, heartbreaking moments. And how much I've learned from my crew, my wonderful crew—all those girls who put careers and normal life on hold to volunteer for ARC overseas duty. And from the men—the Army, the Navy, and our special guys, the GIs. I've learned so much from them all. Enough to know I'll never again judge anybody's intelligence by first appearances—by lack of formal education or extra college degrees, by skin color, speech, or dress. May I always see the person inside the uniform. And may I always remember, as the GIs put it, not to sweat the small stuff of life.

I'm ready to land now and what a wonderful passage it's been—all two years of it.

WESTERN UNION

T.CDU683   FT16=CD NEW YORK NY24
THE LANGHELDTS   1946 APR 24 PM 8 15
BERKELEY CALIF

ARRIVED SAFELY   EXPECT TO SEE YOU SOON   DONT ATTEMPT TO CONTACT OR WRITE ME HERE   LOVE   MISS ROSEMARY LANGHELDT

❧

Journal   Late, April 24, 1946
                                                American University, Washington D.C.

Today we landed and now I can believe it. I'm back in the U.S.A. and it's a glorious feeling. Knew I'd be excited but was totally unprepared for my reactions this morning. Having sailed from a blacked-out New York in the middle of the night on a blacked-out ship, I hadn't anticipated the thrill of sailing into New York on a clear day.

All of us clustered on deck early, laughing with excitement and leaning over the rails as we approached the harbor. Roberta, risen from her bunk, looking as rested and refreshed as though she'd been on a tropical cruise, started to brief me, other Easterners constantly chiming in to make sure this Westerner didn't miss anything. "Staten Island's there on the left, Rosie—Brooklyn's way over that way, why do you ask? You can't possibly see it from here. Look! There goes the Staten Island ferry—that's Jersey over there."

Soon we could see the Manhattan skyline in the distance, looming higher and ever more marvelous as we got nearer. And then the Statue of Liberty rose up ahead, far more moving seen from the water than any picture postcard can begin to suggest. Already I was fumbling around in my purse for a handkerchief as a cluster of smaller craft approached from both sides of the harbor to circle us, flags, pennants, and welcome banners flapping in the breeze. Music and messages blared from loud speakers. A Transportation Corps vessel passed in review displaying a huge Welcome Home, Well Done sign. By then I was having trouble with goosebumps as well as wet eyes. I felt like bursting into a chorus of "God Bless America," when one of the circling boats did just that.

And then we were docking, grab your luggage, hurry-up-and-wait time, until the gangway finally slipped across the gap. As we filed ashore, a blast of such energy, noise, and sheer vitality surged around us I wanted to stop and gawk at my fellow countrymen. To my startled eyes they all looked rich.

Clean, so clean, even dockers in jeans spattered with dirt and grease, but jeans obviously clean beneath the stains. And the shoes, of good quality, some even polished. And the hair, the shiny clean hair of men and women of all ages. And the teeth, bright and white (even the false ones) as they smiled, which they did often as they waved us on. Everyone looked fresh and healthy—and alive. They laughed easily and moved with energy and purpose, destinations in mind. It was as exhilarating as a gust of fresh air.

The contrast between this and the war-worn countries I've just left filled me with wonder at differences I'd forgotten, or never thought about before. I gawked like an immigrant as I followed the signs to Customs.

I lost Roberta going through Customs inspections at the long tables, but we'd exchanged addresses before leaving the ship. After I cleared Customs—the agent demanded receipts for my old French maps and by the time I fished them out he didn't even look at my books, hooray!—I rushed to share a cab to Grand Central with other girls catching the train to Washington.

The phone booths in Grand Central were almost hidden by long lines waiting to use them. We soon became commiserating souls, constantly checking our watches and train times, coins and phone numbers ready if we ever got to the front of the line. Several times callers suffered pounding on the door and rude comments from the next-in-lines. The first time that happened I thought it rude. By the time it was finally my turn, I agreed with the tactic completely and was joining in the hoots. All too aware of the long line still trailing out behind me as I entered the booth, I knew I had to be brief. Just check in, I told myself. Three quick calls if I can get through, and tell them I'll call from Washington.

Bob answered on the second ring and I was laughing and crying and completely speechless for a moment as I'd forgotten the marvelous sound of his voice. Don't think either of us said an intelligent word and then we were both talking at once. Bob's soft, sure words—he's already arranging time off for a midsummer wedding—made me overflow again after we hung up. I got right through to Berkeley and Mother's dear voice answered, sounding so close. Dad was still at work so Mom and I cried and talked at the same time as I told her I'd call when we got to Washington. Then I put through a call to Moosup, as I had promised Ski and Tom I would as soon as I landed. The connection was poor, someone I could hardly hear said hello, I asked for Ski and the connection cut off as I was talking. There wasn't time to try again as I heard my train being called and I rushed to the gate.

Tomorrow I sign off and hope to clear and leave for Pittsburgh. The girls here say final clearing is full of details, down to turning in our dog tags. I'm already planning to cheat and only turn in one. The other one I'll stick in my wallet for luck—and for instant recall of memories enough to last a lifetime.

❧

Pittsburgh
Saturday, April 27, 1946

Dearest ones,

Wasn't it fun talking last night, Mom? You should have seen Aunt Stella and the family. They were all laughing and crying at once and so excited they were dancing around the phone when my call to you went through. When Martha Hoge brought me back from the B&O station, Aunt Stella was waiting on the steps crying, surrounded by our relatives. Aunt Tillie, still thin as a stick and wiry as steel, had on one of her good dresses she only wears once every two years. Just like forever.

I've just talked to Bob again. Mother, you know how I love our relatives but even though they slipped into the background and tried to be absolutely silent while Bob and I talked, I knew they were close by, enjoying every word and pause. Their presence may have preserved my decorum, so I didn't gush too much, but it did put a slight crimp in our conversation. Bob's meeting me Monday morning at 8:15 in Chicago. Isn't that wonderful?

I love you all and I'm coming soon.

Roses

P.S. Talked again with Ski's family. Can you believe she was in Grand Central the same night, the same time I was, waiting for a train to Kentucky to join Tom, who's starting back to finish college. If only I had known!

❦

Journal   *Late! April 28, 1946*
                                                              En route Chicago

After the great send-off from Pittsburgh, I'm propped up in my berth staring out the window, too excited to close an eye. Bob will be waiting when the train pulls in just a few hours from now and a thought just hit me: I've never seen him in civilian clothes. In the crush of people at the station, will I recognize him? Will he look the same in a suit? He looks great in uniform, but most men do. Of course, I'll be in uniform so he's bound to spot me eventually. Suddenly I feel like a mail-order bride.

I'm now going to pull down the blind and sleep, with my gold heart charm bracelet still on my wrist—the lovely one Bob brought me back from Paris just a year ago. I put

*it on tonight for luck before leaving for the train. I loved the message in French—
"I love you—always—today more than yesterday—less than tomorrow"—when he
gave it to me and it's sure proved true so far. We've already had our wonderful yester-
days. In the morning, we finally get to start off together on the most important part—
all the tomorrows, the always part.*

WESTERN UNION

MR AND MRS HB LANGHELDT   1946 MAY 5 PM 9 18
BERKELEY CALIF

ROSEMARY WILL ARRIVE AS SCHEDULED 915AM OAKLAND
LOVE   BOB

Epilogue

As I hoped, we Clubmobile friends, who had shared so much, have kept in touch over the years. Always by phone, checking in from wherever we happen to be, and whenever possible we've rendezvoused in most unlikely places—Muncie, Delray Beach, Sewickley, Chicago, Corpus Christi, Seattle. And yes, we still take up in the middle of a sentence.

Ski and Tom lived in Connecticut for the thirteen years of their marriage and had one son, Thomas Carver, Jr.

Caroline Drane went on to marry Charles Whipple, a Red Cross field director, in Cambridge, Massachusetts.

Harriet Scudder continued to work for the Red Cross in veteran patient rehabilitation before returning to Hyannis to join the family business.

Eloise Reilly, who finished the war with General Bradley's group in Berlin, works and lives in Westport, Connecticut.

Lillian Keit left teaching to go into the family business and remained close friends with Kari Lund Fougner, who married a Norwegian and lives in Oslo.

Barbara Hayes Van Winkelen is an award-winning artist and illustrator and divides her time between a studio in Nantucket and her home in Connecticut.

Bettie Gearhart married tank captain John Brodie to become a farmer's wife and lives in Spirit Lake, Iowa.

Alice Finney returned to her radio and acting career before marrying Dr. James Gabbard. She lives in Corpus Christi, Texas.

Bob and Rosie were married in Berkeley on July 30, 1946. Before and after Martha and Tom were born, Rosie worked as a fashion buyer in St. Louis and then in advertising and public relations in Seattle. She served on the Board of Trustees of the Women's University Club and is an active member of the Association for Women in Communications. After his retirement as executive vice president of Star Machinery Company, Bob was a regional representative for SCORE (Service Corps for Retired Executives) and served on the Advisory Council of the SBA (Small Business Administration). In 1996 they celebrated their fiftieth wedding anniversary in Seattle.